The Sion T

In 1963 a collection of fifty-seven silver vessels was discovered during illegal excavations by villagers in Antalya Province, Turkey. The Sion Treasure, named after the inscription 'Holy Sion' on several vessels in the hoard, is now divided between five collections: Antalya Museum (Turkey), Dumbarton Oaks (United States), a private collection in Geneva, the Digby-Jones collection and Hewett collection (United Kingdom).

This book builds on the studies of the Sion Treasure and examines questions regarding silver mining, manufacture, and the economic and cultural role of the silver vessels. It considers the treasure using the concept of the cultural biography of objects. The vessels from the Sion Treasure have not previously been considered in this context and the book highlights the fact that the value and significance of the objects at the time they were created does not lie exclusively in their visual characteristics and aesthetics since their relationship to, and with, people is also significant. While their functionality lends them one life story, another biography is gained through their users: the producers, patrons and individuals within the church, not only the clergy, who engaged with the objects.

The Sion Treasure Reconsidered will appeal to students and scholars alike interested in Byzantine cultural and material history and medieval material history in general.

Ahmet Arı is a lecturer in Byzantine Studies at Nevsehir Hacı Bektas Veli University, Turkey.

Studies in Byzantine Cultural History
Series Editors: Margaret Mullett, Liz James, and Jim Crow

This series brings the insights of art, archaeology and text to create a new cultural history of Byzantium. Studies in all three disciplines are invited, but especially those works which bring together the three disciplines to create something new. The series includes comparative works with neighbouring subjects, such as classics, medieval studies, Islamic studies, Ottoman studies, Renaissance studies,studies and Modern Greek studies, to allow Byzantine studies to be infused with new energy and to respond to its neighbours.

Experiencing the Last Judgement
Niamh Bhalla

Managing Emotion in Byzantium
Passions, Affects and Imaginings
Edited by Margaret Mullett and Susan Ashbrook Harvey

The Art of Dining in Medieval Byzantium
Lara Frentrop

Power and Representation in Byzantium
The Forging of the Macedonian Dynasty
Neil Churchill

The Sion Treasure Reconsidered
The Biographies and Multivalence of Sacred Silver Objects in Sixth-Century Byzantium
Ahmet Arı

The Sion Treasure Reconsidered

The Biographies and Multivalence of Sacred Silver Objects in Sixth-Century Byzantium

Ahmet Arı

Routledge
Taylor & Francis Group
LONDON AND NEW YORK

First published 2024
by Routledge
4 Park Square, Milton Park, Abingdon, Oxon OX14 4RN

and by Routledge
605 Third Avenue, New York, NY 10158

Routledge is an imprint of the Taylor & Francis Group, an informa business

British Library Cataloguing-in-Publication Data
A catalogue record for this book is available from the British Library

ISBN: 978-1-032-38535-8 (hbk)
ISBN: 978-1-032-38536-5 (pbk)
ISBN: 978-1-003-34550-3 (ebk)

DOI: 10.4324/9781003345503

Typeset in Times New Roman
by MPS Limited, Dehradun

Contents

List of Illustrations — *vi*
Acknowledgements — *xii*
List of Abbreviations — *xiv*

Introduction — 1

1 The Silver Vessels from the Sion Treasure — 5

2 Inscriptions on the Sion Vessels — 102

3 Silver Stamps on the Sion Treasure — 119

4 Questions of Circulation, Production and Cost of the Sion Treasure — 140

5 The Lives and Biographies of the Sion Vessels — 152

Bibliography — *186*
Index — *194*

Illustrations

Tables

1.1 Objects from the Sion Treasure 35
2.1 Inscriptions on Sion Objects 104
3.1 Stamps on Sion Objects 135
4.1 The Cost of the Sion Objects to Their Donors 151

Diagram

5.1 Interrelationships between silverware, people and context 153

Figures

1.1 Paten with gilded, eight-armed Christogram and niello inscription (no. 1). Antalya Museum, Turkey (1020) 47
1.2 Paten with six-armed Christogram and niello inscription (no. 3). Dumbarton Oaks, Byzantine Collection, Washington, DC (DO. BZ. 63.36.1) 48
1.3 Paten with gilded cross and niello inscription (no. 4). Dumbarton Oaks, Byzantine Collection, Washington, DC (DO. BZ. 63.36.2) 49
1.4 Paten with gilded cross and niello inscription (no. 5). Displayed with asterisk (no. 58). Dumbarton Oaks, Byzantine Collection, Washington, DC (DO. BZ. 63.36.3) 50
1.5 Paten with gilded cross and engraved inscription (no. 6). Antalya Museum, Turkey (1021) 51
1.6 Cruciform polycandelon (no. 7). Antalya Museum, Turkey (1051) 52
1.7 Cruciform polycandelon (no. 8). Antalya Museum, Turkey (1052) 53
1.8 Cruciform polycandelon (no. 9). Dumbarton Oaks, Byzantine Collection, Washington, DC (DO. BZ. 65.1.1) 54

1.9 Circular polycandelon (no. 10). Antalya Museum, Turkey (1053) 55
1.10 Circular polycandelon (no. 11). Antalya Museum, Turkey (1054) 56
1.11 Circular polycandelon (no. 12). Dumbarton Oaks, Byzantine Collection, Washington, DC (DO. BZ. 63.36.4) 57
1.12 Rectangular polycandelon with tri-lobed end pieces and paired dolphin decoration (no. 13). Dumbarton Oaks, Byzantine Collection, Washington, DC (DO. BZ. 63.36.5) 58
1.13 Rectangular polycandelon with tri-lobed end pieces and paired dolphin decoration (no. 14). This shows all the detached pieces from both Antalya (two lateral rims and one tri-lobed end piece ANT 1033, 1031 and 1028) and Dumbarton Oaks (central rectangle and one tri-lobed end piece DO. BZ. 63.36.6) 59
1.14 Rectangular polycandelon with semi-circular end pieces and paired dolphin decoration (no. 15). All detached pieces are in Dumbarton Oaks, Byzantine Collection, Washington, DC (DO. BZ.63.36.7 and BZ. 79.14.4 (a-d)) 60
1.15 Rectangular polycandelon with semi-circular end pieces and paired dolphin decoration (no. 16). All detached pieces are in Dumbarton Oaks, Byzantine Collection, Washington, DC (DO. BZ. 65.1.8) 61
1.16 Rectangular polycandelon with semi-circular end pieces and foliate design decoration (no. 17). Detached pieces are from Antalya Museum, Turkey and Dumbarton Oaks, Byzantine Collection, Washington, DC (ANT 1030 and DO. BZ. 65.1.7) 62
1.17a Rectangular polycandelon with semi-circular end pieces and foliate design decoration (no. 18). Antalya Museum, Turkey (2018/74) 63
1.17b Detached semi-circular end piece of no. 18. Dumbarton Oaks, Byzantine Collection, Washington, DC (DO.BZ.79.14.1) 64
1.18a Circular censer with scenes from the life of the Virgin (no. 19). Antalya Museum, Turkey (1019) 65
1.18b Scenes from the life of the Virgin applied on the circular censer (no. 19) 66
1.19a Hexagonal censer supported by four peacocks and decorated with medallions of Christ, St Peter and St Paul (no. 20). Dumbarton Oaks, Byzantine Collection, Washington, DC (DO. BZ. 65.1.5) 67
1.19b Detail of hexagonal censer (no. 20) showing dolphins and imperial stamps 68

1.20 Crushed bowl of a chalice (no. 21). Dumbarton Oaks, Byzantine Collection, Washington, DC (DO. BZ. 63. 36. 19) 69

1.21 Flattened bowl of a chalice with engraved inscription (no. 22). Dumbarton Oaks, Byzantine Collection, Washington, DC (DO. BZ. 79.8) 70

1.22 Bowl and knob of a chalice with engraved inscription (no. 23). Dumbarton Oaks, Byzantine Collection, Washington, DC (DO. BZ. 65.1.11) 71

1.23 Bowl of a chalice with two engraved crosses (no. 24). Dumbarton Oaks, Byzantine Collection, Washington, DC (DO. BZ. 63.36.20) 72

1.24 Bowl of a chalice with pointillé inscription (no. 25). Antalya Museum, Turkey (1043) 73

1.25 Bowl of a chalice with two engraved and gilded crosses and engraved inscription, with its detached bottom (no. 26). Antalya Museum, Turkey (1036–1, 1046) 74

1.26 Chalice with two engraved and gilded crosses (no. 27). Antalya Museum, Turkey (2018/75) 75

1.27 Crushed, detached and folded amphora with niello inscription (no. 28). Dumbarton Oaks, Byzantine Collection, Washington, DC (DO. BZ. 65.1.4) 76

1.28 Amphora with niello inscription and detached body fragment (no. 29). Antalya Museum, Turkey (1049 and 1039) 77

1.29 Crushed and folded ewer (no. 30). Dumbarton Oaks, Byzantine Collection, Washington, DC (DO. BZ. 63.36.14) 78

1.30 Standing lamp with niello inscription and two engraved crosses, crushed and folded (no. 31). Dumbarton Oaks, Byzantine Collection, Washington, DC (DO. BZ. 63.36.15) 79

1.31 Standing lamp with niello inscription and two engraved crosses, crushed and folded (no. 32). Dumbarton Oaks, Byzantine Collection, Washington, DC (DO. BZ. 63.36.16) 79

1.32 Standing lamp with niello inscription and two engraved crosses (no. 33). Dumbarton Oaks, Byzantine Collection, Washington, DC (DO. BZ. 63.36.17) 80

1.33 Standing lamp with niello inscription and two engraved crosses, detached foot and body (no. 34). Antalya Museum, Turkey (1050 and 1042) 81

1.34 Openwork lamp decorated with inverted hearts (no. 35). Dumbarton Oaks, Byzantine Collection, Washington, DC (DO. BZ. 63.36.25 and 63. 36.21) 82

1.35 Fragments of openwork lamp decorated with inverted hearts (no. 36). One foot (upper right) and rim fragment (upper left) in Dumbarton Oaks, Byzantine Collection, Washington, DC (DO. BZ. 63.36.25a/65.1.14), two rim fragments and fragments from the body of the object in Antalya Museum, Turkey (1047 3–7 and 1048 1–2) 83

1.36 Openwork lamp decorated with scales and triangles (no. 37). Dumbarton Oaks, Byzantine Collection, Washington, DC (DO. BZ. 65.1.6) 84

1.37 Fragments of openwork lamp with hexagonal rim (no. 39). One foot and four hexagonal rim fragments. Dumbarton Oaks, Byzantine Collection, Washington, DC (DO. BZ. 65.1.19 a-c/79.11 and 63.36.22) 85

1.38 Fragments of openwork lamp with hexagonal rim (no. 40). Dumbarton Oaks, Byzantine Collection, Washington, DC (DO. BZ. 79.10 a-d/63.36.23 and 63.36.32) 86

1.39 Openwork lamp with openwork inscription (no. 41). Dumbarton Oaks, Byzantine Collection, Washington, DC (DO. BZ. 65.1.12) 87

1.40 Fragments of openwork lamp with openwork inscription (no. 42). Dumbarton Oaks, Byzantine Collection, Washington, DC (DO. BZ. 65.1.15) 88

1.41 Cross-shaped suspension bracket for five lamps (no. 43). Dumbarton Oaks, Byzantine Collection, Washington, DC (DO. BZ. 65.1.18 and 63.36.31) 89

1.42 Pair of book covers with crosses (no. 44). Dumbarton Oaks, Byzantine Collection, Washington, DC (DO. BZ. 63.36.9–10) 90

1.43 Fragments of the pair of book covers (no. 45). Two fragments in Dumbarton Oaks, Byzantine Collection, Washington, DC (DO. BZ. 63.36.8 and 65.1.3) and multiple fragments in Antalya Museum, Turkey (1034 1–3) 90

1.44 Fragments of third pair of book covers (no. 46). Antalya Museum (1034 and 1055) 91

1.45 Lampstand with acanthus capital and column (no. 47). Dumbarton Oaks, Byzantine Collection, Washington, DC (DO. BZ. 63.36.13 and 65.1.9) 92

1.46 Lampstand with crushed and torn acanthus capital, column and column base (no. 48). Dumbarton Oaks, Byzantine Collection, Washington, DC (DO. BZ. 63.36.12, 63.36.18 and 65.1.23) 93

1.47 Fragments of candlestick (no. 49). Antalya Museum, Turkey (1036–3, 1040 1–2, 1041 1–4, 1035). Dumbarton Oaks, Byzantine Collection, Washington, DC (DO. BZ. 63.36.38) 94

1.48	Fragment of candlestick (no. 50). Dumbarton Oaks, Byzantine Collection, Washington, DC (DO. BZ. 65.1.20)	95
1.49a	Rim sheets for an altar table (no. 51) from Antalya Museum, Turkey (1037 1–2, 1045 1–6 and 1038 1–2)	96
1.49b	Rim sheets for an altar table (no. 51) from Dumbarton Oaks, Byzantine Collection, Washington, DC (DO. BZ. 65.1.10 a-g/63.36.11 a-d)	97
1.50a	One of the plain sheets for the top of the altar table (no. 52) from Dumbarton Oaks, Byzantine Collection, Washington, DC (DO 65.1.10 h, i, j, k, l)	97
1.50b	One of the plain sheets for the top of the altar table (no. 52) from Antalya Museum, Turkey (1024)	98
1.51	Inscribed plain sheet (no. 53). Dumbarton Oaks, Byzantine Collection, Washington, DC (DO. BZ. 79.4)	99
1.52	Inscribed plain sheet (no. 54). Antalya Museum, Turkey (1025 and 1044)	100
1.53	Silver bowl with five imperial stamps (no. 55). Dumbarton Oaks, Byzantine Collection, Washington, DC (DO. BZ.63.36.24)	101
3.1	Irregular or non-imperial stamps applied on standing lamp (no. 34). Antalya Museum, Turkey (1042)	120
3.2	Imperial stamps applied on circular polycandelon (no. 10). Antalya Museum, Turkey (1053)	124
3.3	Imperial stamps applied on rectangular polycandelon (no. 17). Dumbarton Oaks, Byzantine Collection, Washington, DC (DO.BZ.65.1.7)	125
3.4	Imperial stamps applied on circular censer (no. 19). Antalya Museum, Turkey (1019)	126
3.5	Imperial stamps applied on a bowl (no. 55). Dumbarton Oaks, Byzantine Collection, Washington, DC (DO. BZ.63.36.24)	127
3.6	Imperial stamps applied on hexagonal censer (no. 20). Dumbarton Oaks, Byzantine Collection, Washington, DC (DO.BZ.65.1.5)	128
3.7	Imperial stamps applied on standing lamp (no. 33). Dumbarton Oaks, Byzantine Collection, Washington, DC (DO.BZ.63.36.17)	129
3.8	Hexagonal stamp cut in half during the making of the monogram of Eutychianos on the rectangular polycandelon (no. 13). Dumbarton Oaks, Byzantine Collection, Washington, DC	131

5.1 Detail of cruciform polycandelon (no. 7) showing ancient restoration by silver soldering. Antalya Museum, Turkey (1051) 173
5.2 Photo showing the designated altar table with sheeting for altar table, lamps, patens, chalice, censer and book covers possibly from 3 m away. Dumbarton Oaks, Byzantine Collection, Washington, DC 176

Acknowledgements

This book has its origin in my PhD dissertation "The Biography and Multivalence of Sacred Silver Objects in the Sixth-Century Sion Treasure" which I completed in 2019 (University of Sussex). Since then, I have conducted further research on this subject to revise the thesis and turn it into a book which examines the Sion objects with more comprehensive study. I have revisited collections and re-examined the objects, especially the objects in Antalya Museum. I have also conducted research on the elemental composition of Sion objects to add to the information given by Dumbarton Oaks scholars who carried out research on the elemental compositions of objects from Dumbarton Oaks. As a result of this new study, I was able to revise and rewrite my doctoral dissertation in these three years. Although the research was suspended and interrupted many times owing to the pandemic, I was able to finish research on objects from the Byzantine Collection at Dumbarton Oaks and the Antalya Museum.

During these three years a lot of people and institutions made this manuscript possible. Therefore, I am in debt to many individuals and institutions. My greatest gratitude is to two people who gave the greatest support to this project. First of all, I should like to thank Liz James who read through various drafts of this book and gave really important feedback on turning the thesis into a book. Whenever I had queries about the book or needed someone to read my drafts, she was always happy to help me. She read the drafts much faster than I had expected, giving me more time to work on her comments. This book would not be possible without her help. And my other angel, who helped and supported me during the preparation of the manuscript is my wife Büşra Mercan Ari. She always tried to calm me when I was anxious and worried about the book. She always had time to hear about the progress of the book. I am also grateful to her for helping me to design the photographs which I have used in the book.

I give special thanks to Antalya Museum Director Mustafa Demirel, archaeologists Süleyman Atalay, Fatma Nur Direr Konukman and Mehmet Ali Saçi and restorer Özgür Gemici for their kindness and help during the examination of objects in Antalya Museum and for giving permission to use the photographs of objects in the book. I should also like to thank the

Museum staff in Dumbarton Oaks, especially Gudrun Bühl, Elizabeth Dospel Williams and Carla Galfano, since they provided me with all the necessary photographs and information on the objects for the book and permission to reproduce the photographs of these objects in my book. I am also grateful to my colleagues Tolga Uyar, Ayşe Budak, Savaş Maraşli, Alper Altin, Enes Kavalçalan and Can Erpek.

This book would not have been possible without the financial support provided by anonymous donors who sponsored the color illustrations. Finally, I am grateful to Margaret Mullett for her helpful feedback on both thesis and several versions of the manuscript for the book. She was one of the people who advised me to turn the thesis into book.

Abbreviations

ArtB	The Art Bulletin
ArtH	Art History
BMGS	Byzantine and Modern Greek Studies
CAH	The Cambridge Ancient History
CH	Church History
CSCO	Corpus Scriptorum Christianorum Orientalium
CSHB	Corpus Scriptorum Historiae Byzantinae
CSL	Comes Sacrarum Largitionum
DOP	Dumbarton Oaks Papers
DOS	Dumbarton Oaks Studies
ETAM	Ergänzungsbände zu den Tituli Asiae Minoris
GOTR	The Greek Orthodox Theological Review
JAC	Journal of Aesthetics and Culture
JAE	The Journal of Aesthetic Education
JAMT	The Journal of Archaeological Method and Theory
JEChS	Journal of Early Christian Studies
JMC	The Journal of Material Culture
JRS	The Journal of Roman Studies
JRSM	Journal of Roman Studies Monographs
NPNF	Nicene and Post Nicene Fathers
OCA	Orientalia Christiana Analecta
ODB	A.P. Kazhdan, A.M. Talbot, A. Cutler, T.E. Gregory and N.P. Ševčenko, eds, *Oxford Dictionary of Byzantium*, 3 vols (New York and Oxford, 1991).
PG	Ed. J.P. Migne, Patrologia Cursus Completus: Series Graeca (Paris, 1857–1866)
PO	Patrologia Orientalis
RN	Revue Numismatique
SBHC	Studies in Byzantine History and Civilization
SGKIO	Studien zur Geschichte und Kultur des Islamischen Orients
SH	Subsidia Hagiographica

SPBS	Society for the Promotion of Byzantine Studies
TAPA	Transactions and Proceedings of the American Philological Association
TMM	The Medieval Mediterranean
TTH	Translated Texts for Historians
TU	Texte und Untersuchungen
XRF	X Radiography Fluorescence

Introduction

The 'Sion Treasure', a collection of fifty-seven silver vessels, alongside various unidentified fragments and pieces, was discovered during illegal excavations in 1963 in Büyük Asar Hill in the north of Hacıveliler village of the Kumluca district of Antalya Province in Turkey.[1] This place where the objects were found is an ancient town in Lycia called Korydalla during the Roman and Byzantine era. Following the discovery of the objects, some were taken to Antalya Museum, but others were sold to private collections, which means that the Treasure is now divided between five collections: Antalya Museum in Turkey; Dumbarton Oaks in the United States of America; George Ortiz collection in Geneva; and the Digby-Jones and Hewett Collection in London.

This book presents a record of the pieces of the Sion Treasure in Antalya Museum and in the Dumbarton Oaks collection. Susan Boyd also recorded one paten in a private collection in Geneva (the George Ortiz Collection), an openwork lamp in the Digby-Jones Collection and a few fragmentary pieces of silverware in the Hewett Collection, both in London.[2] The paten has been

1 According to Susan Boyd, there were between fifty-three and fifty-eight objects, excluding twenty-two revetments and chains, but she also counted the miscellaneous unidentified objects and detached pieces. S.A. Boyd, 'A "metropolitan" treasure from a church in the provinces: an introduction to the study of the Sion Treasure', in S.A. Boyd and M.M. Mango (ed.), *Ecclesiastical Silver Plate in Sixth-Century Byzantium* (Washington, DC, 1992), 5–38. According to examinations I made in both collections (Antalya and Dumbarton Oaks), when the identified objects and fragments come together (including the sheets to cover the altar table), the number of the objects is 57. This book will therefore consider the number of objects as 57 and exclude the detached pieces and fragments which could not be identified.

2 Since Boyd wrote, both the Digby Jones and the Hewett Collection appear to have been dispersed and I have been unable to track down what happened to the Sion pieces, though I would welcome any information. Boyd did not give any detail about these collections, so it is hard to know whose collection they are. The Hewett Collection probably belong to Kenneth John Hewett who was an art collector and active possibly between 1940s and 1990s. Many of the objects from his collection are in the British Museum, though the fragments belonging to Sion objects are not there. The Digby-Jones collection probably belonged to Kenelm Digby-Jones whose collection can be seen in many museums around the world, but I have been unable to track the openwork lamp. Mr. Hewett died in 1994 and Mr. Digby-Jones died in

DOI: 10.4324/9781003345503-1

published in the exhibition called *Byzance En Suisse* held in Rath Museum in Geneva from 4 December 2015 to 13 March 2016 which has gathered together 600 pieces of Byzantine art, covering a large proportion of public and private collections in Switzerland.[3]

A large number of the silver vessels from the Sion Treasure were published in 1992 in a Dumbarton Oaks symposium book *Ecclesiastical Silver Plate in Sixth-Century Byzantium*.[4] This was an incomplete publication as it did not include many of the material in Antalya. Since then, nothing new on the Sion Treasure has been published. By building on these studies, this book provides fresh information about the vessels in the Sion Treasure. It brings into the discussion the pieces in the Antalya Museum as well as Dumbarton Oaks, providing detailed information about the objects in both collections in detail, considering their form, condition, measurements, elemental compositions and manufacturing process, bringing new information about the fragments of silverware and about the weights of the objects. It also suggests a revised number of the pieces of silverware found, as a result of my being able to marry together fragments across the collections and discovering new objects which were not mentioned earlier.

I shall also take a different approach to the silverware from that of the Dumbarton Oaks publication, one which considers it in material culture terms. In order to understand the value of the objects in the Byzantine era, I shall show that these objects had lives as people do and had multiple values. In their life, these objects moved from one context to another context: in these different settings they carried different values. Ideas about the cultural biography of objects, material culture, agency and cognition enable me to approach the Treasure as made up of objects with social lives, and with biographies that changed in different contexts, social, political and economic.[5] However, these factors were only one element, as the functions of the vessels, and their functionality in certain performances, also had an important effect on their

2011. See S. Boyd, 'A bishop's gift: openwork lamps from the Sion Treasure', in F. Baratte (ed.), *Argenterie romaine et byzantine: Actes de la table ronde* (Paris, 1988), 192–3, nos 2 and 4.

3 The exhibition catalogue can be seen on the website of Musée d'art et d'histoire en Genève: http://institutions.ville-geneve.ch/fileadmin/user_upload/mah/documents/Expositions/2015/Byzance_Visuels-exposition.pdf (Accessed 27.03.2023), Paten no. 10, Inv. Ortiz_257. Along with this exhibition, a book was also published about Byzantine art in Switzerland. See M. Martiniani-Reber (ed.), *Byzance En Suisse 4 Decembre 2015 – 13 Mars 2016* (Milan and Geneva, 2015), no. 10. See also the website of George Ortiz collection; https://www.georgeortiz.com/objects/byzantine/257-large-paten-with-engraved-chrismon/ (Accessed 27.03.2023).

4 S.A. Boyd and M. M. Mango (ed.), *Ecclesiastical Silver Plate in Sixth-Century Byzantium* (Washington, DC, 1992).

5 For the concept of 'cultural biography of objects', see A. Appadurai, 'Introduction: commodities and the politics of value', in A. Appadurai (ed.), *The Social Life of Things: Commodities in Cultural Perspective* (Cambridge, 1986), 3–63; I. Kopytoff, 'The cultural biography of things: commoditization as process', in *The Social Life of Things,* ed. Appadurai, 64–91.

biography. In this context, I consider what the objects were really for, how they came into existence, their function, how they were used, and how all of these aspects affected the different functions of the silverware.[6]

The vessels from the Sion Treasure have not previously been considered in this way. They can give us clues and empirical evidence to discuss the value given to the silverware by its producers and donors and those who came into contact with it inside the church of Holy Sion. This book highlights the fact that the value and significance of the objects at the time when they were created and used does not lie only in their visual characteristics and sensual affordances, since their relationship to and with people is also significant; while their functionality lends them one life story, another biography is gained through their users, in terms of their producers, patrons, and the individuals within the church, not only the clergy, who engaged with them. The silverware also possessed a biography in certain contexts that affected both their usage, and individuals' perception. Therefore, this book will highlight three main aspects, all of which are closely related. One is the question of the changing functions of the silverware: as commodities for sale; as gifts to God; as items used within the church during the liturgical performance; or as functional and decorative church revetments. The second is the interrelationship between people and objects and how this affected the biography of the silverware. The third is that these objects were used in different contexts: their production; their usage as gifts to God; and their role as liturgical objects or church revetments inside the church. These varying contexts enabled the users of the Treasure to perceive the vessels in different ways, and to give them life-stories, or biographies. When a worshipper in church engaged with a paten, the function and value of that paten was not the same as that which the donors believed it had when they gave it as a gift. I shall argue that a study of the form and morphological features of the objects alone does not provide a sufficient understanding of the biographies and value of objects placed on them by their contemporaries. Rather, it is necessary to align their morphological features with their functions and materiality, and to

6 For these concepts see J.M. Skibo and M.B. Schiffer, *People and Things: A Behavioral Approach to Material Culture* (New York, 2008); M.B. Schiffer, *Behavioral Archaeology: First Principles* (Salt Lake City, 1995); C. Knappett, *Thinking through Material Culture: An Interdisciplinary Perspective* (Philadelphia, 2005); Knappett, 'The neglected networks of material agency: artefacts, pictures and texts', in C. Knappett and L. Malafouris (ed.), *Material Agency: Towards a Non-Anthropocentric Approach* (New York, 2008), 139; S.E. Van der Leeuw, 'Agency, networks, past and future', in *Material Agency*, ed. Knappett and Malafouris, 220; L. Malafouris, 'At the potter's wheel: an argument for material agency', in *Material Agency,* ed. Knappett and Malafouris, 22; C. Gosden, 'What do objects want?', *Journal of Archaeological Method and Theory,* 12.3 (2005), 193–211; P. Bloom, 'Intention, history, and artifact concepts', *Cognition,* 60 (1996), 1–29; S. Küchler and T. Carroll, *A Return to the Object: Alfred Gell, Art, and Social Theory* (New York, 2021); B. Preston, 'The functions of things: a philosophical perspective on material culture', in P.M. Graves-Brown (ed.), *Matter, Materiality and Modern Culture* (London, 2000), 22–49.

consider the intentions behind their creation and use, in order to understand the value given to these objects by their contemporaries.

This book first examines the objects in the Sion Treasure with their form, measurements, inscriptions, stamps and their circulation and monetary value, and then moves on to discuss how we can use the concept of 'cultural biography' of objects as a way to understand the value of the Sion Treasure. The aim of this book then is twofold: an updating, emending, correcting and expansion of the original checklist; and a discussion of the Treasure and its changing biography during its lives in Chapter 5.

In this context, my key questions are: what happens when we examine these objects in three stages of their life, from their production, through their usage as a gift to God, to their use in the church context? And what happens when we examine the objects in the different contexts of their production, donation and usage in church? What was the purpose of these silver objects? What did they mean to their producers? What did they mean to their donors? And what was their value and biography for worshippers? Did their biography change throughout their life, or by gaining new biographies, did they become multivalent, and gain multi-biographies? What are the implications that lie behind saying 'these objects were to be used in a church', or 'they were given as a gift'? This book seeks to understand the value and life story of these silver vessels in early Byzantium by examining the value given to them by the early Byzantine Christians who created and donated the objects, and engaged with them within the church.

1 The Silver Vessels from the Sion Treasure

The Discovery, Division and Number of the Objects in the Sion Treasure

What happened to the so-called Sion Treasure after its discovery during illegal excavation in 1963 by the villagers in the ancient town of Korydalla in Lycia and how it was divided between five different collections are interesting questions.[1] As a result of discussions with archaeologist Suleyman Atalay in Antalya Museum and investigation of the documents in the museum archive, it is clear that the silverware was found during illegal excavations. The museum reports make it clear that some of the Treasure was confiscated and taken to the Antalya Museum. Some vessels, however, had already been sold to collectors by villagers before the police and museum curators reached the area of excavation. There does not appear to be any information about who found and sold these objects to the collectors. But putting together the acquisition history of the objects in the Dumbarton Oaks Collection and the acquisition report of the objects in Antalya Museum, it seems likely that the Greek collector George Zacos, who was a dealer based in the Grand Bazaar in Istanbul, working between Switzerland, London and Istanbul, bought objects from Sion from the villagers and then sold most of them to Mrs Robert Woods Bliss, who later gave these objects to Dumbarton Oaks. Zacos is also the most likely person to have sold other pieces to the collections in London and Switzerland. Dumbarton Oaks seems to have been given parts of the Treasure over time. For example, a book cover (no. 44), three patens (nos 3–5), fragments from lampstands (nos 47 and 48) and the altar table covers (nos 51 and 52) were given in 1963 whilst a censer (no. 20), an openwork lamp with openwork inscription (no. 41) and a cross-shaped polycandelon (no. 9) were donated

1 S.A. Boyd, 'A "metropolitan" treasure from a church in the provinces: an introduction to the study of the Sion Treasure', in S.A. Boyd and M.M.Mango (ed.), *Ecclesiastical Silver Plate in Sixth-Century Byzantium* (Washington, DC, 1992), 5–38; M. Acara-Eser, *Bizans Maden Sanatı: Dini Törenlerde Kullanılan (Litürjik) Eşyalar* (Ankara, 2020), 160–226; M. Acara, 'Kumluca/Corydalla Definesi', *Sanat Tarihi Araştırmaları Dergisi*, 6 (1989), 74–6.

DOI: 10.4324/9781003345503-2

by Mrs Bliss in 1965, and the flat sheeting with cross and inscription (no. 53) was given in 1979 again by Mrs Bliss.[2] The documents detailing the illegal excavation preserved in the Antalya Museum and in the Ministry of Culture in Ankara make it clear that all of the Sion silver in Antalya Museum were confiscated in 1963, and represented whatever was left by the time officials from the museum and police arrived on the scene.[3]

The exact number of vessels and other objects discovered in the Treasure is not entirely certain. During my examinations of the objects in Antalya Museum, and in the Dumbarton Oaks Collection, it was possible to marry some of the fragments across the collections by comparing their measurements and forms. Two of the five rectangular polycandela in Dumbarton Oaks which are in fragmentary condition can be completed with fragments in the Antalya Museum (Table 1.1, nos 14 and 17), and the one rectangular polycandelon in a fragmentary condition preserved in Antalya Museum can be completed with fragments in the Dumbarton Oaks Collection (Table 1.1, no. 18), for example. As far as it is now possible to reconstruct the Treasure, it consisted of at least fifty-seven identifiable objects, along with various unidentified fragments and pieces that are now detached from the vessels and cannot be matched with other fragments.[4] Some of the identified objects are complete, while others are in a fragmentary condition.

2 S. Zwirn, *Book Cover with a Cross Flanked by Cypress Trees*, Dumbarton Oaks, http://museum.doaks.org/objects-1/info/27043 (accessed 3 February 2022); *Paten with Cross*, Dumbarton Oaks, http://museum.doaks.org/objects-1/info/27040 (accessed 3 February 2022); *Paten with Cross and Inscription*, Dumbarton Oaks, http://museum.doaks.org/objects-1/ianfo/27470 (accessed 3 February 2022); *Paten with Christogram and Repousse Border*, Dumbarton Oaks, http://museum.doaks.org/objects-1/info/27039 (accessed 3 February 2022); *Revetment for Altar Table*, Dumbarton Oaks, http://museum.doaks.org/objects-1/info/46000 (accessed 3 February 2022); J. Hanson, *Sheathing for a Column*, Dumbarton Oaks, http://museum.doaks.org/objects-1/info/35133 (accessed 3 February 2022); *Sheathing for an Acanthus Capital*, Dumbarton Oaks, http://museum.doaks.org/objects-1/info/35134 (accessed 3 February 2022); *Circular Polycandelon*, Dumbarton Oaks, http://museum.doaks.org/objects-1/info/35130 (accessed 3 February 2022); S. Zwirn, *Openwork Lamp with Openwork Inscription*, Dumbarton Oaks, http://museum.doaks.org/objects-1/info/35148 (accessed 3 February 2022); *Hexagonal Censer with Christ, Peter and Paul*, Dumbarton Oaks, http://museum.doaks.org/objects-1/info/27473 (accessed 3 February 2022); G. Bühl, Cross-Shaped Polycandelon, Dumbarton Oaks, http://museum.doaks.org/objects-1/info/35140 (accessed 3 February 2022); J. Hanson, Flat Sheathing with Cross and Inscription, Dumbarton Oaks, http://museum.doaks.org/objects-1/info/35151 (accessed 3 February 2022).

3 Oral communication with villagers and the director of Antalya Museum, Mustafa Demirel.

4 According to Susan Boyd, there were between fifty-three and fifty-eight objects, excluding twenty-two revetments and chains, but she also counted the miscellaneous unidentified objects and detached pieces. Boyd, 'A "metropolitan" treasure from a church in the provinces', 5–38. According to the examinations I made in both collections (Antalya and Dumbarton Oaks), when the identified objects and fragments are brought together (including the sheets to cover the altar table), the number of the objects becomes fifty-seven. On the basis of this work, this book considers the number of objects as fifty-seven and excludes the detached pieces which could not be identified and miscellaneous pieces such as silver nails and asterisk. I considered

Taken together, what we know of the Treasure consists of six patens (one with an asterisk, no. 5), twelve polycandela, two censers, seven chalices,[5] two amphorae, one ewer, four standing lamps, eight openwork lamps that can be employed in either suspended or standing form, one suspension bracket, three pairs of book covers, two lampstands, a rim sheeting set for an altar table, a set of plain sheets for the top of an altar, two inscribed plain sheets, pieces of two candlesticks and a bowl. Along with these there are also one pincer, two gold staffs and one silver ring set. All of the objects from the Treasure are silver (except for the pincer which is bronze and silver-plated and the gold staffs) and some are gilded. Antalya Museum holds two patens, five polycandela, one censer, three chalices, one amphora, one standing lamp, pieces of a candlestick, some rim sheeting fragments, plain sheet fragments for an altar table and one inscribed plain sheet. There are also the fragments that can be associated with objects in the Dumbarton Oaks collection, including the fragments of polycandela, book cover and openwork lamp.[6] In addition to these associated fragments, there are also miscellaneous pieces, including one base of an unidentified vessel, various fragments of unidentified objects and one chalice base.[7] Meanwhile, the Dumbarton Oaks collection holds three patens (one with asterisk, no. 5), seven polycandela, one censer, four chalices, one amphora, one ewer, three standing lamps, seven openwork lamps, one suspension bracket, two book covers, two lampstands, rim sheeting fragments and plain sheet fragments for an altar table, pieces for candlestick, one bowl, one pincer and two staffs. In addition, there are also miscellaneous pieces, including twenty-eight silver nails, four chalice bases and one silver ring set. One paten is in George Ortiz collection in Geneva, one openwork lamp is in the Digby-Jones collection in London, and some fragments of two objects are in the Hewett collection in London.[8]

---

the asterisk as a detached piece, even though it is displayed with a paten (no. 5) since we are not certain if it belonged to this paten.

5 According to Boyd, there were six chalices, but she did not count one chalice in Antalya. See Boyd, 'A "metropolitan" treasure', 20–1; and Table 1.1, no. 27 in this book.

6 See Table 1.1, nos 14, 16, 36, 45. For other studies on the objects on display in Antalya Museum see Acara-Eser, *Bizans Maden Sanatı,* 160–226; Acara, 'Kumluca/Corydalla Definesi', 74–6; C. Arıkan, 'Lykia'da erken Bizans Devri'ne ait bir define: Korydalla Hazinesi', in N.E. Akyürek Şahin and A.V. Çelgin (ed.), *Eskiçağ Yazıları* (İstanbul, 2012), 129–87; N. Fıratlı, 'Un trésor du VIe siècle à Kumluca en Lycie', *Akden Des VII. Internationalen Kongresses für Christliche Archäologie, Trier 5-11 September 1965* (Vatican City, 1969), 523–5.

7 This chalice base might belong to one of the chalices in Dumbarton Oaks without a foot. See Table 1.1, nos 21-24.

8 For paten in George Ortiz collection see the website of George Ortiz collection, https://www.georgeortiz.com/objects/byzantine/257-large-paten-with-engraved-chrismon/ (accessed 27 March 2023); also see the exhibition catalogue on the website of Musée d'art et d'histoire en Genève, http://institutions.ville-geneve.ch/fileadmin/user_upload/mah/documents/Expositions/2015/Byzance_Visuels-exposition.pdf (accessed 27 March 2023), Paten no. 10, Inv. Ortiz_257. Along with this exhibition, a book was also published about Byzantine art in Switzerland. See M. Martiniani-Reber (ed.), *Byzance En Suisse 4 Decembre 2015 – 13 Mars 2016* (Milan and Geneva, 2015), no. 10.I have been unable to track down what happened to the Sion pieces in Digby Jones

Many of the Sion Treasure objects bear inscriptions, stamps, monograms and decoration. In total, forty-five of the fifty-seven objects are inscribed, with thirty-nine of the inscribed objects bearing the names of their original donors, and the name of the individuals in whose memory the objects were given.[9] Of these thirty-nine objects inscribed with the names of their donors, the twelve inscribed polycandela have the monogram of their donor, instead of a full name. In total, there were four specific donors: bishop Eutychianos, bishop Paregoros, the priest Zacharias and bishop Theodore. Twenty-nine of the fifty-seven objects were donated by bishop Eutychianos, including three patens, all of the polycandela, two censers, four standing lamps, two amphorae, six of the openwork lamps and one suspension bracket for lamps. The rim sheeting for an altar table, and the plain sheet were donated by bishop Paregoros, and one plain sheet was donated by a priest, Zacharias.

The Condition of the Objects

Some of the objects, mostly the flatter ones, were found in good condition, such as the patens (nos 1–6), the circular and cross-shaped polycandela (nos 7–12) and the censers (nos 19 and 20). Others were found crushed, folded and rolled up. The rectangular polycandela (nos 14–18) are in a fragmentary condition except one (no. 13) which was restored in Dumbarton Oaks. The state of the polycandela indicates that they might have been crushed during burial. Two of the book covers (nos 44 and 45) are crushed and one of them is in a fragmentary condition (no. 45); the third book cover exists in several pieces (no. 46). Only one chalice was found in one piece but still there are cracks on its body (no. 27). The other chalices from the Antalya Museum were not folded but detached from their feet and flattened (nos 25–26). Two chalices from Dumbarton Oaks survive only as the body, without feet (nos 23 and 24). Two other chalices in Dumbarton Oaks were folded and are detached from their foot (nos 21 and 22). Two of the standing lamps were also flattened and rolled up (nos 31 and 32). One further standing lamp in Antalya is detached from its foot (no. 34). The last example is in Dumbarton Oaks and is in good condition (no. 33). There are also other examples of

and Hewett collections in London. For these see S. Boyd, ‘A bishop’s gift: openwork lamps from the Sion Treasure’, in F. Baratte (ed.), *Argenterie romaine et byzantine: Actes de la table ronde* (Paris, 1988), 192–3, nos 2 and 4. I am also grateful to Robin Cormack for sharing his ideas when I was trying to track down the pieces in Digby Jones and Hewett collections. He advised me to check Ernst Kitzinger Collection; however, the pieces I was looking for were not there.

9 Four inscribed chalices and one inscribed base of a candlestick do not bear the names of donors. See Tables 1.1 and 2.1 , nos 22, 23, 25, 26 and 49. And six objects (nos 4, 5, 6, 39, 40, 45), have names inscribed on them; however, since the names of these people are preceded by the formula ‘for the memory of’, they might have been given by someone else for the memory of those whose names written on the objects. The detailed discussion of this will be made after the description of the inscriptions.

objects which were folded. These include the ewer (no. 30) and the amphora (no. 28) which were folded like a towel. The plain altar table sheets were rolled up (no. 52). The lampstands were also detached and folded (nos 47–48). The other surviving objects in the treasure were all crushed and are now in a fragmentary condition. Three of the openwork lamps were restored at Dumbarton Oaks, but still have missing fragments (nos 35, 37 and 41). The other five openwork lamps are in fragmentary condition. When all of these folded and rolled up objects are examined, they give an indication of intentional folding. The traces of nails on the altar table sheets, for example, indicate that they were removed carefully without ripping them off. They might have been folded to be put in a storage case to fit them, though there is no evidence again to explain whether these objects were buried with a storage case or buried randomly. Perhaps they were folded and rolled before being carried to wherever they were buried. Some of the objects, especially the flat ones, might have been stacked on top of one another and the others which did not fit in the bag might have been folded to create more space.

Attribution, Date and Burial

Because several of the inscriptions bear the formula 'Holy Sion', the accepted view is that these objects belonged to the Sion monastery.[10] According to the *Vita* of St Nicholas of Sion, the monastery was founded in a place that God showed Nicholas to be the counterpart of the Holy Sion in Jerusalem.[11] Based on this evidence, another view is that those who donated vessels to the Sion monastery are likely to have considered it to be the counterpart of the shrine in Holy Sion in Jerusalem. If Nicholas of Sion was a mediator between individuals and 'Holy Sion', making a donation to his monastery was perhaps seen as equal to making a donation to Holy Sion in Jerusalem.[12] It is also evidenced in the *Vita* that Nicholas 'produced many (miraculous) signs and cures for those who believed through him in Holy Sion'.[13] Therefore, the monastery which these objects were donated was very likely the monastery of Sion which was mentioned in the vita.

The most recent studies on the *Vita* of Nicholas of Sion, together with those concerning the topography of Lycia, have indicated that the monastery of Nicholas of Sion is situated in Karabel-Asarcık village.[14] The village is

10 I. Ševčenko, 'The Sion Treasure: the evidence of the inscriptions', in *Ecclesiastical Silver Plate*, ed. Boyd and Mango, 50–2; Boyd, 'A "metropolitan" treasure from a church in the provinces', 5–8.

11 Nicholas of Sion, *Βίος τοῦ Ἁγίου Νικολάου τῆς Ἁγίας Σιών*, c. 10, ed. tr. I. Ševčenko and N.P. Ševčenko, *The Life of Saint Nicholas of Sion* (Brookline, MA, 1984), 31–3.

12 Ševčenko, 'The Sion Treasure: the evidence of the inscriptions', 51.

13 Nicholas of Sion, c. 14, ed. tr. Ševčenko and Ševčenko, 35.

14 R.M. Harrison, 'Churches and chapels of central Lycia', *Anatolian Studies*, 13 (1963), 131–5. For recent topographical studies in Lycia, see M. Alkan, 'Parerga to the Stadiasmus

situated a few kilometres north of the well-known monastery of Nicholas of Myra, the modern town of Demre, and 40 km from Kumluca, where the objects were found. In the course of his topographical research, Martin Harrison discovered a monastery with a triconch church that was situated in a location possibly mentioned in the *Vita* of the saint.[15] And building on the discoveries made by Harrison, during his later topographical survey in Karabel-Asarcık village, Bülent İşler also discovered additional buildings related to monastery and created up-to-date plan of the monastery complex with its church and other buildings. According to this plan, he argues that the plan of the church and monastery complex and the site where the monastery situated correspond to the place and church mentioned in the *Vita.*[16] Within this monastery complex, there is a mausoleum and a reliquary chapel adjacent to the south side of the church which can be reached through the door inside the church. The mausoleum includes three sarcophagi while the reliquary chapel includes an altar in front of the apse, a reliquary and three sarcophagi. The reliquary has been found in situ carved into the wall of the apse in the chapel. İşler argued that one of these three sarcophagi in reliquary chapel might have belonged to Nicholas of Sion, since according to the *Vita*, Nicholas of Sion was buried in 'Holy and glorious Sion', the monastery he founded. By considering the phrase in the vita which says that Nicholas of Sion was buried in the place where the remains of holy martyrs are deposited, he also argued that the other two sarcophagi in the chapel might have been belonged to martyrs and the other one belongs to Nicholas of Sion.[17] Moreover, an inscription in the baptistery of the monastery bearing the name 'Nicholas' discovered by Harrison is also helpful to suppose that Nicholas of Sion founded the monastery here and buried in one of these sarcophagi.[18]

Since the objects that constitute the Sion Treasure were found buried on the hill of Buyuk Asar, Kumluca, 40 km from the Sion monastery, some have suggested that they might have belonged to a church in Kumluca and have

Patarensis (8): on the named places in the journeys of sacrifice recorded in the Vita of Saint Nicholas of Holy Sion', *Gephyra*, 8 (2011), 99–124.

15 Harrison, 'Churches and chapels of central Lycia', 131–5.

16 B. İşler, 'Likya bölgesi Karabel Asarcık'taki erken Bizans dönemi yerleşimi' (Unpublished PhD diss. Hacettepe University, 2009); İşler, 'Likya Bölgesi'ndeki Karabel-Asarcık yerleşimi yapılarının plan ve işlev özellikleri üzerine gözlemler', *International Young Scholars Conference I: Mediterranean Anatolia Symposium Proceedings 4–7 November 2009*, (İstanbul, 2012), 165.

17 For the sarcophagi in the mausoleum see İşler, 'Karabel Asarcık'taki Sion Manastırı mezar odası ve Bizans Lahitleri, (the burial chamber and early Byzantine sarcophagi in the Sion monastery at Karabel Asarcık)', *Seleucia*, 7 (2017), 161–82; İşler, 'Sionlu Aziz Nikolaos'un Batı Asarcık yerleşimindeki mezar yapısı', in S. Doğan and M. Kadiroğlu (ed.), *Bizans Ve Çevre Kültürler: Prof. Dr. S. Yıldız Ötüken'e Armağan* (İstanbul, 2010), 186–96. For the information on where Nicholas of Sion was buried see Nicholas of Sion, c. 80, ed.tr. Ševčenko and Ševčenko, 113.

18 Harrison, 'Churches and chapels of central Lycia', 134.

connected Holy Sion with Buyuk Asar.[19] However, there is little evidence for this, and there are no traces of a church on the hill. The inscriptions on some of the silver objects mention 'Holy Sion' but there is no church with the name 'Holy Sion' in Kumluca.[20] Since all of the silver vessels were found together, it presumably belonged to the same church, and this church might have been in the Sion Monastery. In his study, Harrison attempted to locate empirical evidence that the objects could be carried from the village of Karabel to Kumluca, noting that the track from Karabel to Kumluca takes one day to walk, and he himself travelled this road with a donkey bearing a load of at least 100 kilograms.[21] This proved that it would be entirely possible to transport the silver objects from the church in this way. He also interviewed a villager who used to travel from Karabel to the mosque in Kumluca for prayers on Fridays, departing the village on Thursday evening, and returning on Friday evening.[22] It is plausible that this track was also a viable route during the Byzantine era, and it seems likely that the Treasure was transported to Kumluca by donkey, and buried there.

The dating of the objects in the Sion Treasure is based on the silver stamps on many of the vessels and the letter forms of the inscriptions. There are twenty-four stamped objects with imperial stamps in the Treasure. All the stamps bear the monograms and busts of Justinian I and can be dated to the second half of the sixth century.[23] The date of the unstamped objects is generally felt to be the same. In addition, Ihor Ševčenko compared the writing style of the inscriptions on the silver objects with that on other treasures from the sixth century, and argued that both the ligatures and the use of certain letters, such as the style of the alpha and omega forms, are similar.[24] However, he also noted that this evidence is not sufficient for epigraphists, and that the form of the inscriptions, the date of the Sion monastery and the inscriptions bearing the name of the Holy Sion should also be considered.[25] As a result of taking all these into account, I treat all of the objects in the Sion Treasure as being from the sixth century, or the beginning of the seventh century, since there is also a possibility that some of them may have been donated to the church some years after its foundation.

19 H. Hellenkemper, 'Ecclesiastical silver hoards and their findspots: implications for the treasure found at Korydella, Lycia', in *Ecclesiastical Silver Plate*, ed. Boyd and Mango, 65–70.

20 Ševčenko, 'The Sion Treasure: the evidence of the inscriptions', 51.

21 M. Harrison, *Mountain and Plain: From the Lycian Coast to the Phrygian Plateau in the Late Roman and Early Byzantine Period* (Ann Arbor, MI, 2001), 38, note 47.

22 Harrison, *Mountain and Plain*, 38.

23 For stamps on objects, see Table 3.1 For an explanation of imperial stamps see Chapter 3. And for dating of the objects, see E.C. Dodd, 'The question of workshop: evidence of the stamps on the Sion Treasure', in *Ecclesiastical Silver Plate*, ed. Boyd and Mango, 57–64; Dodd, 'The location of silver stamping: evidence from newly discovered stamps', in *Ecclesiastical Silver Plate*, ed. Boyd and Mango, 217–24.

24 Ševčenko, 'The Sion Treasure: the evidence of the inscriptions', 39–40.

25 Ševčenko, 'The Sion Treasure: the evidence of the inscriptions', 40–1.

It is not known when the Treasure was buried. It is most likely that it was the act of monks from the church, following the Arab invasions that commenced in the second half of the seventh century. The first confrontation between the Byzantine and Arab navies that occurred near Lycia was the so-called 'Battle of the Masts', near Phoenix, Lycia, in 655 CE, in which the Byzantine fleet was defeated by the Arabs.[26] This is considered to mark the commencement of the Arab invasions of Lycia, and the defeat engendered other invasions and attacks that continued from the seventh century to the beginning of the ninth century, with the Arab fleet settling in the port of Phoenix in 715 CE, and Harun al-Rashid attacking Myra in 809 CE.[27] It has been suggested that the first Arab incursion near Phoenix Bay, which is 20 km from the Sion monastery, might have prompted the removal of important objects from the church for burial in a secure place. However, the defeat of the Byzantine fleet, and the loss of Syria and Antioch, a decade before the invasions, may also have promoted the concealment.[28] Those who buried the Sion Treasure were most plausibly those who were responsible for safe-keeping of these objects or responsible for the administration of the church and monastery property in the Sion monastery.

Since there is no specific information about when exactly the Arabs captured the city of Myra, it is also possible that the objects were buried following other attacks, and while Harrison proposed that the objects may have been buried for safekeeping after Myra was attacked by Harun al-Rashid in 809 CE, he also noted that the silver vessels could have been stolen by the Arabs and buried in Kumluca.[29] However, since the condition of the objects is good, with some rolled up intentionally, and none ripped off in removal, with even nails preserved with their objects, it is unlikely that they were buried by the Arabs. It seems likely that the Treasure was buried for safekeeping sometime before the capture of Myra, probably at some point in, or after, the end of the eighth century. If this was the case, then the objects were used between the second half of the sixth century, or the beginning of the seventh century and the end of the eighth century.

The Silver Objects from the Sion Treasure

Although the studies already carried out on the Sion silver vessels provide important information about the objects from both the Antalya Museum and the Dumbarton Oaks collections, in terms of their decoration, inscriptions, stamps, form, manufacture and donors, they do not describe the vessels in

26 C. Foss, 'The Lycian coast in the Byzantine age', *DOP*, 48 (1994), 3.

27 Theophanes, *Χρονογραφία*, ed. C. de Boor, *Theophanis Chronographia*, 1 (Leipzig, 1883), 345, 385 and 483, tr. C. Mango and R. Scott, *The Chronicle of Theophanes Confessor* (Oxford, 1997), 482, 535, 663; cited in Harrison, 'Churches and chapels of central Lycia', 121.

28 For the discussions about the Sion treasure and their find spots, see Boyd, 'A "metropolitan" treasure from a church in the provinces', 7; Hellenkemper, 'Ecclesiastical silver hoards', 68.

29 Harrison, *Mountain and Plain*, 31–40.

Antalya Museum fully. The measurements and forms of these objects, and the description of their decoration, have not previously been fully presented. This is because Susan Boyd, one of the foremost scholars of the Treasure, was never able to view the objects fully, or to examine them first hand since she did not have the opportunity to visit Antalya. Instead, Nezih Fıratlı, director of Antalya Museum in the 1990s, and Ihor Ševčenko and Erica Cruickshank Dodd, who visited Turkey, photographed the objects and sent the photographs, along with some brief information, to her. As she said herself, these photographs were not enough to correlate any fragmentary objects between Antalya and Dumbarton Oaks.[30] Consequently, a key aspect of this section is to provide detailed, comprehensive and new information about form, condition, measurements, elemental compositions and manufacturing process of the objects from both Antalya Museum and the Dumbarton Oaks collection.

My first-hand examination of the Sion Treasure silverware in the Antalya Museum and Dumbarton Oaks, which I compared with Boyd's checklist of the objects from Antalya Museum, Dumbarton Oaks, the private collection in Geneva and London and Hewett collections in London, revealed inaccuracies in Boyd's list.[31] With the help of the current archaeologists in the Antalya Museum, Fastma Nur Direr Konukman and Süleyman Atalay, I was able to connect fragments of various objects, and to reconsider the number of pieces in the collection and their measurements. As a consequence of this I have prepared a revised table of the objects in the collection, Table 1.1, at the end of this chapter. This table records the museum's accession number of each object, together with its dimensions, condition, material and form, inscription, donor and silver stamp. The fragmentary objects are also listed, together with the detached objects that it was not possible to associate with others. I have added the weights of all chalices in the Antalya Museum. In addition, I have also added the objects' thickness, in terms of the silver sheet used, and the dimensions of the inscriptions.

Information on the manufacturing process, type of decoration techniques and materials used on the objects comes from the results on the x-radiography and technical examinations done on the Antalya objects by the author and done earlier on the Dumbarton Oaks silver by Henry Lie, Richard Newman, Clifford Crane, John R. Dennis, Eugene Farrell and Pieter Meyers. Twelve objects in the Antalya collection have been analysed by XRF to see the make-up of the metal. These are two patens (nos 1 and 6), five polycandela (nos 7, 8, 10, 11, 18), one censer (no. 19), one standing lamp (no. 34), two chalices (26–27) and one amphora (29).[32] For all of the objects in Dumbarton Oaks, neutron

30 Boyd, 'A "metropolitan" Treasure', 6.

31 Boyd, 'A "metropolitan" Treasure', 19–34.

32 For this examination, a Vanta C Series model X Radiography Fluorescence Spectrometer was used. It was not applied to some fragments and altar table sheets because of unsuitable conditions and time restrictions for laboratory staff.

activation analysis has been used to look at the elemental compositions.[33] Technical studies have been applied to the eleven objects from Dumbarton Oaks by using stereo binocular microscope and XRF analysis.[34] For the Antalya objects, XRF analysis looked for elemental compositions, those used during the manufacture of the objects. For the technical examinations of Antalya objects XRF analysis showed in which parts silver soldering or gilding was used, the percentage of silver used and ancient restorations on objects. To determine how the objects were shaped and decorated, and the tools used for the production, silver expert Özgür Gemici was consulted. With the results of technical examinations and XRF analysis applied to the objects in Dumbarton Oaks and in Antalya, most of the objects from the Sion Treasure have now been analysed.[35]

To summarise the current knowledge of the Treasure resulting from this new study, I shall start with the patens, then continue with the polycandela, censers, chalices, amphorae, the ewer, standing lamps, openwork lamps (both standing and hanging lamps), the suspension bracket for hanging lamps, book covers, lamp stands and altar table sheets.

The Patens

In total, there are six patens in the Sion Treasure. Two are currently located in Antalya Museum, three in the Dumbarton Oaks collection, and one in the George Ortiz collection in Geneva. All of the patens are inscribed and one (in Antalya Museum) is stamped with imperial stamps (no. 1). Each of these six patens was produced from a single sheet of silver, by being worked on a lathe, compressing and stretching the metal with a hammer. The traces of the lathe and hammering are evident on the bottom of the objects. The patens were decorated using repoussé, chasing and engraving techniques, and although their forms are similar, they differ in their types of decoration. The centres of the patens are encircled by inscriptions, and their borders are raised from their centre. Three of the six patens were donated by bishop Eutychianos,

33 P. Meyers, 'Elemental compositions of the Sion Treasure and other Byzantine silver objects', in *Ecclesiastical Silver Plate*, ed. Boyd and Mango, 169.

34 R. Newman and H. Lie, 'The technical examination and conservation of objects in the Sion Treasure', in *Ecclesiastical Silver Plate*, ed. Boyd and Mango, 77.

35 The results of this examination will be explained while presenting each object; reports on the process and general results of the XRF examination was discussed in detail elsewhere in Turkish. See A. Arı, 'Bir hazine, beş koleksiyon: Sion (Kumluca) Hazinesi'nin toplu olarak yeniden değerlendirilmesi', in M. Demirel et al. (ed.), *Antalya Müzesi 100 Yaşında: Antalya'nın Arkeolojik Mirası*, 2 vols (Ankara, 2022), vol. 2, 124–146; see also A. ARI, 'Byzantine control stamps applied on the silver objects from the Sion Treasure', *Nevşehir Hacı Bektaş Veli Üniversitesi SBE Dergisi*, 12.1 (2022), 34–55. The XRF examination for Antalya objects has been done by Antalya Conservation and Laboratory Department. I am grateful to the director of the Antalya Museum who arranged this examination and provided space and plenty of time to examine the objects in the museum.

according to their inscriptions (nos 1, 2 and 3). They have a similar type of decoration but differ from one another in terms of the form of their decoration, and their measurements. They all have a gilded Christogram in their centre surrounded by a niello inscription and a gilded cusped border which has floral decoration.

The paten in the Antalya collection (no. 1) has an eight-armed Christogram in its centre (Figure 1.1). It measures 31.5 × 35.5 cm. This huge Christogram almost fills the centre, and is gilded, with the two gilded lines separating the niello inscription from the centre and the border. It has a cusped border, and its decoration is divided into three separate rows, with the first row after the inscriptions, and a wider space of approximately 30 mm used for the decoration. In this space, there are twenty-nine concavities decorated with vine leaves. This row is followed by one that is decorated with vine leaves, and the last is decorated with classical egg and dart motifs. The paten is 61 cm in diameter, with a foot of 1.6 cm in diameter, and it weighs 5,400 grams. There are six stamps applied on the bottom of the paten. There is a crack on its rim which extends about 30 mm inside. The object is 5 cm high from the bottom. The thickness of the rim is 2 mm and the thickness of the body is 4 mm.

The Geneva paten has a six-armed Christogram at its centre (no. 2), smaller than that on the Antalya paten (no. 1). This Christogram is encircled by a bordered niello inscription, which is identical to the inscription on the Antalya paten (no. 1), although Boyd suggested that the style of the inscription is different, because there is an abbreviation on one of the letters from *θεῷ* to *θῷ*.[36] The Geneva paten also has a cusped border divided into three rows of decoration, commencing with leaves that alternate with 'Sasanian palmettes', filling twenty-six concavities, followed by vine leaves, and finally egg and dart motifs. It is 73.5 cm in diameter, which makes it bigger than the other two patens with Christograms in the centre.[37]

The Dumbarton Oaks paten (no. 3, Figure 1.2) also has a six-armed Christogram at its centre and is surrounded by a niello inscription. The style of the inscription is similar to that of the paten in the Antalya collection, with a cusped border decorated with leaves, alternating with Sasanian palmettes, filling twenty-four concavities, surrounded by leaves, and egg and dart motifs. This paten weights 5,200 grams, and measures 60.5 cm in diameter, which is very similar to the Antalya paten. But it differs from the Antalya paten in terms of the measurements of the Christogram and the decoration on its rim. The Antalya paten is decorated on obverse and reverse only with vine leaves,

36 For this and discussion of patens also see Boyd, 'A "metropolitan" treasure', 14.

37 For the paten in the George Ortiz collection in Geneva see Martiniani-Reber, ed., *Byzance en Suisse*, no. 10, http://institutions.ville-geneve.ch/fileadmin/user_upload/mah/documents/Expositions/2015/Byzance_Visuels-exposition.pdf (accessed 27 March 2023), Paten no. 10, Inv. Ortiz_257. See also the website of George Ortiz collection, https://www.georgeortiz.com/objects/byzantine/257-large-paten-with-engraved-chrismon/ (accessed 27 March 2023).

while the other two are decorated with Sasanian palmettes. The Dumbarton Oaks object is 2 mm thick in its rim and its body 4 mm. The height of the letters varies between 17 and 18 mm.

The other three patens, two of which are in the Dumbarton Oaks collection (nos 4 and 5), and one in Antalya Museum (no. 6), all have a gilded cross at their centre, surrounded by a nielloed inscription. The Dumbarton Oaks patens have identical decoration, with gilded crosses and gilded fluted borders. Paten no. 4 (Figure 1.3) measures 58 cm in diameter, and weighs 4,537 grams, and paten no. 5 (Figure 1.4) is displayed with an asterisk and measures 58.5 cm in diameter, and weighs 4,234 grams. According to its inscription, paten no. 4 was donated in memory of Angeleuos Roufinos, while no. 5 was donated in memory of John. Both are 2 mm thick in their rim and 4 mm in their body. The height of the letters varies between 16 and 17 mm.

These patens (nos 4 and 5), in Dumbarton Oaks, have weight marks on their bottom that differ from their actual weights, which might be because of a loss of weight during their manufacture. The marks might have been applied when the silver was in the form of bullion and then the object might have been shaped. The progress of shaping the object might cause the difference between the weight of silver bullion and the object produced from it. When the decoration was applied to the object, it might also have made the object lose its original weight, because decoration of the paten includes engraving. For example, the fluted border and cross were made by using engraving techniques.

The Antalya paten (no. 6, Figure 1.5) also has a gilded cross at its centre, surrounded by an engraved inscription, and gilded bands. There is no decoration other than the large cross. An engraved technique was employed for the inscription in which the abbreviation was also used, and its plain decoration makes this paten distinct from the others. It measures 77.5 cm in diameter, and weight 8,000 grams. The height of the letters on this paten varies between 25 and 26 mm. The object is 8 cm high from the bottom, and its thickness is 3 mm in rim and 6 mm in body.

When it comes to elemental composition of silver used in the manufacture of these objects, the two patens from Antalya show similar results. In the case of no. 1, eighteen stations were examined on this object: gilded surfaces, deformed surfaces and undamaged surfaces. Gilded surfaces mostly present the highest percentage of gold and mercury. Station 1 is from the gilded arm of the Christogram. It indicates a mix of 42.93% gold, 32.87% silver, 12.18% mercury and 9.392% iron. We came across iron on all surfaces. The purest silver is from the stations on the reverse of the object with 88.722% silver, 9.091% iron and 1.12% gold.[38] The nielloed letters show a high percentage of copper: 63.323%

38 The surfaces which gave the highest percentages of silver were the undamaged surfaces. The examination which made for Antalya objects was not only from one station, we categorised the stations according to the condition of the surfaces to receive reliable results. Even though

silver, 23.754% copper, 9.516% iron and 1.2% lead. No. 6 has similar percentages in terms of silver percentage in undamaged and ungilded surfaces. On the reverse of the object one surface presents 89.392% silver, 9.144% iron. On the gilded surface, for example the surface on the arm of the cross, 48.94% gold, 33.06% silver, 9.664% iron and 5.69% mercury are found.

Examination for elemental composition for the Dumbarton Oaks patens reveals the different percentage of silver. The samples, taken from the exterior of the patens, are between 95.1% and 96.3%, copper is between 3.10% and 4.21%, and gold is between 0.594% and 0.649%.[39]

Polycandela

In total, the Sion Treasure includes twelve polycandela, each of which was produced from a single sheet of silver, shaped by hammering and decorated using openwork and engraving. All of them were burnished after the shaping and decorating stages. They share a similar type of decoration. In form, three of the polycandela are cruciform (nos 7, 8 and 9), three are circular (nos 10, 11 and 12) and six are rectangular (nos 13, 14, 15, 16, 17 and 18). All twelve of the polycandela have an inscription and a monogram identifying their donor as Eutychianos the bishop (ƐΠΙCΚΟΠΟΥ), and all of them bear imperial stamps.

The three cruciform polycandela, two of which are in Antalya Museum (nos 7 and 8), and one in the Dumbarton Oaks collection (no. 9), are identical in shape and decoration (Figures 1.6–1.8). These three are in the form of a cross, with arms of equal length, designed to hold twelve lamps, with three holes in each arm. The donors' monograms are at the centre of the polycandela and are surrounded by niello inscriptions. Dolphins flank the centre and connect the openwork arms and the centre. Their eyes and the side fins are decorated with chased and engraved lines, and their tails connect to fleurs-de-lys at the centre. The three lamp holes on each arm are supported by dolphins and palmette motifs and culminate with the fleurs-de-lys. Each of the four suspension loops is attached by two rivets on the upper side of the end of each cross arm. The location of the stamps on the polycandela differs; while no. 7 (Figure 1.6) has five imperial stamps surrounding its centre, between the dolphins, the stamps on nos 8 and 9 (Figures 1.7 and 1.8) are located one on each arm, between the rivets, with one more at the centre, between the tails of the dolphins. On one of these

the other surfaces in Dumbarton Oaks objects were examined, only the surfaces which gave higher percentage of silver is shared in the table. See Meyers, 'Elemental Compositions', 169.

39 Objects analysed by Pieter Meyers in or around 1980s by using neutron activation analysis show different results from the results we reached in Antalya. This might be because of the methods used. Neutron activation analysis could not analyse the lead, which appears in Antalya patens at about 1%. They might have also not seen the percentage of copper and iron correctly. See Meyers, 'Elemental compositions', 169, especially Table 1.1, nos 2–4. And for the detailed explanation on the neutron activation analysis, see Newman and Lie, 'The technical examination', 78.

three polycandela, there is also evidence of ancient silver soldered repairs (no. 7, Figure 1.6). In addition, the monograms of Eutychianos on the polycandela are slightly different in their style of script.[40] These polycandela are identical in terms of their weight and measurements: each is 57 cm in diameter, and weighs 2,800 grams. The silver is 3 mm thick at the centre of each, and the height of the letters in the inscriptions on each is 11 mm.

Two of these polycandela which are preserved in Antalya Museum were examined for their elemental compositions. Eighteen stations were beamed to examine no. 7. They present different percentages. The highest percentage of silver is again from the undamaged surface. Some surfaces were deformed and turned black. There are also ancient restorations where a high amount of copper was used. The results from the surface which shows the highest percentage of silver are 88.362% silver, 9.2% iron, 1% copper and 1% gold. On the surface with ancient repairs the results are 64.19% silver, 16.43% copper, 9.26% iron, 9% zinc. Seventeen stations were beamed to examine polycandela no. 8. The highest percentage of silver is from the reverse of the object with 88.695% silver, 9.168% iron. There are no ancient repairs on this object, so the results are not dramatically different. The lowest amount of silver is from the surface which its colour is darker than the other surfaces, the results are 84.232% silver, 9.119% iron, 4.248% copper and 1.043% lead. The cruciform polycandelon in Dumbarton Oaks again shows different results from the Antalya ones. As with patens, results show that 96.9% silver, 2.57% copper and 0.678% gold were detected in the polycandelon.

The three circular polycandela are also identical in shape and decoration. Two of the circular polycandela are in Antalya Museum (nos 10 and 11, Figures 1.9 and 1.10), and one is in the Dumbarton Oaks collection (no. 12, Figure 1.11). Each of these three was also produced from one single sheet of silver, and shaped by hammering, with engraving and openwork techniques employed for decoration. These polycandela were designed to hold sixteen lamps. There are rivets for loops on the back of each to enable them to be hung. Each bears imperial stamps, and in the centre of each is a cross, the arms of which terminate in four open circles to hold the lamps. These circles are flanked by dolphins, in the same form of decoration as on the cruciform polycandela: the tail of each dolphin connects with that of the other dolphins, and a fleur-de-lys motif. The dolphins face vegetal scrolls surrounding the openwork monograms of 'Eutychianos Episcopos, ЄΥΤΥΧΙΑΝΟΥ ЄΠΙϹΚΟΠΟΥ'. The centre is enclosed by an openwork border, with a niello inscription. The stamps on these polycandela are identical to the stamps on the cruciform polycandela. These circular polycandela are 56 cm in diameter, and each weighs 3,500 grams. The thickness of each varies from 4 to 5 mm, and the height of the letters is 11 mm.

40 Boyd also mentioned this difference, see Boyd, 'A "metropolitan" treasure', 10. Bouras also described one of these polycandela, see M.G. Parani and L. Bouras, *Lighting in Early Byzantium* (Washington, DC, 2008), 88.

Nos 10 and 11 were examined for evidence of their elemental composition. Fifteen stations were beamed to examine no. 10. The results did not change dramatically. Only the darker surfaces show 85.34% silver, 9.091% iron, 2.284% copper, 1.7% lead and 1.034% gold. The highest amount of silver in this object is 86.683% silver, this is followed by 9.111% iron, 1.934% copper and 1.234% lead. Similar results can be seen in no. 11. In total, fourteen stations were beamed to examine this object. The highest amount of silver is 87.902% and this is followed by 9.205% iron and 1.443% copper. The darker surfaces show a lower percentage of silver. For example, on station 13, the results are 84.232% silver, 9.119% iron, 4.248% copper and 1.043% lead. The nielloed letters were also examined, for example, the nielloed letter I presents 76.879% silver, 12.202% copper and 9.594% iron. According to the results of examinations made in Dumbarton Oaks, the percentage of silver in the reverse of the circular polycandelon (no. 12) is 96.5%, copper 3.02% and gold 0.452%.[41]

The remaining six polycandela are all rectangular in shape, and only survive as fragments, with the exception of that in the Dumbarton Oaks collection (no. 13), and exist only as, for example, centre or end pieces. These fragments are divided between the Dumbarton Oaks Collection and Antalya Museum. Table 1.1 explains this further, and details which pieces belong to which object (nos 14, 15, 16, 17 and 18). Despite their fragmentary condition, it is possible to recreate their decoration.

All of these polycandela were shaped from single sheets of silver and shaped by hammering, with engraving and openwork techniques employed for decoration. There are openwork monograms of Eutychianos on the centre of each polycandelon that are encircled by niello inscriptions. They have a central rectangle and this rectangle is stepped up to the two rectangular lateral rims on the sides and the end pieces. These objects have two different shapes and forms of decoration: two have tri-lobed end pieces and fourteen holes for lamps, of those eight on the lateral rims (four on each) and six on the end pieces (three on each) (nos 13 and 14), while the other four were designed with semi-circular end pieces and have twelve holes for lamps, of those eight are on the lateral rims (four on each) and four on the end pieces (two on each) (nos 15, 16, 17 and 18).

The central rectangle of each polycandelon with tri-lobed end pieces is decorated with two pairs of dolphins and heart motifs between each pair, flanking the monogram of Eutychianos surrounded by a niello inscription (nos 13 and 14, Figures 1.12 and 1.13). The central rectangle is connected to lateral rims and tri-lobed end pieces via an openwork band. Each of the lateral rims has holes to hold lamps and each hole is flanked by openwork palmette motifs. And the holes in the tri-lobed end pieces were also flanked by paired dolphins and hearts. Both polycandela have imperial stamps with same names and monograms. Loops are riveted to each corner, with stamps near

41 Meyers, 'Elemental compositions', Table 1.1, no. 6.

each of them. No. 13 was restored and it is in good condition while no. 14 has six detached pieces. Therefore, it is only possible to calculate the weight and measurements of one polycandelon correctly (no. 13), which is 57 cm in length, 37 cm in width and weighs 2,647 grams. No. 14 has fragments in both Antalya Museum and Dumbarton Oaks Collection, its weight in total, including Antalya fragments, is 2,562.5 grams, which is close to the weight of no. 13. It is possible that this difference is due to the small fragments which have not survived. The thickness of these rectangular polycandela is also similar: it varies between 2 and 4 mm, with the height of the letters being 21 mm.

The other four rectangular polycandela with semi-circular end pieces have two different kinds of decoration. On the central rectangle of those two there are also two pairs of dolphins and hearts between each pair flanking the monograms surrounded by niello inscription (nos 15 and 16, Figures 1.14 and 1.15). The only difference from the previous polycandela with tri-lobed end pieces is that the central rectangle of each polycandelon is stepped up to the semi-circular end piece on which there is a floral motif surrounded by two holes for lamps. These two polycandela only survive in fragments. No. 15 has nine detached pieces; central rectangle, two semi-circular end pieces and six fragments of lateral rim. This polycandelon is 47 cm in length, 29 cm in width, and in total it weighs 2,098 grams. No. 16 has four detached pieces: a central rectangle, two fragments of lateral rim and one semi-circular end piece. The other parts are missing. Because of these missing fragments the measurements are different from the other rectangular polycandela. Its length is 27.5 cm, and width is 20 cm. and it weighs 981 grams.

Another two rectangular polycandela with semi-circular end pieces have a different type of decoration than the other four rectangular polycandela. On the centre rectangle of these, the monograms of Eutychianos and the inscriptions are surrounded by palmette and fleur-de-lys motifs, in a foliate design (nos 17 and 18, Figures 1.16 and 1.17a–1.17b). The other parts and the form of the objects are similar to the other rectangular polycandela. No. 17 has nine detached pieces and most of the fragments are preserved in Dumbarton Oaks. They are the central rectangle, one semi-circular end piece, five fragments of another semi-circular end piece, and two lateral rims. One lateral rim is now preserved in Antalya Museum. Its length is 42.5 cm, width 26.4 cm and it weighs 1,759 grams. No. 18 has two detached pieces. Fragment with one semi-circular end piece, central rectangular and two lateral rims is preserved in Antalya Museum (Figure 1.17a) while the other semi-circular end piece is preserved in Dumbarton Oaks (Figure 1.17b). Its length is 37 cm, width 21 cm, and it weighs 1,200 grams.

Among the rectangular polycandela, no. 18 underwent XRF examination for elemental composition. Only four stations were beamed to examine this object because of its fragile condition. The results show 86.366% silver, 9.151% iron, 2.691% copper as the highest silver content. There is not too much difference between the results from these stations. Only the surface with a darker colour presents 79.01% silver, 9.823% iron and 9.835% copper.

Five other rectangular polycandela underwent elemental analysis in Dumbarton Oaks. The percentages of elements in these polycandela are really close. Results show that the percentage of silver is between 96.9% and 97.5%, copper is between 2.03% and 2.33, gold is between 0.496% and 0.634%.

These polycandela were designed in a similar form and decorated with similar motifs. All of them are inscribed, and all bear the monograms of their donor. Nevertheless, despite the apparently identical form and dimensions of the three cruciform polycandela, or the three circular polycandela, there are differences between them, like the lettering of the monograms, and the location of their silver stamps.[42] And the stamps which were applied on the rectangular polycandela with semi-circular end pieces are different from the ones applied on the other polycandela.[43]

Censers

The Sion Treasure includes two censers, one of which is in Antalya Museum (no. 19), and the other in the Dumbarton Oaks collection (no. 20). They have not previously been discussed in any detail. Both of the censers were produced by casting them in a mould, and both are decorated using repoussé, chasing and silver soldering techniques. These objects were also donated by bishop Eutychianos. The Antalya censer (no. 19, Figure 1.18a–1.18b) is circular in shape, and is attached to its chain by three hooks that are silver soldered to the rim of the censer. The body of the censer rests on a ring-shaped foot that is 11.5 cm in diameter. There are three lines of decoration on this censer, the first of which, at the bottom, is decorated with ribbing-type decoration with stylised eggs and fleurs-de-lys. In the centre, there are five scenes from the life of the Virgin, namely the Annunciation, the Trial by Water, the Visitation, the Journey to Bethlehem and the Nativity. The scenes start with the Annunciation. On the Annunciation scene, we can see the Virgin and the archangel. The figures and draperies are in relief; faces and other parts are engraved. We can see detailed work on the draperies and fingers in all scenes especially in the fingers of the archangel. This scene is followed by the Trial by Water: the Virgin is tested by bitter water as proof of her virginity; in this scene we see her drinking water from the cup held by Zachariah. The following scene is the Visitation, in which we see Elizabeth and the Virgin embracing. This scene is followed by the Journey to Bethlehem in which the Virgin is sitting on the donkey, depicted as pregnant. On the front, Joseph is leading the donkey and, on the back, there is an angel accompanying them. The final scene is the Nativity. This scene is given in four separate parts, perhaps because of the space required. In the beginning of the scene, Joseph is sitting on a rock in front of the building. Next to him, the Virgin is lying down, the washing

42 For the discussion of the lettering of monograms see Boyd, 'A "metropolitan" treasure', 10.
43 For detailed discussion see Chapter 3 on stamps.

of Christ by servants is depicted and this is followed by the part depicting Christ in the middle with donkey and ox. One of the Wise Men points to the star which is above Christ and a shepherd looks up, possibly at the angel announcing to him the birth of Christ (Figure 1.18b).

The final level of decoration is a niello inscription surrounding the rim. This object is 17 cm in diameter, 11.6 cm in high and weighs 1,520 grams. The thickness of the censer is 7 mm, and the height of the letters is 9 mm.

The censer in Antalya Museum underwent XRF examination for elemental composition. Eight stations were beamed to examine this object. The results are 89.07% silver and 9.189% iron. These results are taken from an ungilded and undamaged surface on the bottom of the object. Gilded surfaces show a high percentage of gold. For example, the fourth and fifth stations are from the gilded surfaces where the figures from the life of the Virgin are depicted. The results from the fourth station are 65.05% gold, 22.362% silver and 9.209% iron. The results from the fifth station are 48.65% gold, 34.96% silver, 9.210% iron and 4.13% mercury. The results from the gilded surfaces show that the percentage of mercury is less than the percentage of mercury from the gilded surfaces of patens. The mercury might have evaporated. The eighth station is from the hook for attaching the chain on the rim of the object. The results are 89.506% silver and 9.244% iron. This shows the highest percentage of silver found among the objects preserved in Antalya Museum.

The Dumbarton Oaks censer (no. 20, Figure 1.19a) is decorated with figural, animal and vegetal motifs,[44] and is hexagonal in shape, and supported by three standing peacocks. Like the censer in Antalya Museum, the niello inscription encircles the rim of the censer. In the middle register are medallions of figures of Christ, St Paul and St Peter, separated by peacocks. These medallions are encircled by vegetal motifs, and are flanked by palmette motifs, and the tails of standing peacocks that are attached to the body of the censer using silver soldering. The object has three feet in the form of peacock feet and at the bottom of the censer, these feet are supported by dolphins functioning as a bridge between the foot and the base (Figure 1.19b). This object is 15 cm high, 20.2 cm in diameter and weighs 1,725 grams. The height of the letters varies from 5 to 6 mm. Both are stamped with five similar imperial stamps. The elemental composition of this censer is 97.1% silver, 2.31% copper and 0.569% gold.[45]

Chalices

There are seven chalices in the Sion Treasure (nos 21, 22, 23, 24, 25, 26 and 27), four of which are inscribed, and provide important examples of inscriptions without the names of their donors. Most of the seven survive

44 Boyd, 'A "metropolitan" treasure', cat. no. 18.
45 Meyers, 'Elemental compositions', Table 1.1, no. 51.

only as bowls, detached from their bases. There are also five detached chalice bases but it is not possible to marry these bases with surviving bowls. The bowl and foot of each chalice were produced from a single sheet of silver and attached together by silver soldering. In the case of no. 21 (Figure 1.20), in the Dumbarton Oaks collection, only the crushed bowl of the chalice is preserved. It is not decorated and inscribed. This chalice weighs 273 grams. And in the case of no. 22 (Figure 1.21), which is also in the Dumbarton Oaks collection, again, only the flattened bowl is preserved, and there is an engraved inscription and zigzag letters between the engraved bands encircling the rim. This chalice measures 22.5 cm in diameter and weighs 222 grams. The bowl was produced from a single sheet of silver and was burnished following its completion. Meanwhile, the bowl of chalice no. 23 (Figure 1.22), which is also in the Dumbarton Oaks collection, is preserved together with the knob of the foot. Its diameter is 17 cm, and its weight is 341 grams. It has a hemispherical body and was produced from a single sheet of silver. There is an engraved inscription encircling its rim. In the case of no. 24 (Figure 1.23), which is in the Dumbarton Oaks collection, only the broad bowl is preserved; it is not inscribed, but there are two engraved crosses on its body, and two gilded bands encircling the rim. Meanwhile, chalice no. 25 (Figure 1.24) is in Antalya Museum, and only its body survives. This was also produced from a single sheet of silver. Its foot might have been attached using silver soldering, as evidenced by the traces of silver solder on the bottom of the bowl. It has a *pointillé* inscription, and is 9.5 cm high, 16 cm in diameter and weighs 500 grams. The thickness of the rim is 2 mm and of the body 0.5 mm. Chalice no. 26 (Figure 1.25) is also in Antalya Museum. Again, only the bowl is preserved. It has gilded bands encircling the rim with an engraved inscription. The base of the bowl is also detached, but can be completed with the survived piece of the base. On this base, there is a trace of silver soldering which indicates the foot attached to it. The thickness of the rim is 4 mm, and the thickness of the body is 1 mm. There are two engraved and gilded crosses on its body, and it measures 14 cm in height, 22.5 cm in diameter and weights 930 grams. The seventh chalice (no. 27, Figure 1.26), is also in Antalya Museum. It is complete, with a broad bowl and a conical foot. This bowl was produced from a single sheet of silver, with its foot attached using silver soldering. The chalice is not inscribed. Two gilded bands encircle its rim, and there are two gilded crosses on its body. It measures 32.5 cm in height, 22.5 cm in diameter and weighs 1,040 grams. This chalice was not examined by Dumbarton Oaks scholars and was not presented in Susan Boyd's checklist. The thickness of the rim is 4 mm and the thickness of the body is 1 mm.

Two chalices from Antalya Museum were examined for their elemental compositions. For no. 26, only surfaces on the bottom of the bowl, which is detached, were beamed. The highest amount of silver on this object is 87.762% and this followed by 9.091% iron and 1.471% copper on the same surface. On the silver soldering part where the foot and body attached, the results show 83.65% silver, 9.152% iron, 2.798% lead and 1.960% copper.

The other chalice is no. 27; eight stations on this object were beamed. The highest amount of silver in this object is 87.70% silver, with 9.123% iron and 1.753% copper. On the surface from the gilded cross, the results are 47.89% gold, 28.23% silver, 11.98% mercury and 9.263% iron. The reading from the station at the silver solder, which might be modern restoration, shows 67.003% silver, 17.011% copper, 6.062% zinc and 9.215% iron.

The percentages of elements in chalices preserved in Dumbarton Oaks are 92.5–94.6% silver, 4.64–6.79% copper, 0.613–0.747% gold.[46]

Amphorae

There are two amphorae in the Sion Treasure: one is preserved in the Dumbarton Oaks collection (no. 28, Figure 1.27), and the other is preserved in Antalya Museum (no. 29, Figure 1.28). Both were also donated by bishop Eutychianos. The amphora in Dumbarton Oaks is crushed and folded, with the rim detached from the body of the amphora. It has a fluted neck and is decorated with a band of palmettes below this, with a niello inscription encircling the body. The decoration is engraved, and the amphora bears five imperial stamps. It is 32 cm in height and weighs 2,954 grams. The thickness of the rim is 2 mm, body 1 mm and foot 4 mm. The height of the letters is 15 mm. The percentage of silver in this amphora is 97%, of copper is 2.30% and of gold is 0.690%.[47]

According to Boyd, this amphora has two detached handles, also part of the Dumbarton Oaks collection. However, there are no traces of the handles on the body of this object. If it had handles, there should be traces on the body or rim indicating that something had become detached. Further, the forms of the handles do not fit the body of the amphora, since they seem relatively small for the amphora. Presumably the handles must belong to another vessel – one which has not survived, or which is unknown to us. The amphora in Dumbarton Oaks Collection is, in form and decoration, identical to the amphora which is preserved in Antalya Museum. This amphora does not have handles or any traces indicating it had handles; this also enables me to argue that the amphora in DO also did not have handles.[48]

The second amphora, which was not presented in detail in previous publications, has the same niello inscription and foliate design decoration (no. 29, Figure 1.28). It is in a fragmentary condition, with the body, a fragment completing the body with niello inscription and a rim fragment in Antalya Museum, and a fragments of the base and fluted rim are possibly in the London Hewett collection.[49] It is unknown if this object was stamped because of the missing fragments of the bottom. It is 30 cm in height and

46 Meyers, 'Elemental compositions', Table 1.1, nos 29–32.

47 Meyers, 'Elemental compositions', Table 1.1, no. 52.

48 See also Boyd, 'A "metropolitan" treasure', cat. no. 15.

49 I was not able to track down the fragment in Hewett collection. For this information see Boyd, 'A "metropolitan" treasure', cat. no. 16 and 16a.

weighs 1,350 grams. The thickness of the rim is 2 mm, body 1 mm and foot 4 mm. The height of the letters of the inscription is 15 mm.

The amphora from Antalya Museum underwent XRF examination for elemental composition. Six stations were beamed. The highest percentage of silver is from the undamaged surface. The results are 87.773% silver, 9.161% iron and 1.333% copper. One example is also taken from the niello inscription, but the niello has almost disappeared. The results are 85.94% silver, 9.427% iron and 2.377% copper.

Ewer

There is one ewer in the Sion Treasure that is now in the Dumbarton Oaks collection (no. 30, Figure 1.29). It has a gilded repoussé decoration, is not inscribed, and is crushed and folded. As I explained in the introduction, the folding of the object indicates that it was folded intentionally, like folding a towel. It is 36 cm in height and weighs 822 grams.[50] The percentage of silver in this ewer is 97.4%, of copper is 1.96% and of gold is 0.665%.[51]

Standing Lamps

There are four standing lamps in the Sion Treasure, three of which are in the Dumbarton Oaks collection (nos 31, 32 and 33), and one in Antalya Museum (no. 34). Lamps (nos 31 and 32, Figures 1.30 and 1.31) were flattened and rolled up. They are all similar in form, shape and decoration, and their niello inscriptions are identical. Lamp (no. 31) weighs 1170 g, and no. 32 weighs 1,291 grams.

Lamp no. 33 (Figure 1.32) is in good condition. It was shaped from a single sheet of silver using hammering, and has a cup-shaped body, and a ring foot. It is not clear whether the ring foot was attached later by silver soldering, or whether the foot and body were shaped together.[52] It bears the same inscription as the standing lamps (nos 31 and 32). The niello inscription encircles the rim, and there are two engraved crosses on its body. It measures 18.5 cm in height, with a 17.2-cm rim diameter, and an 18.4-cm ring foot diameter. It weighs 1,150 grams and bears five imperial stamps. The percentage of silver in these standing lamps varies between 96.5% and 99.7%, of copper is 0.142–2.83% and of gold is 0.166–0.710%. The 99.7% of silver in nos 32–33 is the highest percentage of silver used in any of the objects in the Sion Treasure.[53]

Lamp no. 34 (Figure 1.33), which is in Antalya Museum, is identical in every way to the others, in terms of its decoration, form and inscription, although the foot and body of this object are separated from one another.

50 Boyd, 'A "metropolitan" treasure', cat. no. 17.
51 Meyers, 'Elemental compositions', Table 1.1, no. 53.
52 Newman and Lie, 'The technical examination', 82.
53 Meyers, 'Elemental compositions', Table 1.1, nos 26–8.

The foot of this object was not presented in Boyd's checklist and its measurements were not considered. The foot is on display in Antalya Museum and the body is in storage. When I examined these two fragments, I was able to find its foot and measure the object as complete. The height of the body is 18.5 cm and 17.5 cm in diameter, the foot 10 cm. They weigh 1200 g in total. The thickness of the rim is 4 mm, the body is 1 mm and the foot is 2 mm. The height of the letters is 11 mm. These measurements are the same as in other standing lamps in Dumbarton Oaks. There are traces of silver soldering on the foot which might indicate that the foot and body of the object are silver soldered together. This might also suggest that the other standing lamps were made in the same way as the Antalya object.

No. 34 was examined for its elemental composition. Since it was separated from its foot, the foot and body were examined separately. Four stations were beamed to examine the foot. Except for one station, the stations showed close results. The first station was from the surface with a dark colour, which is from the bottom. It shows 56.87% silver, 20.503% lead, 9.679% tin, 9.208% iron and 2.291% copper. The highest percentage of silver is 87.637% silver, and this is followed by 9.142% iron and 1.621% copper. For the examination of the body of the object, five stations were beamed. The highest amount of silver is from an undamaged surface; the results are 89.917% silver and 9.402% iron. This is one of the highest silver results from the objects we examined. On the Dumbarton Oaks standing lamp Meyers found 99.7% of silver. This might be due to the different methods and machines used. Some machines only focus on the silver and other primary materials, such as gold and copper. It might not have recognised iron.

Openwork Lamps (Both Standing and Hanging Lamps)

There are eight openwork lamps in the Sion Treasure, seven of which are in the Dumbarton Oaks collection, and one in the Digby-Jones collection in London (no. 38).[54] These objects have both feet and loops on the rim for chains, and therefore may have been used as both standing and hanging lamps. They were originally designed to hold glass lamps. There are different styles of decoration on these objects; inverted hearts, scales and triangles, diaper patterns with convex petals, openwork architectural design and bisected scale design, and two types of inscription: niello and openwork. All of them are decorated using openwork. The inscription on one of the lamps is illegible (no. 42). Six of the lamps are stamped with imperial stamps.

54 This lamp which according to Boyd was from Digby-Jones collection. Boyd did not give any detail about these collections, so it is hard to know whose collection they are. The Digby-Jones collection probably belonged to Kenelm Digby-Jones whose collection can be seen in many museums around the world, but I have been unable to track the openwork lamp. Therefore, the information gained about this object is from the article published by Boyd. See S. Boyd, 'A bishop's gift', 193, no. 4.

Lamp no. 35 has a hemispherical bowl, a baluster foot and a plain rim that thickens at the top. There is no indication of how the foot was attached to the body.[55] The loops are attached to the rim using silver soldering, and the plain rim is encircled with a niello inscription, in which the letters epsilon and omega are decorated with crosses.[56] The body of the lamp is decorated with inverted hearts. It measures 15.5 cm in height, with a rim diameter of 18 cm, foot diameter of 6 cm and weighs 663 grams. The rim is 3 mm thick (Figure 1.34).

Lamp no. 36 survives in a fragmentary state but bears the same inscription as lamp no. 35. Its form and decoration are also similar which can be understood from the fragments of the body of the object. The rim, some fragments and the foot of this object are in Dumbarton Oaks, parts of the rim and body fragments are in the Antalya Museum and one rim fragment is in the Hewett collection in London (Figure 1.35).[57]

Lamp no. 37 has a hemispherical body, and a stemmed baluster foot, which is longer than the feet of the other openwork lamps. The niello inscription is identical to that of the previous lamps, but the lettering is different, as the omega and epsilon are not decorated with crosses,[58] and at 2.1 cm, the letters are taller than those on the previous two lamps, which are only 1.1 cm tall. The rim of the lamp is not plain like the previous two, and projects outward, while the body is decorated with openwork scales, alternating with triangles. The lamp is 17 cm tall, with a rim diameter of 21 cm, and a foot diameter of 7 cm, and it weighs 1,112 grams. The rim thickness is 3 mm (Figure 1.36).

Lamp no. 38, which is in the Digby-Jones Collection in London, has a plain rim, a hemispherical bowl, and a baluster foot. Its niello inscription encircles the rim, and its bowl is decorated with an openwork bisected scale design. It is 10.5 cm tall, with a rim diameter of 14.3 cm. Its weight is unknown. In design and shape, it resembles lamps nos 35, 36 and 37, but the decoration is different.[59]

Lamp no. 39 has a different decoration and shape, and a different inscription from the other lamps, and is in a fragmentary condition, with the body, rim and foot detached from one another. It has a hemispherical body, a hexagonal rim and a baluster foot. A niello inscription encircles the rim, and the body is decorated with openwork 'diaper patterns' and convex petals.[60] The lamp is 11.4 cm tall, with a rim and flange diameter of 21.4 cm,

55 Newman and Lie, 'The technical examination', 83.
56 Boyd, 'A bishop's gift', 192, no. 1.
57 As in the openwork lamp, I was not able to track down the fragment in Hewett collection. For this information see Boyd, 'A bishop's gift', 192, no. 2.
58 Boyd, 'A bishop's gift', 193, no. 3.
59 Boyd, 'A bishop's gift', 193, no. 4.
60 Boyd, 'A bishop's gift', 194.

and a foot diameter of 6 cm and weighs 566 grams. The height of letters varies between 1 and 1.2 cm, and the rim thickness is 3 mm (Figure 1.37).

Lamp no. 40 is of a similar shape and decoration to no. 39, although its inscription cites a different person, 'Himeria'. It is also in fragmentary condition. It is possible to complete its rim with the rim fragment held in the Hewett collection in London.[61] Although it is not possible to determine its height, because of missing fragments, the diameter of the rim and flanges is 22.4 cm, and its weight is 565 g (Figure 1.38).

Lamp no. 41 has a cylinder-shaped body, its openwork decoration consists of a colonnade and arcades, and it is inscribed with an openwork style inscription. Its rim diameter is 15.5 cm, it weighs 480 g, and the height of the letters in the inscription is 1.2 cm (Figure 1.39).

Lamp no. 42 is of a similar shape and style of decoration, but is crushed, folded, and in multiple fragments, which in total weigh 231.7 g (Figure 1.40).

The openwork lamps in Dumbarton Oaks were tested for their elemental composition. The percentage of silver in these lamps varies between 96.7% and 98%; the copper content is 1.81–2.65%, and gold is 0.162–0.444%.[62]

Five of these lamps were donated by bishop Eutychianos, and the other two were donated in memory of Himeria and Eutychianos, though this Eutychianos is not called 'bishop'. They represent three different types of form and four different types of openwork decoration. Four of the lamps are in the shape of a hemispherical bowl, with a squat-stemmed foot. Two of these are decorated with inverted hearts (nos 35 and 36), while the other two are decorated with scales and triangles (nos 37 and 38). Two of the lamps (nos 39 and 40) have a hemispherical body, and a hexagonal rim decorated with six flanges in a triangle form. The body of these lamps is decorated with openwork 'diaper patterns'.[63] The other two lamps (nos 41 and 42) are cylindrical in shape and are decorated with an architectural design; their inscriptions are also in an openwork style.

Suspension Bracket for Hanging Lamps

This bracket is in the Dumbarton Oaks collection (no. 43). It is in the shape of a cross, with one vertical, and four horizontal crossed arms. It can be hung using the bracket on the top of the vertical arm. Each arm has a bracket for suspending lamps, five in total. The reverse and the obverse of the arms are inscribed with niello inscriptions (Figure 1.41). This bracket was also donated by bishop Eutychianos. The percentage of silver in this object is 97%, of copper is 2.37% and of gold is 0.590%.[64]

61 Boyd, 'A bishop's gift', 194, no 8.
62 Meyers, 'Elemental compositions', Table 1.1, nos 12–20.
63 Boyd, 'A bishop's gift', 194.
64 Meyers, 'Elemental compositions', Table 1.1, no. 21.

Book Covers

There are three pairs of book covers from the Sion Treasure. Two of them are in the Dumbarton Oaks collection, one of which is decorated with a cross and geometric motifs (no. 44), while the decoration of the other is figurative (no. 45). Meanwhile, Antalya Museum has small fragments of one book cover that complete the figurative cover in the Dumbarton Oaks collection (no. 45). And there are fragments of a third book cover with no matches in Antalya Museum or Dumbarton Oaks. These fragments possibly belong to one piece of another pair of book covers (no. 46).

The pair decorated with crosses (no. 44) was discussed in detail by Kitzinger, including a detailed description, and a discussion of the meaning of the iconography of the cross depicted with teardrops and flanked by palm trees.[65] Its decoration was created using a repoussé technique, and the plaques are bordered with meander motifs between beaded edges. There are quatrefoils on the corners, while inside the frame, there is an arcade that is supported by spiral fluted columns and divided by vertical flutings. This arcade surrounds the cross, which is flanked with palm trees, which Kitzinger identified as trees of life. By considering the other book covers and art objects, he observed that the depiction of the tree of life had become a common feature of decorated objects by the time the book covers were made.[66] On the spandrels, there are palmette leaves flanking the pediment (Figure 1.42). The percentage of silver in this book cover is 91%, of copper is 8.31% and of gold is 0.660%.[67]

The other book cover (no. 45) is framed with overlapping leaves, or birds' wings, between beaded edges. Again, it has quatrefoils on the corners, and floral medallions at the centre of the lines. Within the frame, there is an arcade whose spandrels are decorated with fleurs-de-lys and peacocks pecking the vines. The arcade is supported by spirally-fluted columns with acanthus capitals. Inside the pediment, which is also framed by overlapping leaves between beaded edges, there is a conch shell, and three six-pointed stars on the angles. At the centre of each panel, Christ stands between two saints, holding a book in his left hand, while the right is raised in a gesture of blessing. The centre is framed by a *pointillé* inscription. The piece with a peacock in Antalya Museum completes the cover in Dumbarton Oaks which lacks the corner with a peacock. John Lowden discussed both book covers in the Treasure, in order to understand the relationship between the decoration and the objects, arguing that the decoration on the covers provided information about the function of the book. Consequently, he argued that the book cover depicting Christ and two saints was used to cover the gospel book, and the cover with the cross was

65 E. Kitzinger, 'A pair of silver book covers in the Sion Treasure', in U.E. McCracken et al. (ed.), *Gatherings in Honour of Dorothy E. Miner* (Baltimore, 1974), 3–17.
66 Kitzinger, 'A pair of silver book covers', 8.
67 Meyers, 'Elemental compositions', Table 1.1, no. 1.

used for the Acts of the Apostles, because the cross was flanked by two trees of life, representing Christ transfigured between Moses and Elijah (Figure 1.43).[68]

Both sets of book covers are gilded. There are rectangular cuttings on the sides; some nails between the fragments and traces of nails might suggest that these pairs of book covers were attached to each other with nails. The pair with crosses measures 37.2 × 30 cm and 37.5 × 27.6 cm, and weighs 917 grams. Since the other pair has detached fragments, it is not possible to measure them accurately, but the estimated measurements are 25 × 2.8 cm, and the surviving fragments weigh 317 grams.

In addition to these pairs, and the fragments belonging to them, there are also fragments in Antalya Museum that cannot be matched with either of the other two pairs (no. 46). This may suggest that there was another pair of book covers that has not survived. This fragment is decorated with an apostle and on his left-hand side; there is possibly Christ. The iconography could be Christ between apostles. But the gestures of the apostles are different from that on book cover no 45. It cannot be a fragment of either of the other two pairs. The other fragments are a small fragment with a gilded hand giving a blessing, a fragment of a foot, and various gilded fragments with beaded edges and overlapping leaves possibly from the arch surrounding the figures or outer frame surrounding rim of the cover. This means that, given these fragments in Antalya Museum, there were three pairs of book covers in the Sion Treasure (Figure 1.44).

Lampstands

The lampstands from the Sion Treasure are in a fragmentary state, and the fragments are preserved only in the Dumbarton Oaks collection. There are two capitals, of which one is crushed and torn; one column base; and two column shafts. Since there are two column shafts and two capitals, the total number of lampstands can be presumed to be two (nos 47 and 48, Figures 1.45–1.46).[69] The capitals are both decorated with an acanthus leaf decoration. The capital of no. 47 is the most complete and well-preserved, therefore its measurements are likely to be more accurate. It is 8.1 cm in diameter, 15–15.5 cm high and 15.5–16.2 cm wide. It weighs 872 g, and is 0.6 mm thick at the bottom, and 1.2 mm thick at the top. It was created by hammering out a single sheet of silver. The bottom of the capital is circular; it flares outwards and is square at the top. The plate, which is decorated with a foliate design, was silver soldered at the top. There are also signs of silver soldering on the plate, which might indicate that lamps were attached to this lampstand using silver soldering. The decoration was made using

68 J. Lowden, 'The Word made visible: the exterior of the early Christian book as visual argument', in W.E. Klingshirn and L. Safran (ed.), *The Early Christian Book* (Washington, DC, 2007), 28–29.

69 For more discussion about the number of objects, see Boyd, 'A "metropolitan" treasure', 31–2.

chasing and engraving, and the object was burnished. The silver soldering appears at the bottom of the object, indicating that it was attached to the shaft using silver soldering.[70] The column shaft is inscribed with a repoussé inscription. This shaft is cylindrical in shape, was formed from a single sheet of silver and connected using silver soldering. It is 1 mm thick, 43.7 cm high and 8.8 cm in diameter. It was decorated using hammering, chasing and engraving. This column shaft fits with the column capital,[71] and they are displayed together in Dumbarton Oaks Museum, but it lacks its base (Figure 1.45). The column shaft measures 43.7 cm in height and 8.8 cm in diameter.

The capital of the lampstand (no. 48, Figure 1.46) is detached and crushed. It has a similar decoration to that of the capital of lamp stand (no. 47), and weighs 435 grams. In addition, the same type of manufacture and form are evident in the shaft as in the shaft of the lampstand (no. 47). This shaft is decorated with rosettes and flanking crosses in two bands on the centre of the shaft. This shaft fits with the column base, and they are displayed together. This column base was formed from a single sheet of silver by hammering, with the square bottom rising to a vertical rim and circular top. It is attached to the column shaft using silver soldering. It is 0.8–1.1 mm thick at the bottom, and 2–2.5 mm thick at the top. The column shaft and base together weigh 1,400 grams. It is 68.6 cm high.[72] The percentage of silver in these lampstands varies between 94.5% and 96%, of copper 3.45% and 5.04%, and of gold 0.488% and 0.504%.[73]

Candlesticks

There are possibly two candlesticks in the Sion Treasure, and they only survive in fragments (nos 49 and 50).[74] Most of the pieces of one candlestick (no. 49) are preserved in Antalya Museum, and they match one foot fragment in Dumbarton Oaks (Figure 1.47). It has squashed base fragments, knobs, sticks and fragments of the upper parts. When one of the detached base fragments was examined, it was possible to determine that it is the base of a candlestick. The base of a candlestick stands on three feet; of these one is detached and now preserved in Dumbarton Oaks. Each foot is in the form of a knob. There is a *pointillé* inscription surrounding the bottom of the base, but it lacks an ending,[75] indicating that the foot of the candlestick on which it

70 The technical examination of this object was carried by Newman and Lie, and detailed examination of the object can be found in their paper. See Newman and Lie, 'The technical examination', 83.

71 Newman and Lie, 'The technical examination', 83.

72 Newman and Lie, 'The technical examination', 84.

73 Meyers, 'Elemental compositions', Table 1.1, nos 38–41.

74 I owe many thanks to Gudrun Bühl who was museum director in Dumbarton Oaks when I was studying the Treasure for her recommendations and time taken to discuss this object by comparing it with other candlesticks.

75 The inscription of this object was examined and translated by the author. See Table 1.1, no. 49.

stood was larger. The missing fragments, traces of detachment and missing inscription support this assumption. It seems that the foot of the candlestick had three corners; on each corner there is a foot and rosette decoration above the foot. It is decorated with a foliate design. This piece was considered as a cup fragment, but its feet and the direction of the inscription suggest that this object is a base fragment of a candlestick. If we were to suppose that this were a cup with handles, then the letters would be upside down. The inscription was written on the bordered frieze at the bottom between the feet. This makes it impossible to consider this as a cup fragment. The form of the object bears similarities with other lampstand bases, for example those in the Lampsacus Treasure.[76] The other flat pieces which have a similar decoration might have been the pieces from the connection part between the base and the sticks. There are also some fragments suggesting that they are pieces of the upper part of a candlestick.

In Dumbarton Oaks there is one knob pierced by an opening from a shaft identical to the one preserved in Antalya Museum (no. 50, Figure 1.48). There are no base fragments but the fragments that do survive suggest that there may have been another candlestick in the treasure.[77]

Altar Table Sheets

There are fourteen separate sheets that would have been used as sets to cover the rim and top of the altar. These sheets are divided between the collections in the Antalya Museum and Dumbarton Oaks. When the sheets connected, it is evident that they would have covered the rim and top of the altar (no. 51) and (no. 52) (Figures 1.49a–1.49b and 1.50a–1.50b).[78] It is possible to reconstruct the altar table using the measurements of the sheeting. In total, the front and back of this altar table are 225 cm in length, and it can be gleaned from the traces of folding that the thickness of the rim is 5 cm. Meanwhile, the left and right edges are 116 cm in length. The total measurements of each piece are presented in Table 1.1. When completed, the total measurement of the table sheets is 225 × 116 cm, including the rim sheets and the plain sheets for the top of the altar. Therefore, this measurement also indicates the total measurement of the altar table. The rim sheets for the front and right edge of the altar are inscribed using a repoussé technique, with the inscription commencing at the left side of the front panel, and ending at the right end of the right edge. There are signs of silver soldering and riveting on these objects, indicating that they were

76 M.M. Mango, 'Three illuminating objects in the Lampsacus Treasure', in C. Entwistle (ed.), *Through a Glass Brightly: Studies in Byzantine and Medieval Art and Archaeology Presented to David Buckton* (Oxford, 2003), fig. 9.1.

77 Boyd, 'A "metropolitan" treasure', cat. nos 59, 74. Also see Table 1.1, no. 50 in this book.

78 All 14 sheets were combined in two numbers as a set of rim sheeting and a set of sheets for the top of the altar.

possibly riveted to the table, and later silver soldered together, overlapping one another. In Dumbarton Oaks Museum staff made a reconstruction of the altar with the pieces in Dumbarton Oaks. With the pieces in Antalya this reconstruction can be completed.[79] Three rim sheets in five pieces and two plain sheets for the top of the altar are preserved in Antalya Museum, together with fragments completing either the rim sheeting or plain sheets for the top of the altar. The percentage of silver in the altar table sheet fragments in Dumbarton Oaks varies between 93.8% and 97.4%; the percentage of copper is 1.92–5.62%, and of gold is 0.548–0.730%.[80]

Inscribed Plain Sheets

There are also two decorated and inscribed sheets, but it is uncertain whether these belonged to the altar table, or were placed elsewhere in the church, such as on a templon screen. It is also possible that they (no. 53, Figure 1.51 in the Dumbarton Oaks collection, and no. 54, Figure 1.52 in Antalya Museum) were placed on the altar table. Traces of silver soldering on both sides of the rims of the plain sheets indicate that they may have been silver soldered to the plain sheets that cover the top of the table. However, the measurements do not fit the altar table, as both of the objects are 97 cm in length, and 39 cm wide, which means there would be a gap of approximately 19 cm in width and 140 cm in length. There are two possible solutions: either they were placed elsewhere in the church, or there may have been another two or more sheets for the top of the altar that have not survived. As is apparent in the illustration of the altar table, the top of the altar is covered with rivets and silver soldering, and the rim sheets are positioned on the plain sheets (Figure 1.50a). Furthermore, there are also traces of the silver soldering on the edges of the rim sheets and on these two inscribed sheets. There may have been additional materials that covered these rivets and silver solder marks; possibly these two objects functioned as covers for the rivets and on the altar. These two plain sheets were inscribed with repoussé inscriptions; no. 53 was donated by the priest Zacharias, and no. 54 was donated by bishop Paregoros, who was also the donor of the rim sheets.

Bowl

There is one bowl in the Sion Treasure and it is preserved in Dumbarton Oaks (no. 55, Figure 1.53). In earlier studies, this vessel was considered as a base of an object, but its rim is carefully shaped and there is no trace of any

79 For this reconstruction see Zwirn, *Revetment for Altar Table*, http://museum.doaks.org/objects-1/info/46000 (accessed 3 February 2022); also see Boyd, 'A "metropolitan" treasure', fig. S61.1–4.

80 Meyers, 'Elemental compositions', Table 1.1, nos 12–20.

detachment which suggests that this was an individual object not a detached fragment.[81] It is circular and broad and there are five imperial stamps applied to this object. The stamps on this object were applied inside not outside as was the case for all other objects from the Sion Treasure. This object was produced from a single sheet of silver and formed by hammering. After it was formed, the surface of the object was burnished. This object might have been used for drinking wine or water. It might also have been used for pouring water, possibly when the priest washed his hands before the Eucharist or in baptism. There is another silver bowl which is identical to this one; it was found in the Hama Treasure.[82] It measures 13 cm in diameter and weighs 304 grams. The percentage of silver used in the production of this object is 97.2%, the percentage of copper is 2.19% and of gold is 0.648%.[83]

81 Boyd defined this as base of a vessel, see Boyd, 'A "metropolitan" treasure', cat. no. 20.
82 M.M. Mango, *Silver from Early Byzantium: The Kaper Koraon and Related Treasures* (Baltimore, MD, 1986), no. 16.
83 Meyers, 'Elemental compositions', Table 1.1, no. 35.

Table 1.1 Objects from the Sion Treasure

No.	*Object*	*Museum Inv. No.*	*Material, Form and Condition*	*Measurements*	*Inscription*	*Donors*	*Stamps*
1	Paten	ANT. 1020	Silver. Circular dish with foot. Centre: eight-armed gilded Christogram. Rim: decorated with vine leaves and gilded with gold. In good condition, small crack on the rim (Figure 1.1)	Diam. 61 cm; diam foot: 1.6 cm. Letters: H. 2 cm. Thickness: rim: 2 mm; body: 4 mm. Height: 6 cm (from bottom to top). Wt. 5,400 grams.	Niello inscription encircling the rim	Eutychianos	Four imperial stamps
2	PATEN	Geneva, George Ortiz Collection. Inv. no: Ortiz_257	Silver. Circular dish with foot. Centre: six-armed gilded Christogram. Rim: gilded vine leaves and Sasanian palmette decoration. In good condition	Diam. 73.5 cm. For this paten, see https://www.georgeortiz.com/objects/byzantine/257-large-paten-with-engraved-chrismon/ (accessed 27 March 2023)	Niello inscription encircling the rim	Eutychianos	Unstamped
3	Paten	DO. BZ.63.36.1	Silver. Circular dish with foot. Centre: gilded six-armed Christogram. Rim: gilded vine leaves and Sasanian palmette decoration. In good condition (Figure 1.2)	Diam. 60.5 cm. Letters: 1.7–1.8 cm. Thickness: rim: 2 mm; body: 4 mm. **Wt.** 5,200 grams.	Niello inscription encircling the rim	Eutychianos	Unstamped
4	Paten	DO. BZ.63.36.2	Silver. Circular dish with foot. Centre: gilded cross. Rim: fluted and gilded border. In good condition (Figure 1.3)	Diam. 58 cm. Letters: 1.6–1.7 cm. Thickness: rim: 2 mm; body: 4 mm. **Wt**. 4,537 grams.	Niello inscription encircling the rim	For the memory of Angelous Roufinos	Weight marks: 13.50 lb
5	Paten	DO. BZ.63.36.3, BZ.79.5	Silver. Circular dish with foot. Centre: gilded cross. Rim: fluted and gilded border. In good condition, displayed with asterisk. (DO. BZ.79.5) in	Diam. 58.5 cm. Letters: 1.6–1.7 cm. Thickness: rim: 2 mm; body: 4 mm. **Wt.** 4,234 grams.	Niello inscription encircling the rim	For the memory of John and his daughter	Weight marks: 13 lb 1 oz

(*Continued*)

Table 1.1 (Continued)

No.	*Object*	*Museum Inv. No.*	*Material, Form and Condition*	*Measurements*	*Inscription*	*Donors*	*Stamps*
			Dumbarton Oaks (Figure 1.4)				
6	Paten	ANT. 1021	Silver. Circular dish with foot. Centre: gilded cross. Rim: gilded cusped and undecorated border. In good condition (Figure 1.5)	Diam. 77.5 cm; foot: 1.9 cm. Letters: H. 2.5–2.6 cm. Thickness: rim: 3 mm; body: 6 mm. Height: 8 cm (from bottom to top). Wt. 8,000 grams.	Engraved inscription encircling the rim	For the memory of Maria	Unstamped
7	Polycandelon	ANT. 1051	Silver. Cruciform. Designed for holding twelve lamps. Decorated with dolphins flanking holes and foliate design. In good condition (Figure 1.6)	57 × 57 cm. Letters: 1.3 cm. Thickness: 2.5–4 mm. **Wt**. 2,800 grams.	Niello inscription and openwork monogram	Eutychianos	Five imperial stamps
8	Polycandelon	ANT. 1052	Silver. Cruciform. Designed for holding twelve lamps. Decorated with dolphins flanking holes and foliate design. In good condition (Figure 1.7)	57 × 57 cm. Letters: 1.3 cm. Thickness: 2.5–4 mm. **Wt**. 2,800 grams.	Niello inscription and openwork monogram	Eutychianos	Five imperial stamps
9	Polycandelon	DO. BZ.65.1.1	Silver. Cruciform. Designed for Holding twelve lamps. Decorated with dolphins flanking holes and foliate design. In good condition (Figure 1.8)	57 × 57 cm. Letters: 1.3 cm. Thickness: 2.5–4 mm. **Wt.** 2,800 grams.	Niello inscription and openwork monogram	Eutychianos	Five imperial stamps
10	Polycandelon	ANT. 1053	Silver. Circular. Designed for holding sixteen lamps. Decorated with dolphins flanking holes and foliate design. In good condition (Figure 1.9)	Diam. 56 cm. Letters: 1.3 cm. Thickness: 5–6 mm. **Wt.** 3,500 grams.	Niello inscription and openwork monogram	Eutychianos	Five imperial stamps

11	Polycandelon	ANT. 1054	Silver. Circular. Designed for holding sixteen lamps. Decorated with dolphins flanking holes and foliate design. In good condition (Figure 1.10)	Diam. 56 cm. Letters: 1.3 cm. Thickness: 5–6 mm. **Wt.** 3,500 grams.	Niello inscription and openwork monogram	Eutychianos	Five imperial stamps
12	Polycandelon	DO. BZ.63.36.4	Silver. Circular. Designed for holding sixteen lamps. Decorated with dolphins flanking holes and foliate design. In good condition (Figure 1.11)	Diam. 56 cm. Letters: 1.3 cm. Thickness: 5–6 mm. **Wt**. 3,500 grams.	Niello inscription and openwork monogram	Eutychianos	Five imperial stamps
13	Polycandelon	DO. BZ.63.36.5	Silver. Rectangular with tri-lobed end pieces. Paired dolphin decoration. Designed for holding fourteen lamps. Restored. In good condition (Figure 1.12)	L. 57 cm. W. 37 cm. Letters: 1–1.2 cm. Thickness: 3–6 mm. **Wt.** 2,647 grams.	Niello inscription and openwork monogram	Eutychianos	Six imperial stamps
14	Polycandelon	DO. BZ.63.36.6 and ANT. 1033, 1031 and 1028	Silver. Rectangular with tri-lobed end pieces. Paired dolphin decoration. Designed for holding fourteen lamps. Six detached pieces, three in DO, three in Antalya. Nos: 1033, 1031, 1028 (Figure 1.13)	L. 54 cm. W. 31 cm (due to loss of some fragments). Letters: 1–1.2 cm. Thickness: 3–6 mm. **Wt**. 2,562.5 grams. (Including Antalya fragments)	Niello inscription and openwork monogram	Eutychianos	Five imperial stamps
15	Polycandelon	DO. BZ.63.36.7	Silver. Rectangular. With semi-circular end pieces. Paired dolphin decoration. Designed for holding twelve lamps. Five detached pieces. Central rectangle, two semi-circular end pieces, two fragments of lateral rim. Might be completed with the lateral fragments in DO. DO.79.14.4 (a-d) (Figure 1.14)	L. 47 cm. W. 29 cm (due to loss of some fragments). Letters: 1–1.2 cm. Thickness: 3–6 mm. **Wt**. 2,098 grams.	Niello inscription and openwork monogram	Eutychianos	Five imperial stamps

(*Continued*)

Table 1.1 (Continued)

No.	*Object*	*Museum Inv. No.*	*Material, Form and Condition*	*Measurements*	*Inscription*	*Donors*	*Stamps*
16	Polycandelon	DO.BZ.65.1.8	Silver. Rectangular with semi-circular and pieces. Paired dolphin decoration. Designed for holding twelve lamps. Three detached pieces. Central rectangle and two joining fragments of lateral rim. Other pieces are missing (Figure 1.15)	L. 27.5 cm. W. 20 cm. Letters: 1–1.2 cm. Thickness: 3–6 mm. **Wt.** 981 grams.	Niello inscription and openwork monogram	Eutychianos	One imperial stamp
17	Polycandelon	DO. BZ. 65.1.7 and ANT. 1030	Silver. Rectangular with semi-circular end pieces. Foliate design decoration. Designed for holding twelve lamps. Nine detached pieces. Central rectangle, one semi-circular end piece, five fragments for semi-circular end piece and one fragment of lateral rim. Can be completed with lateral rim in Antalya no. 1030 (Figure 1.16)	L. 42.5 cm. W. 26.4 cm. Letters: 1–1.2 cm. Thickness: 3–6 mm. **Wt.** 1,759 grams.	Niello inscription and openwork monogram	Eutychianos	Four imperial stamps
18	Polycandelon	ANT. 2018/74	Silver. Rectangular with semi-circular end pieces. Foliate design decoration. Designed for holding twelve lamps. Possibly completed with the fragment of semi-circular end piece in DO. No: DO 79.14.1 (Figure 1.17a–1.17b)	L. 37 cm. W. 21 cm. Letters: 1–1.2 cm. Thickness: 3–6 mm. **Wt.** 1,200 grams.	Niello inscription and openwork monogram	Eutychianos	Six imperial stamps

19	Censer	ANT. 1019 and 1022	Silver. Circular. With chain. Circular foot. Decorated with five scenes from life of Virgin: Annunciation, Trial by Water, Visitation, Journey to Bethlehem, Nativity. Gilded. In good condition (Figure 1.18a–1.18b)	Chain: L. 43 cm. Wt. 320 g. Censer: H. 11.6 cm. Diam. (rim) 17 cm; (foot) 11.5 cm. Letters: 9 mm. Thickness: 7 mm. **Wt**. 1,520 grams.	Niello inscription encircling the rim	Eutychianos	Five imperial stamps
20	Censer	DO. BZ.65.1.5	Silver. Hexagonal. Foot supported by four peacocks. Each square decorated with medallions of Christ, St Peter and St Paul. In good condition (Figure 1.19a–1.19b)	H. 15 cm (with rings and feet). Diam. (corner to corner): 20. 2 cm (side to side), 17.7 cm. Letters: 5–6 mm. Thickness: rim: 5 mm; body: 1.2 mm. **Wt.** 1,725 grams.	Niello inscription encircling the rim	Eutychianos	Five imperial stamps
21	Chalice	DO. BZ.63.36.19	Silver. Incomplete. Only flattened bowl preserved (Figure 1.20)	Height cannot be measured. **Wt.** 273 grams.	Uninscribed	–	Unstamped
22	Chalice	DO. BZ.79.8	Silver. Only flattened and folded bowl preserved (Figure 1.21)	Diam. 22.5 cm. Letters: 1.2–1.4 cm. Thickness: Rim: 2 mm; interior of bowl: 0.5–0.7 mm. Height cannot be measured. Wt. 222 grams.	Engraved inscription encircling the rim		Unstamped
23	Chalice	DO. BZ.65.1.11	Silver. Hemispherical bowl. Only bowl and knob of foot preserved (Figure 1.22)	H. (bowl) 10.2 cm. Diam. 17 cm. Thickness: rim: 2 mm; body: 0.4–0.7. Wt. 341 grams.	Engraved inscription encircling the rim		Unstamped
24	Chalice	DO. BZ.63.36.20	Silver. Broad cup. Only bowl is preserved. Decorated with two engraved crosses (Figure 1.23)	H. 10.5 cm. Diam. 15.5 cm. Wt. 257 grams.	Uninscribed		Unstamped
25	Chalice	ANT. 1043	Silver. Bowl of the chalice is preserved. Foot is lost. No decoration (Figure 1.24)	H. 9.5 cm; Diam. rim: 16 cm. Letters: 8–9 mm. Thickness: rim: 2 mm; body: 0.5 mm. Wt. 500 grams.	Pointillé inscription encircling the rim		Unstamped

(*Continued*)

Table 1.1 (Continued)

No.	*Object*	*Museum Inv. No.*	*Material, Form and Condition*	*Measurements*	*Inscription*	*Donors*	*Stamps*
26	Chalice	ANT. 1036–1 and 1046	Silver. Bowl of the chalice is preserved. Foot is lost. Decorated with two engraved crosses (Figure 1.25)	H. 14 cm. Diam. rim: 22.5 cm. Letters: 1.1 cm. Thickness: rim 4 mm; body 1.2 mm. Wt. 930 grams.	Engraved inscription encircling the rim		Unstamped
27	Chalice	ANT. 2018/75	Silver. Broad body, conical foot. Body and foot both preserved, but some fragments are lost. Two engraved crosses (Figure 1.26)	H. 32.5 cm. Diam. (rim) 22.5 cm; foot: 12 cm. Thickness: rim 4 mm. **Wt.** 1,040 grams.	Uninscribed		Unstamped
28	Amphora	DO. BZ.65.1.4	Silver. Fluted at neck and base. Two fragments; body and rim. Rim: fluted decoration. Body: foliate design decoration (Figure 1.27)	H. 41.5 cm. Letters: 1.5 cm. Thickness: rim: 2 mm, body: 1 mm, foot: 4 mm. **Wt.** 2,954 grams.	Niello inscription encircling the body of the object	Eutychianos	Five imperial stamps
29	Amphora	ANT. 1049 and 1039	Silver. Broken in three pieces. One fragment is missing. Probably completed by the piece in London, Hewett Collection. See; Boyd, 'A "metropolitan" treasure', cat. no. 16 and 16a. Foliate design decoration (Figure 1.28)	H. 30 cm. Letters: 1.5 cm. Thickness: rim: 2 mm; body: 1 mm; foot: 4 mm. **Wt.** 1,350 grams.	Niello inscription encircling the body of object	Eutychianos	Unstamped
30	Ewer	DO. BZ.63.36.14	Silver. Flattened and folded (Figure 1.29)	H. 36 cm. Thickness: rim: 2 mm. Wt.: 822 grams.	Uninscribed		Unstamped

31	Standing lamp	DO. BZ.63.36.15	Silver. Possibly cup-shaped. Flattened and rolled up (Figure 1.30)	**Wt**. 1,170.5 grams.	Niello inscription encircling the rim of object	Eutychianos	Unknown
32	Standing lamp	DO. BZ.63.36.16	Silver. Possibly cup-shaped. Flattened and rolled up (Figure 1.31)	**Wt.** 1,291 grams.	Niello inscription encircling the rim of object	Eutychianos	Unknown
33	Standing lamp	DO. BZ.63.36.17	Silver. Cup-shaped body and ring foot. Body: two engraved crosses. Foot: acanthus leaf decoration (Figure 1.32)	H. 18.5 cm. Diam. rim: 17.2–18.4 cm; foot: 9.7–10.4 cm. Letters: 1.1 cm. Thickness: 3 mm. **Wt.** 1,159 grams.	Niello inscription encircling the rim of object	Eutychianos	Five imperial Stamps
34	Standing lamp	ANT. 1050 and 1042	Silver. Cup-shaped body and ring foot. Two detached pieces, foot and body. Body: two engraved crosses. Foot: acanthus leaf decoration (Figure 1.33)	H. 18.5 cm. Diam. rim: 17.5 cm; foot: 10 cm. Letters: 1.1 cm. Thickness: 3 mm. **Wt**. 1,200 grams.	Niello inscription encircling the rim of object	Eutychianos	Two non-imperial stamps
35	Openwork lamp	DO. BZ.63.36.25 and 63.36.21	Silver. Hemispherical bowl decorated with inverted hearts. With squat-stemmed foot. This lamp can be used as both suspension and standing. Some inverted hearts lost (Figure 1.34)	H. 15.5 cm. Diam. rim: 18 cm; foot: 6 cm. Thickness: rim: 3 mm; body: 0.8–0.9 mm. Wt. 663 grams.	Niello inscription encircling the rim of object	Eutychianos	One imperial stamp
36	Openwork lamp	DO. BZ.63.36.25a and foot DO. BZ. 65.1.14. ANT. 1047 3–7, 1048 and 1048–2. And one rim fragment London Hewett collection	Silver. Hemispherical bowl with inverted hearts. Squat-stemmed foot. With rings for chain and foot. This lamp can be used as both suspension and standing. Multiple fragments. Incomplete. Rim fragment: DO. 63.36.25a and foot DO. 65.1.14. Parts of rim and body fragment in Antalya nos 1047 3–7, 1048 and 1048–2. And rim fragment London Hewett collection (Figure 1.35)	Wt. approx. 500 grams. Letters: 1 cm. For this object also see Boyd, 'A bishop's gift', 192, no. 2	Niello inscription encircling the rim of object (Inscription can be completed by marrying the fragments of inscriptions from three collections.)	Eutychianos	One imperial stamp

(*Continued*)

Table 1.1 (Continued)

No.	*Object*	*Museum Inv. No.*	*Material, Form and Condition*	*Measurements*	*Inscription*	*Donors*	*Stamps*
37	Openwork lamp	DO. BZ.65.1.6	Silver. Hemispherical bowl with design of scales and triangles. Squat-stemmed foot. With rings for chain and foot. This lamp can be used as both suspension and standing. Restored, in good condition (Figure 1.36)	H. (without rings) 17 cm. Diam. rim: 21 cm; foot: 7 cm. Letters: 2.1 cm. Thickness: 1–1.5 mm. **Wt.** 1,112 grams.	Niello inscription encircling the rim of object	Eutychianos	Unstamped
38	Openwork lamp	London, Digby-Jones Collection	Silver. Decorated with openwork with bisected scale design. Not examined at first hand. See Boyd, 'A bishop's gift', 193, no. 4.	H. 10.5 cm. Diam. rim: 14.3 cm; foot: 4.7 cm. Weight was not measured	Niello inscription encircling the rim of object	Eutychianos	Six imperial stamps
39	Openwork lamp	DO. BZ.65.1.19, a-c, 79.11 and 63.36.22	Silver. Openwork lamp with everted flanged hexagonal rim and hemispherical body. This lamp can be used as both suspension and standing. Incomplete (Figure 1.37)	H. 11.4 cm. Diam. rim (with flanges): 21.4 cm; foot: 6 cm. Letters: 1–1.2 cm. Thickness: rim: 3 mm. (thickness for body was not measured). Wt. 566 grams.	Niello inscription encircling the rim of object	For the memory of Eutychianos	Five imperial stamps
40	Openwork lamp	DO. BZ.79.10 a-d, 63. 36.23 and 63.36.32	Silver. Openwork lamp with everted flanged hexagonal rim and hemispherical body. This lamp can be used as both suspension and standing. Rim completed with the rim fragment from London Hewett collection. Incomplete, some fragments are lost (Figure 1.38)	Diam. rim: 22.4 cm; foot: 6 cm. Wt. 565 grams.	Niello inscription encircling the rim of object	For the memory of Himeria	Three imperial stamps

41	Openwork lamp	DO. BZ.65.1.12	Silver. Openwork lamp. Cylinder-shaped body. Decorated with openwork architectural design. This lamp can be used as both suspension and standing (Figure 1.39)	H. (without rings) 10.1–13 cm. Diam. rim: 14.4–15.5 cm; foot: 5 cm. Letters: 1 cm. Thickness: 3 mm. Wt. 480 grams.	Openwork inscription encircling the rim of object	Eutychianos	Five imperial stamps
42	Openwork lamp	DO. BZ.65.1.15	Silver. Openwork lamp. Crushed, folded and in multiple fragments (Figure 1.40)	Wt. 231.7 grams.	Openwork inscription. Cannot be read		Unknown
43	Suspension bracket for five lamps	DO. BZ.65.1.18 AND 63.36.31	Silver. Cross-shaped. For five lamps. In good condition. Two vertical and two lateral rods (Figure 1.41)	H. 89 cm. W. 36.5 cm. Letters: 5–6 mm. **Wt**. 2,014.6 grams.	Two Niello inscriptions. Obv: vertical rod and lateral rod. And rev: vertical rod and lateral rod	Eutychianos	Unstamped
44	Book cover	DO. BZ.63.36.9- 10	Silver. Pair of book covers. Each cover decorated with crosses flanked by cypress trees. In good condition (Figure 1.42)	Front cover: 37.2 × 30 cm. Wt. 495 g. Back cover: 37.5 × 27.6 cm. **Wt**. 422 grams.	Uninscribed		Unstamped
45	Book cover	DO.BZ.63.36.8 and BZ. 65.1.3; ANT: 1034 1–3.	Silver. Pair of book covers decorated with Christ between apostles. In multiple fragments. Front and back cover completed with the multiple fragments from Antalya, fragment with peacock and small pieces (Figure 1.43)	Front cover: 25 × 23.8 cm. Wt. 317 g. Back cover: 23.4 × 17.5 cm. **Wt**. 250 grams.	Front cover, pointillé inscription. Back cover, pointillé inscription but not complete. Some words on Antalya piece and some words on Dumbarton Oaks piece	For the memory of deacon Prinkipios, Stephane, Leontia and deacon Konon	Unstamped

(Continued)

Table 1.1 (Continued)

No.	*Object*	*Museum Inv. No.*	*Material, Form and Condition*	*Measurements*	*Inscription*	*Donors*	*Stamps*
46	Book cover	ANT. 1055 and 1034	Silver. Detached pieces of book cover. One piece is decorated with a figure of an apostle and the others are small pieces. Including the nails (Figure 1.44)	L. 14 cm, W. 8.5 cm. **Wt**. 230 grams.	Uninscribed		Unstamped
47	Lampstand	DO. BZ.63.36.13, BZ.65.1.9	Silver. This capital and this column shaft fit together and are displayed together in DO collection. Column base is missing. Capital decorated with acanthus leaves (Figure 1.45)	Acanthus capital: H. 15–15.5 cm. Wt. 872 g. Column shaft: H. 43.7 cm. Diam. 8.8 cm. Letters: 2 cm. Thickness: 1–3 mm	Repoussé inscription surrounding the centre of the column shaft	Restored in the time of bishop Theodore	Unstamped
48	Lampstand	DO. BZ.63.36.12, BZ.63.36.18, BZ.65.1.23	Silver. Column shaft and column base are displayed together in DO collection. Lines of rosettes on the shaft. Acanthus capital is detached. Capital is crushed and torn (Figure 1.46)	Capital: Wt. 435 g. Column shaft: H. 52.2 cm. Diam. 8.8 cm. Columnbase: H. 16.4 cm. Thickness: 1–3 mm	Uninscribed		Unstamped
49	Candlestick	ANT. 1036- 3, 1040 1–2, 1041 1–4, 1035. DO. BZ.63.36.38	Silver. In multiple fragments, two flattened and crushed base fragments in Antalya, one base fragment in DO. Four fragments of spirally fluted colonnettes, one knob and two fragments of the upper part. Foliate design decoration (Figure 1.47)	Letters: 5 mm. Thickness: 1 mm. Wt. 930 grams.	Pointillé inscription	Unknown	Unstamped

50	Candlestick	DO. BZ.65.1.20	Silver. Fragment of one knob (Figure 1.48)	Colonnettes: H. 62 cm. Knob: H. 8 cm. Wt. 596 grams.	Uninscribed	Unknown	Unstamped
51	Rim sheets for altar table	DO. BZ.65.1.10 a-g and BZ.63.36.11 a-d. ANT. 1037–1038 and ANT 1045, 1–6	Silver. Rim sheeting from front, left and right edges and back of the altar. In various detached pieces. In multiple fragments (Figure 1.49a–1.49b)	Front panel: L. 2.25 m. H. 19.5 cm; H. (inscribed face) 5 cm. **Wt**. 2,817 grams. Right edge: L. 1.16 m; H. 19.5 cm; H. (inscribed face) 5 cm. Wt. 1,321 grams. Left edge: H. 19.5 cm. L. 1.16 m; **Wt.** 1,445 g. Back of altar: H. 19.5 cm, L. 2.25 cm. **Wt**. 2,968 grams. Letters: 2–2.5 cm. Thickness: 1.1 mm	Starts in front panel and ends in the right edge. Repoussé inscription	Paregoros	Unstamped
52	Plain sheets for top of the altar	DO. BZ.65.1.10 h, i, j, k, l; ANT. 1024 1–2	Silver. Plain sheets used to cover the top of the altar. Folded and in various detached pieces (Figure 1.50a–1.50b)	W. 1.14 m. L. 2.23 m (these measures were reached when all detached objects from the top of altar were put together). Thickness: 1.2 mm. Wt. 16,328 grams.	Uninscribed		Unstamped
53	Inscribed plain sheet	DO. BZ.79.4	Silver. Plain sheet. Small fragments are missing. Decorated with cross. In good condition (Figure 1.51)	L. 97 cm. W. 37 cm. Letters: 2–2.5 cm. Thickness: 1.1 mm. **Wt**. 3,164 grams.	Repoussé inscription.	Zacharias	Unstamped
54	Inscribed plain sheet	ANT 1025 and 1044	Silver. Plain sheet. Completed with small fragment. The other fragments are missing. Decorated with cross (Figure 1.52)	L. 95.5 cm. W. 39 cm. Letters: 2–2.5 cm. Thickness: 1.1 mm. Wt. 2,980 grams.	Repoussé inscription	Paregoros	Unstamped
55	Bowl	DO. BZ.63.36.24	Silver. Circular (Figure 1.53)	Diam. 13 cm. Wt. 304 grams.			Five imperial stamps
56	Pincers	DO. BZ.65.1.22	Silver-plated bronze	L. 13.8 cm			

(*Continued*)

Table 1.1 (Continued)

No.	*Object*	*Museum Inv. No.*	*Material, Form and Condition*	*Measurements*	*Inscription*	*Donors*	*Stamps*
57	Staff/scepter	DO. BZ.63.36.28, BZ.65. 1.2	Gold. Decorated with pearls and emeralds. Thirteen fragments		Uninscribed	Unknown	Unstamped
			Miscellaneous and Detached Pieces				
58	Asterisk	DO. BZ.79.5	Silver. Now displayed with the paten in Dumbarton Oaks, DO. 63. 36.3, no: 6	Wt. 893.5 grams.			
59	Chain	ANT. 1023	Silver. Possibly the chain of polycandelon. Ant. No: 1028.	L. 43 cm. Wt. 230 grams.			
60	Chalice base	DO. BZ.63.36.33	Silver	H. 8.8 cm. Wt. 84 grams.			
61	Chalice base	DO. BZ.63.36.34	Silver	H. 12 cm. Wt. 108 grams.			
62	Chalice base	DO. BZ.63.36.35	Silver	H. 8.5 cm. Wt. 63 grams.			
63	Chalice base	DO. BZ.79.9	Silver	H. 8.5 cm. Wt. 61 grams.			
64	Chalice base	ANT. 1039.2	Silver, conical foot	H. 11.5 cm			
65	Base of vessel	ANT. 1050–2	Silver. Flattened. Base of unidentified vessel	Wt. 1800 grams.			
66	Silver nails	DO. BZ.63.36.30	Silver. Twenty-nine silver nails, twenty-eight in DO, one in London Hewett collection.				
67	Silver ring set	DO. BZ.63.36.39	Decorated with carnelian intaglio.	Diam. 2 cm			

Figure 1.1 Paten with gilded, eight-armed Christogram and niello inscription (no. 1). Antalya Museum, Turkey (1020).

Source: Photograph by the author.

Figure 1.2 Paten with six-armed Christogram and niello inscription (no. 3). Dumbarton Oaks, Byzantine Collection, Washington, DC (DO. BZ. 63.36.1).

Source: Photograph by the author.

Figure 1.3 Paten with gilded cross and niello inscription (no. 4). Dumbarton Oaks, Byzantine Collection, Washington, DC (DO. BZ. 63.36.2).

Source: Photograph by the author.

Figure 1.4 Paten with gilded cross and niello inscription (no. 5). Displayed with asterisk (no. 58). Dumbarton Oaks, Byzantine Collection, Washington, DC (DO. BZ. 63.36.3).

Source: Photograph by the author.

Figure 1.5 Paten with gilded cross and engraved inscription (no. 6). Antalya Museum, Turkey (1021).

Source: Photograph by the author.

Figure 1.6 Cruciform polycandelon (no. 7). Antalya Museum, Turkey (1051).
Source: Photograph by the author.

Figure 1.7 Cruciform polycandelon (no. 8). Antalya Museum, Turkey (1052).

Source: Photograph by the author.

Figure 1.8 Cruciform polycandelon (no. 9). Dumbarton Oaks, Byzantine Collection, Washington, DC (DO. BZ. 65.1.1).

Source: Photograph by Dumbarton Oaks, Byzantine Collection, Washington, DC.

Figure 1.9 Circular polycandelon (no. 10). Antalya Museum, Turkey (1053).

Source: Photograph by the author.

Figure 1.10 Circular polycandelon (no. 11). Antalya Museum, Turkey (1054).

Source: Photograph by the author.

Figure 1.11 Circular polycandelon (no. 12). Dumbarton Oaks, Byzantine Collection, Washington, DC (DO. BZ. 63.36.4).

Source: Photograph by the author.

Figure 1.12 Rectangular polycandelon with tri-lobed end pieces and paired dolphin decoration (no. 13). Dumbarton Oaks, Byzantine Collection, Washington, DC (DO. BZ. 63.36.5).

Source: Photograph by the author.

Figure 1.13 Rectangular polycandelon with tri-lobed end pieces and paired dolphin decoration (no. 14). This shows all the detached pieces from both Antalya (two lateral rims and one tri-lobed end piece ANT 1033, 1031 and 1028) and Dumbarton Oaks (central rectangle and one tri-lobed end piece DO. BZ. 63.36.6).

Source: Photographs of fragments from Antalya Museum by author, Fragments from Dumbarton Oaks by Dumbarton Oaks, Byzantine Collection, Washington, DC.

Figure 1.14 Rectangular polycandelon with semi-circular end pieces and paired dolphin decoration (no. 15). All detached pieces are in Dumbarton Oaks, Byzantine Collection, Washington, DC (DO. BZ.63.36.7 and BZ. 79.14.4 (a-d)).

Source: Photograph by Dumbarton Oaks, Byzantine Collection, Washington, DC.

Figure 1.15 Rectangular polycandelon with semi-circular end pieces and paired dolphin decoration (no. 16). All detached pieces are in Dumbarton Oaks, Byzantine Collection, Washington, DC (DO. BZ. 65.1.8).

Source: Photograph by Dumbarton Oaks, Byzantine Collection, Washington, DC.

Figure 1.16 Rectangular polycandelon with semi-circular end pieces and foliate design decoration (no. 17). Detached pieces are from Antalya Museum, Turkey and Dumbarton Oaks, Byzantine Collection, Washington, DC (ANT 1030 and DO. BZ. 65.1.7).

Source: Photographs of fragments from Antalya Museum by author, fragments from Dumbarton Oaks by Dumbarton Oaks, Byzantine Collection, Washington, DC.

Figure 1.17a Rectangular polycandelon with semi-circular end pieces and foliate design decoration (no. 18). Antalya Museum, Turkey (2018/74).

Source: Photograph by the author.

Figure 1.17b Detached semi-circular end piece of no. 18. Dumbarton Oaks, Byzantine Collection, Washington, DC (DO.BZ.79.14.1).

Source: Photograph by Dumbarton Oaks, Byzantine Collection, Washington, DC.

Figure 1.18a Circular censer with scenes from the life of the Virgin (no. 19). Antalya Museum, Turkey (1019).

Source: Photograph by the author.

Figure 1.18b Scenes from the life of the Virgin applied on the circular censer (no. 19).
Source: Created by the author.

Figure 1.19a Hexagonal censer supported by four peacocks and decorated with medallions of Christ, St Peter and St Paul (no. 20). Dumbarton Oaks, Byzantine Collection, Washington, DC (DO. BZ. 65.1.5).

Source: Photograph by Dumbarton Oaks, Byzantine Collection, Washington, DC.

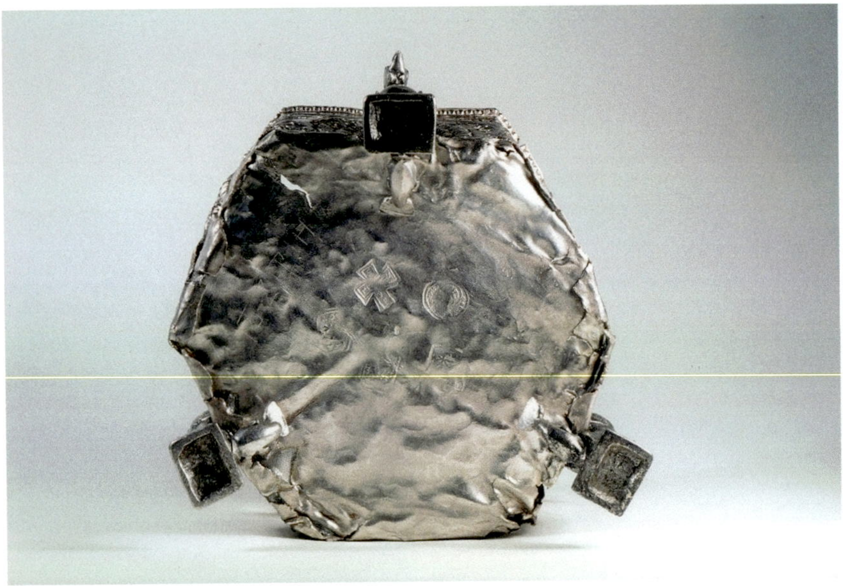

Figure 1.19b Detail of hexagonal censer (no. 20) showing dolphins and imperial stamps.

Source: Photograph by Dumbarton Oaks, Byzantine Collection, Washington, DC.

Figure 1.20 Crushed bowl of a chalice (no. 21). Dumbarton Oaks, Byzantine Collection, Washington, DC (DO. BZ. 63. 36. 19).

Source: Photograph by Dumbarton Oaks, Byzantine Collection, Washington, DC.

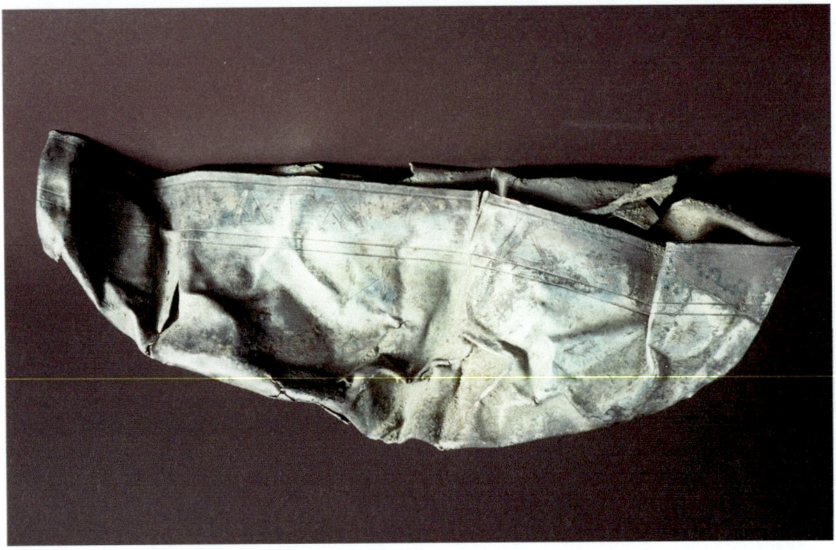

Figure 1.21 Flattened bowl of a chalice with engraved inscription (no. 22). Dumbarton Oaks, Byzantine Collection, Washington, DC (DO. BZ. 79.8).

Source: Photograph by Dumbarton Oaks, Byzantine Collection, Washington, DC.

Figure 1.22 Bowl and knob of a chalice with engraved inscription (no. 23). Dumbarton Oaks, Byzantine Collection, Washington, DC (DO. BZ. 65.1.11).

Source: Photograph by Dumbarton Oaks, Byzantine Collection, Washington, DC.

Figure 1.23 Bowl of a chalice with two engraved crosses (no. 24). Dumbarton Oaks, Byzantine Collection, Washington, DC (DO. BZ. 63.36.20).

Source: Dumbarton Oaks, Byzantine Collection, Washington, DC.

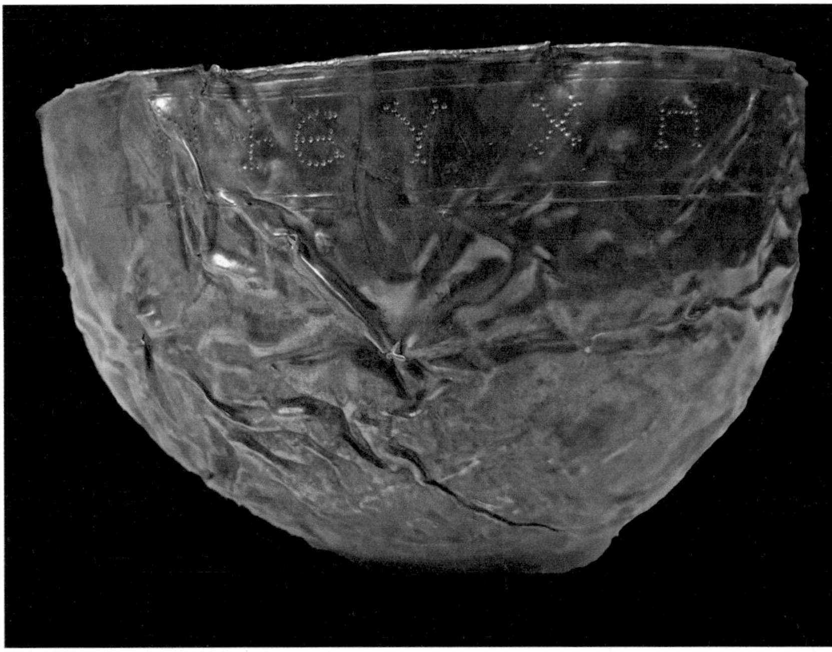

Figure 1.24 Bowl of a chalice with pointillé inscription (no. 25). Antalya Museum, Turkey (1043).

Source: Photograph by the author.

Figure 1.25 Bowl of a chalice with two engraved and gilded crosses and engraved inscription, with its detached bottom (no. 26). Antalya Museum, Turkey (1036–1, 1046).

Source: Photographs by the author.

Figure 1.26 Chalice with two engraved and gilded crosses (no. 27). Antalya Museum, Turkey (2018/75).

Source: Photograph by the author.

Figure 1.27 Crushed, detached and folded amphora with niello inscription (no. 28). Dumbarton Oaks, Byzantine Collection, Washington, DC (DO. BZ. 65.1.4).

Source: Photograph by the author.

Figure 1.28 Amphora with niello inscription and detached body fragment (no. 29). Antalya Museum, Turkey (1049 and 1039).

Source: Photograph by the author.

Figure 1.29 Crushed and folded ewer (no. 30). Dumbarton Oaks, Byzantine Collection, Washington, DC (DO. BZ. 63.36.14).

Source: Photograph by the author.

Figure 1.30 Standing lamp with niello inscription and two engraved crosses, crushed and folded (no. 31). Dumbarton Oaks, Byzantine Collection, Washington, DC (DO. BZ. 63.36.15).

Source: Photograph by Dumbarton Oaks, Byzantine Collection, Washington, DC.

Figure 1.31 Standing lamp with niello inscription and two engraved crosses, crushed and folded (no. 32). Dumbarton Oaks, Byzantine Collection, Washington, DC (DO. BZ. 63.36.16).

Source: Photograph by Dumbarton Oaks, Byzantine Collection, Washington, DC.

Figure 1.32 Standing lamp with niello inscription and two engraved crosses (no. 33). Dumbarton Oaks, Byzantine Collection, Washington, DC (DO. BZ. 63.36.17).

Source: Photograph by Dumbarton Oaks, Byzantine Collection, Washington, DC.

Figure 1.33 Standing lamp with niello inscription and two engraved crosses, detached foot and body (no. 34). Antalya Museum, Turkey (1050 and 1042).

Source: Photographs by the author.

Figure 1.34 Openwork lamp decorated with inverted hearts (no. 35). Dumbarton Oaks, Byzantine Collection, Washington, DC (DO. BZ. 63.36.25 and 63. 36.21).

Source: Photograph by Dumbarton Oaks, Byzantine Collection, Washington, DC.

Figure 1.35 Fragments of openwork lamp decorated with inverted hearts (no. 36). One foot (upper right) and rim fragment (upper left) in Dumbarton Oaks, Byzantine Collection, Washington, DC (DO. BZ. 63.36.25a/65.1.14), two rim fragments and fragments from the body of the object in Antalya Museum, Turkey (1047 3–7 and 1048 1–2).

Source: Photographs by Dumbarton Oaks, Byzantine Collection, Washington, DC and author.

Figure 1.36 Openwork lamp decorated with scales and triangles (no. 37). Dumbarton Oaks, Byzantine Collection, Washington, DC (DO. BZ. 65.1.6).

Source: Photograph by the author.

Figure 1.37 Fragments of openwork lamp with hexagonal rim (no. 39). One foot and four hexagonal rim fragments. Dumbarton Oaks, Byzantine Collection, Washington, DC (DO. BZ. 65.1.19 a-c/79.11 and 63.36.22).

Source: Photographs by Dumbarton Oaks, Byzantine Collection, Washington, DC.

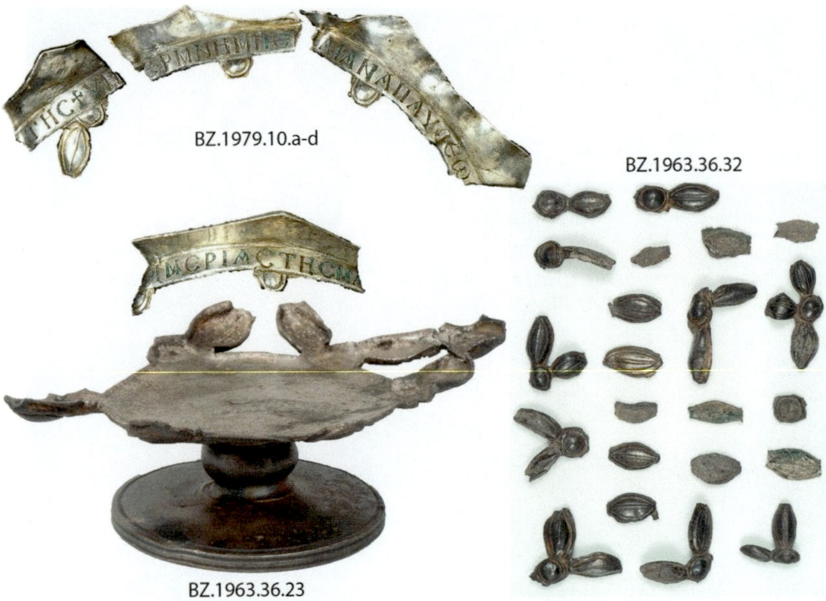

Figure 1.38 Fragments of openwork lamp with hexagonal rim (no. 40). Dumbarton Oaks, Byzantine Collection, Washington, DC (DO. BZ. 79.10 a-d/ 63.36.23 and 63.36.32).

Source: Photographs by Dumbarton Oaks, Byzantine Collection, Washington, DC.

Figure 1.39 Openwork lamp with openwork inscription (no. 41). Dumbarton Oaks, Byzantine Collection, Washington, DC (DO. BZ. 65.1.12).

Source: Photograph by Dumbarton Oaks, Byzantine Collection, Washington, DC.

Figure 1.40 Fragments of openwork lamp with openwork inscription (no. 42). Dumbarton Oaks, Byzantine Collection, Washington, DC (DO. BZ. 65.1.15).

Source: Photograph by Dumbarton Oaks, Byzantine Collection, Washington, DC.

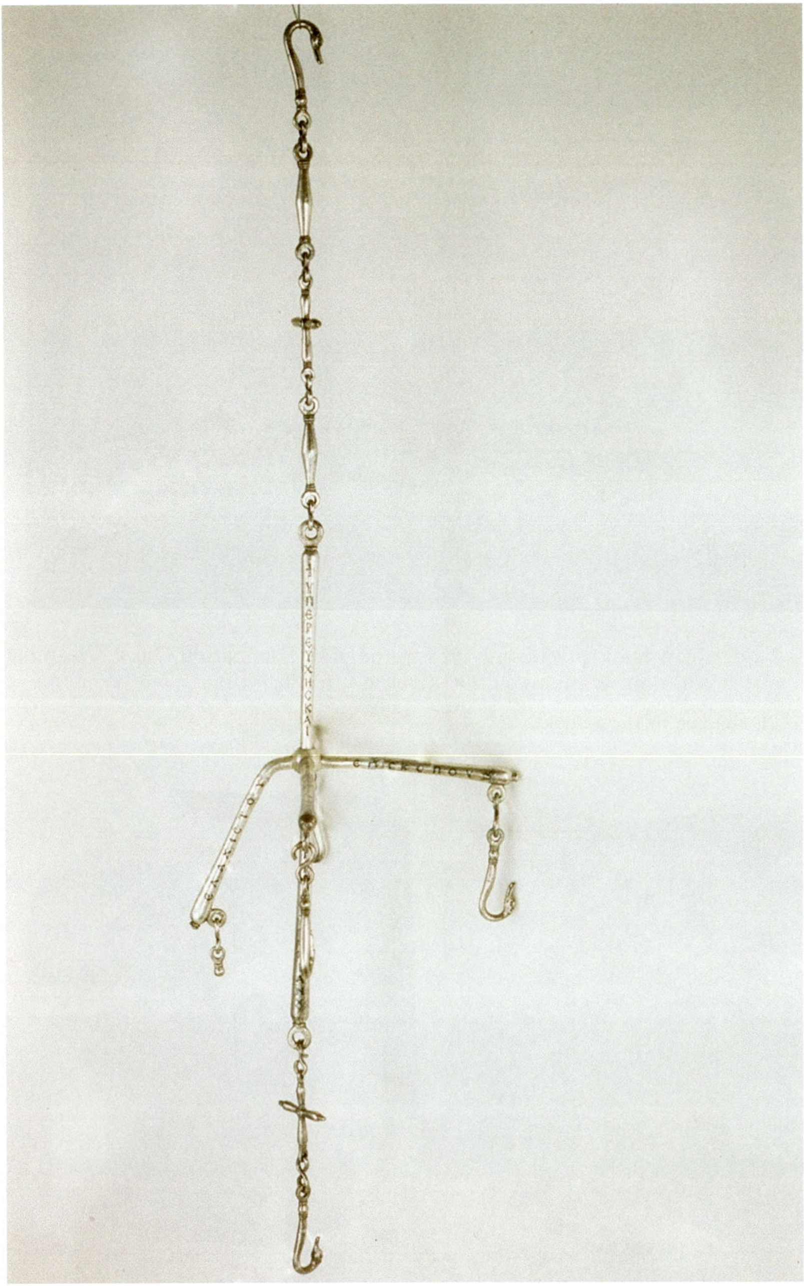

Figure 1.41 Cross-shaped suspension bracket for five lamps (no. 43). Dumbarton Oaks, Byzantine Collection, Washington, DC (DO. BZ. 65.1.18 and 63.36.31).

Source: Photograph by Dumbarton Oaks, Byzantine Collection, Washington, DC.

Figure 1.42 Pair of book covers with crosses (no. 44). Dumbarton Oaks, Byzantine Collection, Washington, DC (DO. BZ. 63.36.9–10).

Source: Photograph by the author.

Figure 1.43 Fragments of the pair of book covers (no. 45). Two fragments in Dumbarton Oaks, Byzantine Collection, Washington, DC (DO. BZ. 63.36.8 and 65.1.3) and multiple fragments in Antalya Museum, Turkey (1034 1–3).

Source: Photographs by Dumbarton Oaks, Byzantine Collection, Washington, DC and the author.

Figure 1.44 Fragments of third pair of book covers (no. 46). Antalya Museum (1034 and 1055).

Source: Photograph by the author.

Figure 1.45 Lampstand with acanthus capital and column (no. 47). Dumbarton Oaks, Byzantine Collection, Washington, DC (DO. BZ. 63.36.13 and 65.1.9).

Source: Photograph by Dumbarton Oaks, Byzantine Collection, Washington, DC.

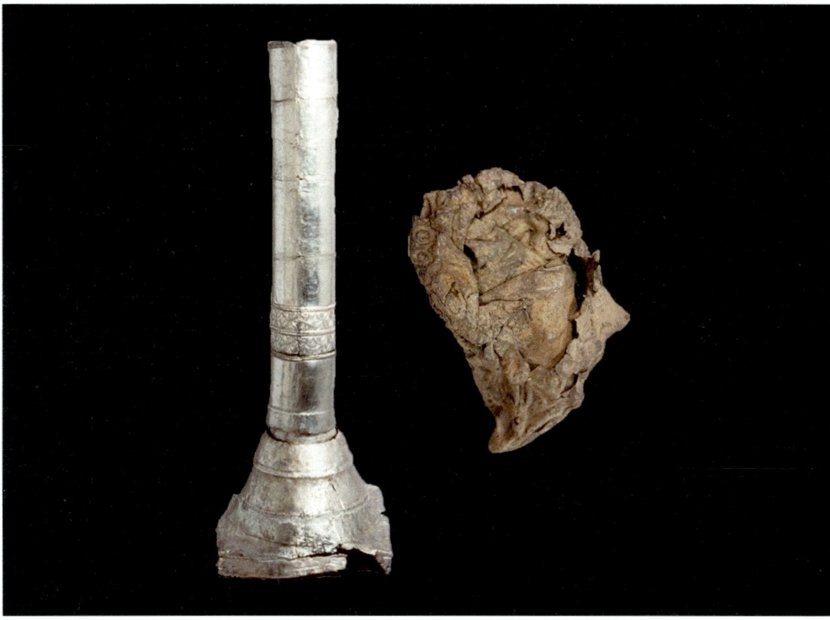

Figure 1.46 Lampstand with crushed and torn acanthus capital, column and column base (no. 48). Dumbarton Oaks, Byzantine Collection, Washington, DC (DO. BZ. 63.36.12, 63.36.18 and 65.1.23).

Source: Photograph by Dumbarton Oaks, Byzantine Collection, Washington, DC.

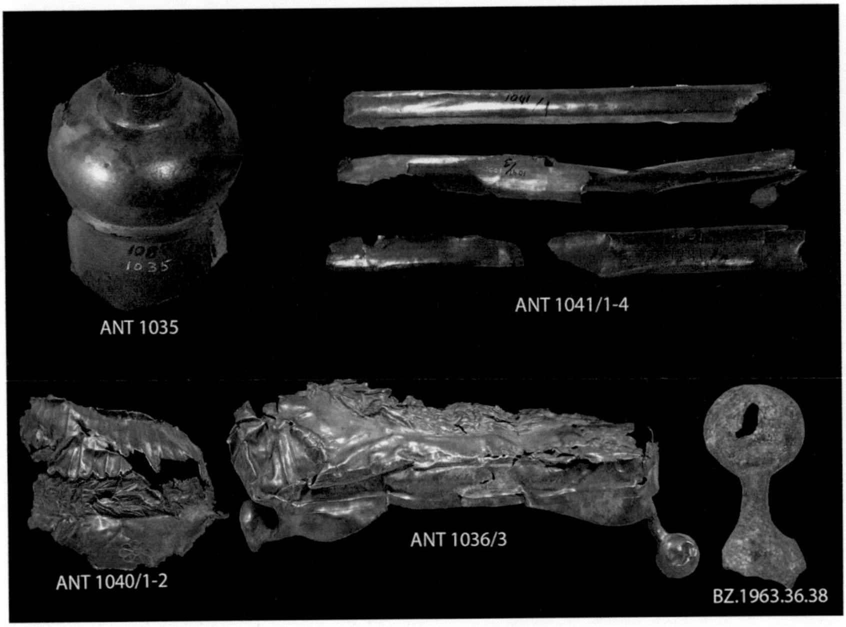

Figure 1.47 Fragments of candlestick (no. 49). Antalya Museum, Turkey (1036–3, 1040 1–2, 1041 1–4, 1035). Dumbarton Oaks, Byzantine Collection, Washington, DC (DO. BZ. 63.36.38).

Source: Designed by the author. Photographs of Antalya pieces by author. Photograph of DO piece by Dumbarton Oaks, Byzantine Collection, Washington, DC.

Figure 1.48 Fragment of candlestick (no. 50). Dumbarton Oaks, Byzantine Collection, Washington, DC (DO. BZ. 65.1.20).

Source: Photograph by Dumbarton Oaks, Byzantine Collection, Washington, DC.

Figure 1.49a Rim sheets for an altar table (no. 51) from Antalya Museum, Turkey (1037 1–2, 1045 1–6 and 1038 1–2).

Source: Photograph and design by the author.

Figure 1.49b Rim sheets for an altar table (no. 51) from Dumbarton Oaks, Byzantine Collection, Washington, DC (DO. BZ. 65.1.10 a-g/63.36.11 a-d).

Source: Photograph and design by the author.

Figure 1.50a One of the plain sheets for the top of the altar table (no. 52) from Dumbarton Oaks, Byzantine Collection, Washington, DC (DO 65.1.10 h, i, j, k, l).

Source: Photograph by the author.

Figure 1.50b One of the plain sheets for the top of the altar table (no. 52) from Antalya Museum, Turkey (1024).

Source: Photograph by the author.

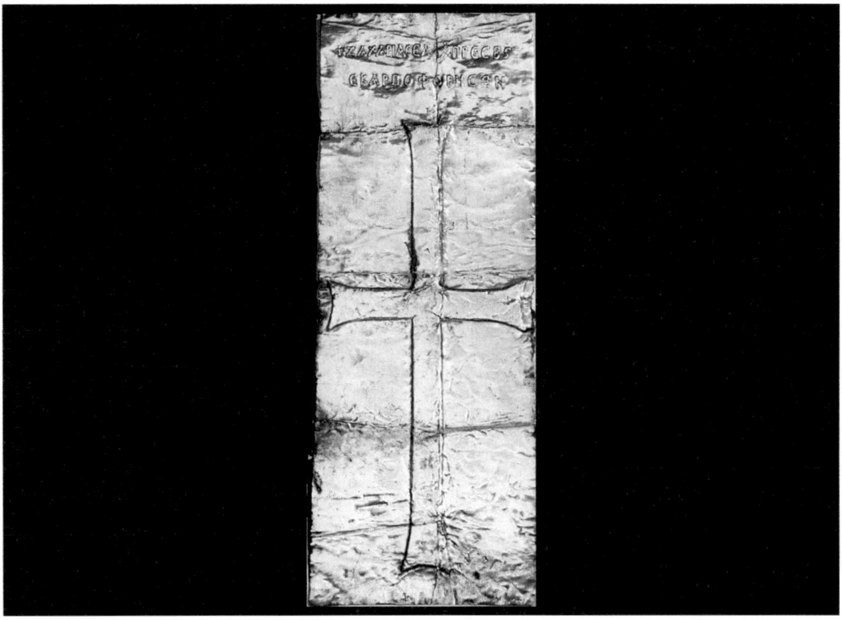

Figure 1.51 Inscribed plain sheet (no. 53). Dumbarton Oaks, Byzantine Collection, Washington, DC (DO. BZ. 79.4).

Source: Photograph by Dumbarton Oaks, Byzantine Collection, Washington, DC.

Figure 1.52 Inscribed plain sheet (no. 54). Antalya Museum, Turkey (1025 and 1044).
Source: Photograph by the author.

Figure 1.53 Silver bowl with five imperial stamps (no. 55). Dumbarton Oaks, Byzantine Collection, Washington, DC (DO. BZ.63.36.24).

Source: Photograph by Dumbarton Oaks, Byzantine Collection, Washington, DC.

2 Inscriptions on the Sion Vessels

Forty-five of the fifty-seven objects in the Treasure were inscribed (Table 1.1). Twelve were not: three of the seven chalices; the ewer; two book covers; one of the lamp stands, the plain silver sheets for the altar table; the silver ring set; the pincers and the staff.[1] Only one of the inscriptions is illegible, that on one of the openwork lamps (no. 42), as a result of its smashed and crushed state. It is not known whether one of the book covers (no. 46) and a candlestick (no. 50) were inscribed, again because of their fragmentary state. The inscriptions take a variety of forms. Many include the names and title of their donor; some bear the names of those in whose memory the vessel was given. The inscriptions generally use phrases such as: 'in fulfilment of a vow'; 'this was presented in the time of'; 'X offers/presents this to the great God/Mother of God'; 'Holy God'; 'Holy Mighty One'; 'Holy Immortal One have mercy on us'; 'Thrice Holy Lord help'; 'Holy Sion help' (see Table 2.1 for details).

The inscriptions indicate that the donors were primarily members of the clergy: three bishops (Eutychianos, who gave most, Paregoros, and Theodore); and one priest (Zacharias).[2] Other names that appear are the deacons Prinkipios and Konon, and Maria, Himeria, John, Angelous Roufinos and Eutychianos (once more, on a lamp without a title), presumably lay people. All of these are commemorated by silverware given for their memory. Whether these people were the actual donors, in the sense that they presented the vessels

1 An explanation of the inscriptions on the objects in the Sion Treasure is provided in Table 2.1 in this chapter; it details writing and translation and thumbnails of inscriptions, and explains which object was given by which donor. Thumbnails of some objects could not be provided owing to the condition of the objects, for example, some chalices which were folded do not provide clear enough photographs to put into thumbnails. And for others, it was not possible to take enough photographs to create the entire inscription since they were both circular and could not be taken out of the case in the museum.

2 For detailed examination on the donors see I. Ševčenko, 'The Sion Treasure: the evidence of the inscriptions', in S. A. Boyd and M. M. Mango (ed.), *Ecclesiastical Silver Plate in Sixth-Century Byzantium* (Washington, DC, 1992), 46–58.

DOI: 10.4324/9781003345503-3

themselves, or whether others gave the objects on their behalf is unknown.[3] The inscription on the rim sheeting (no. 51) reads: 'Paregoros, most humble bishop, offers this to Christ the true God for the memory and repose of his parents, and brothers and their children and Nicholas, Severus, and Apphianos, the lector' and indicates that bishop Paregoros offered it in memory of his family, not himself.

The lamp (no. 39) that mentions the name of Eutychianos without a title is problematic. All other inscriptions mentioning Eutychianos include his title of bishop, so these might be two different people. Moreover, the inscription reads 'In memory of Eutychianos': the lamp was not donated by Eutychianos, but by someone else in Eutychianos's memory. In terms of its technique and style, the lamp is comparable to the other lamps given by bishop Eutychianos. This led Susan Boyd to suggest that this lamp, like the others, was given by bishop Eutychianos in memory of another Eutychianos, a relative.[4] The silver stamps of the lamp suggest that it was one of the earliest lamps presented to the Sion monastery, which would make it one of bishop Eutychianos's first gifts.[5] But there is no proof of this; we cannot be sure who this Eutychianos was.

Boyd also suggested that the openwork lamp (no. 40) given 'in memory of Himeria' was for another member of bishop Eutychianos's family since its silver stamps suggest that it was given to the church at the same time when the lamp for the memory of Eutychianos was given. Again, this cannot also be proven. Although the other five lamps were donated by bishop Eutychianos, the others might have been given by someone else; that these openwork lamps are similar in style and decoration does not mean that they were given by the same donor. The resemblances may just tell us that the lamps came from the same workshop. Further, when silver was stamped and when it was used are two different stages in the production of silverware, and we cannot assume that the objects bearing the same stamps and similar decoration were donated at the same time.

Of the forty-four inscriptions, only five do not mention an individual by name. Four of these anonymous inscriptions are on the chalices (nos 22, 25, 26, 28), and one is on the base of a candlestick (no. 49). They read: 'a vow/or prayer of those whose names are known to God'; 'having given thanks I made it'; 'for the most holy hymn this was presented'.

3 For discussion of the act of giving an object in someone's memory see; S. Boyd, 'A bishop's gift: openwork lamps from the Sion Treasure', in F. Baratte (ed.), *Argenterie romaine et byzantine: Actes de la table ronde* (Paris, 1988), 194.

4 Boyd, 'A bishop's gift', 194.

5 E.C. Dodd, 'The question of workshop: evidence of the stamps on the Sion Treasure', in *Ecclesiastical Silver Plate*, ed. Boyd and Mango, 61.

Table 2.1 Inscriptions on Sion Objects

No.	*Object*	*Inscription*	*Thumbnails*	*Translation*
1	Paten	εΥΤΥΧΙΑΝΟϹ εΛΑΧΙϹΤΟϹ εΠΙϹΚΟΠΟϹ Τω ΜεΓΑΛω Θεω ΥΠεΡ ΑΦεϹεωϹ ΑΜΑΡΤΙωΝ		Eutychianos, most humble bishop (presents or offers this) to the Great God, for the forgiveness of his sins
2	Paten	ƐΥΤΥΧΙΑΝΟϹ ƐΛΑΧΙϹΤΟϹ ƐΠΙϹΚΟΠΟϹ Τω ΜƐΓΑΛω ΘƐω ΥΠƐΡ ΑΦƐϹƐωϹ ΑΜΑΡΤΙωΝ		Eutychianos, most humble bishop, presents this to the Great God, for the forgiveness of his sins
3	Paten	ƐΠΙ ΤΟΥ ΟϹΙωΤΑΤΟΥ Κϛ ΜΑΚΑΡΙωΤΑΤΟΥ ΗΜωΝ ƐΠΙϹΚϛ ƐΥΤΥΧΙΑΝΟΥ ΚΑΤƐϹΚƐΥΑϹΘΙ		This was presented in the time of our most holy and blessed bishop Eutychianos

4	Paten	ΥΠΕΡ ΜΝΗΜΗC ΚΑΙ ΑΝΑΠΑΥCΕωC ΑΓΓΕΛΕΥΟΥ ΡΟΥΦΙΝΟΥ ΤΟΥ ΤΗC ΛΑΜΠΡΑC ΜΝΗΜΗC		For the memory and repose of Angelouos Roufinos of illustrious memory
5	Paten	ΥΠΕΡ ΜΝΗΜΗC Κ … ΑΝΑΠΑΥCΕωC ΙωΑΝΝΟΥ ΤΟΥ ΤΗC ΘΕΟΦΙΛ … ΜΝΗΜΗC Κ … ΠΡΟΚΛΗC ΤΗC ΑΥΤΟΥ ΘΥΓΑΤΡΟC		For the memory and repose of John, of God-loving memory, and Procle his daughter
6	Paten	ΥΠΕΡ ΜΝΗΜΗC ΜΑΡΙΑC ΛΑΜΠΡΟΤΑς	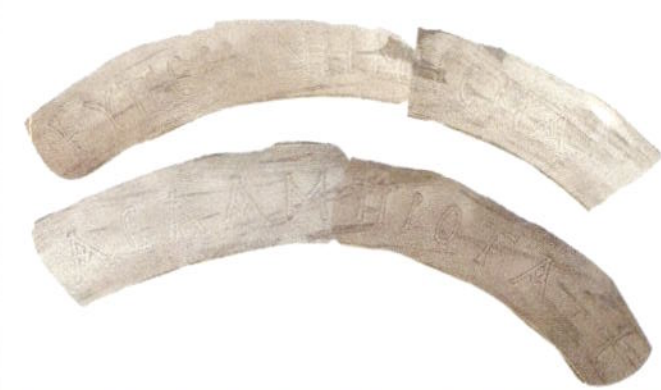	For the memory of Maria the illustrious

(*Continued*)

Table 2.1 (Continued)

No.	*Object*	*Inscription*	*Thumbnails*	*Translation*
7	Polycandelon (Cruciform)	Inscription: TRICAΓIƐ KƐ BOHΘI, monogram: ƐYTYXIANOY ƐΠΙCKOΠOY		Inscription: Thrice Holy Lord help, Monogram: bishop Eutychianos
8	Polycandelon (Cruciform)	Inscription: TRICAΓIƐ KƐ BOHΘI, monogram: ƐYTYXIANOY ƐΠΙCKOΠOY		Inscription: Thrice Holy Lord help, Monogram: bishop Eutychianos

9	Polycandelon (Cruciform)	Inscription: TRICAΓIЄ KЄ BOHΘI, monogram: ЄYTYXIANOY ЄΠICKOΠOY		Inscription: Thrice Holy Lord help, Monogram: bishop Eutychianos
10	Polycandelon (Circular)	Inscription: YΠЄP ЄYXHC KAI CωTHPIAC ЄYTYXIANOY ЄΛAXICTOY ЄΠICKOΠOY, monogram: ЄYTYXIANOY ЄΠICKOΠOY		Inscription: In fulfilment of a vow and for the salvation of Eutychianos, most humble bishop. Monogram: bishop Eutychianos
11	Polycandelon (Circular)	Inscription: YΠЄP ЄYXHC KAI CωTHPIAC ЄYTYXIANOY ЄΛAXICTOY ЄΠICKOΠOY, monogram: ЄYTYXIANOY ЄΠICKOΠOY		Inscription: In fulfilment of a vow and for the salvation of Eutychianos, most humble bishop. Monogram: bishop Eutychianos

(*Continued*)

Table 2.1 (Continued)

No.	*Object*	*Inscription*	*Thumbnails*	*Translation*
12	Polycandelon (Circular)	Inscription: ΥΠƐΡ ƐΥΧΗC ΚΑΙ CωΤΗΡΙΑC ƐΥΤΥΧΙΑΝΟΥ ƐΛΑΧΙCΤΟΥ ƐΠΙCΚΟΠΟΥ, monogram: ƐΥΤΥΧΙΑΝΟΥ ƐΠΙCΚΟΠΟΥ		Inscription: In fulfilment of a vow and for the salvation of Eutychianos, most humble bishop. Monogram: bishop Eutychianos
13	Polycandelon (Rectangular)	Inscription: ΑΓΙΑ CΙωΝ ΒΟΗΘΙ, Monogram: ƐΥΤΥΧΙΑΝΟΥ ƐΠΙCΚΟΠΟΥ		Inscription: Holy Sion help. Monogram: bishop Eutychianos
14	Polycandelon (Rectangular)	Inscription: ΑΓΙΑ CΙωΝ ΒΟΗΘΙ, Monogram: ƐΥΤΥΧΙΑΝΟΥ ƐΠΙCΚΟΠΟΥ		Inscription: Holy Sion help. Monogram: bishop Eutychianos

15	Polycandelon (Rectangular)	Inscription: ΑΓΙΑ CIωN ΒΟΗΘΙ, Monogram: ƐΥΤΥΧΙΑΝΟΥ ƐΠΙCΚΟΠΟΥ		Inscription: Holy Sion help. Monogram: bishop Eutychianos
16	Polycandelon (Rectangular)	Inscription: ΑΓΙΑ CIωN ΒΟΗΘΙ, Monogram: ƐΥΤΥΧΙΑΝΟΥ ƐΠΙCΚΟΠΟΥ		Inscription: Holy Sion help. Monogram: bishop Eutychianos

(*Continued*)

Table 2.1 (Continued)

No.	*Object*	*Inscription*	*Thumbnails*	*Translation*
17	Polycandelon (Rectangular)	Inscription: ΑΓΙΑ CIωN ΒΟΗΘΙ, Monogram: ƐΥΤΥΧΙΑΝΟΥ ƐΠΙCΚΟΠΟΥ		Inscription: Holy Sion help. Monogram: bishop Eutychianos
18	Polycandelon (Rectangular)	Inscription: ΑΓΙΑ CIωN ΒΟΗΘΙ, Monogram: ƐΥΤΥΧΙΑΝΟΥ ƐΠΙCΚΟΠΟΥ		Inscription: Holy Sion help. Monogram: bishop Eutychianos

19	CENSER	ƐΥΤΥΧΙΑΝΟϹ ƐΛΑΧΙϹΤΟϹ ƐΠΙϹΚΟΠΟϹ ΤΗ ΔƐϹΠΟΙΝΗ ΤΗ ΘƐΟΘΟΚω		Eutychianos, most humble bishop (offers this) to our lady, the Mother of God
20	CENSER	ΥΠƐΡ ƐΥΧΗϹ ΚΑΙ ϹωΤΗΡΙΑϹ ΚΑΙ ΑΦƐϹƐωϹ ΑΜΑRΤΙωΝ εΥΤΥΧΙΑΝ… … ΑΧΙϹΤΟΥ ƐΠΙϹΚΟΠΟΥ ΑΜΗΝ		In fulfilment of a vow and for the salvation of and the forgiveness (of the sins) of Eutychianos, most humble bishop. Amen
22	CHALICE	… ΝΟΜΑΤΑ ΟΙΔƐ …		A vow/a prayer of those whose names are known to God.
25	CHALICE	ƐΥΧΗ ωΝΟ ΘƐΟϹ ΤΑ ΟΝΟΜΑ … ΟΙΔƐΝ	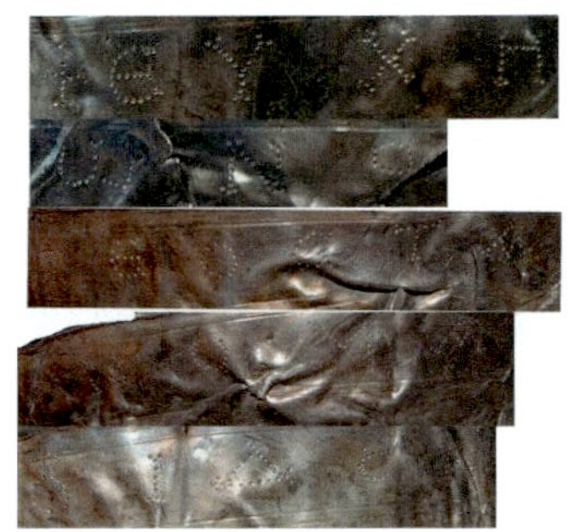	A vow/a prayer of those whose names are known to God

(*Continued*)

Table 2.1 (Continued)

No.	*Object*	*Inscription*	*Thumbnails*	*Translation*
26	CHALICE	ƐYXA … Tω N ΠƐΠO..	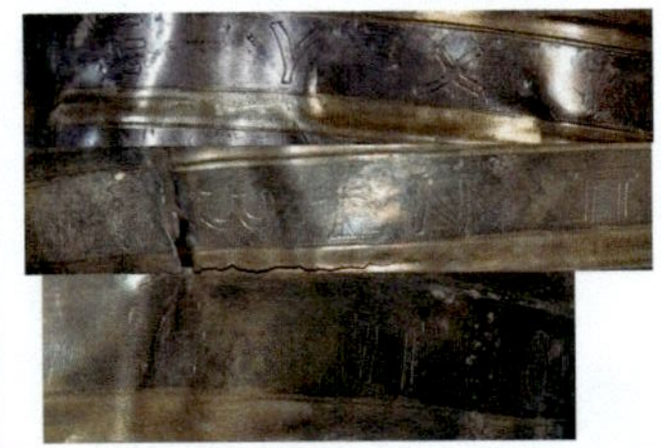	Having given thanks, I made (it)
28	AMPHORA	AΓIA CIωN BOHΘ ƐYTYXIANOY Ɛ …		Holy Sion helps bishop Eutychianos
29	Amphora	AΓIA CIωN BOHΘI ƐYTYXIANOY ƐΠICKOΠOY		Holy Sion helps bishop Eutychianos

31	Standing lamp	… XIANOC ƐΛAXICTOC ƐΠICKOΠOC Tω MEΓA …		Eutychianos, most humble bishop (offers this) to the great God
32	Standing lamp	..C ƐΛAXIC CKOΠOC Tω MƐΓAΛ …		Eutychianos, most humble bishop (offers this) to the great God
33	Standing lamp	ƐYTYXIANOC ƐΛAXICTOC ƐΠICKOΠOC Tω MEΓAΛω ΘƐω		Eutychianos, most humble bishop (offers this) to the great God
34	Standing lamp	ƐYTYXIANOC ƐΛAXICTOC ƐΠICKOΠOC Tω MEΓAΛω ΘƐω	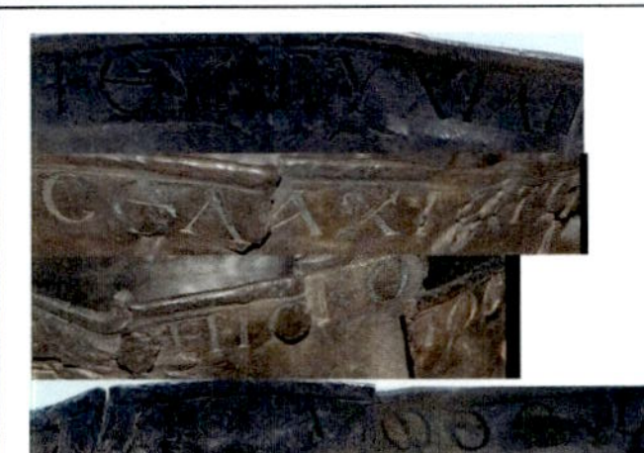	Eutychianos, most humble bishop, (offers this) to the great God

(*Continued*)

Table 2.1 (Continued)

No.	*Object*	*Inscription*	*Thumbnails*	*Translation*
35	Openwork lamp	ƐΥΤΥΧ..ΑΝΟC ƐΛΑΧΙCΤΟC ƐΠΙCΚΟΠΟC Τω ΜƐΓΑΛω ΘƐω		Eutychianos, most humble bishop (offers this) to the great God
36	Openwork lamp	ΕΥΤΥΧΙΑΝΟS ƐΛΑΧΙCΤΟC ƐΠΙCΚΟΠΟC Τ … … ..ω ΘƐω		Eutychianos, most humble bishop (offers this) to the great God
37	Openwork lamp	ƐΥΤΥΧΙΑΝΟC ƐΛΑΧΙCΤΟC ƐΠΙCΚΟΠΟC Τω ΜƐΓΑΛω ΘƐω		Eutychianos, most humble bishop (offers this) to the great God
38	Openwork lamp	ΥΠƐΡ ƐΥΧΗC ƐΥΤΥΧΙΑΝΟΥ ƐΛΑΧΙCΤΟΥ ƐΠΙCΚΟΠΟΥ		In fulfilment of a vow of Eutychianos, most humble bishop

39	Openwork lamp	ΥΠƐΡ ΜΝΗΜΗC Κ.. ΑΝΑΠΑΥCƐωC ƐΥΤΥΧΙΑΝΟΥ ΤΟΥ ΤΗC ΜΑΚΑΡ … S ΜΝΗΜΗC.		For the memory and repose of Eutychianos of blessed memory
40	Openwork lamp	ΥΠƐΡ ΜΝΗΜΗC ΚΑΙ ΑΝΑΠΑΥCƐωC ΙΜƐΡΙΑC ΤΗC ΜΑ … .ΤΗC		For the memory and repose of the most blessed Himeria
41	Openwork lamp	ƐΥΤΥΧΙΑΝΟC ƐΛΑΧΙCΤΟC ƐΠΙCΚΟΠΟC ΤΗ ΔƐCΠΟΙΝΗ ΤΗ ΘƐΟΘΟΚω		Eutychianos, most humble bishop, offers this to our lady, the Mother of God

(*Continued*)

Table 2.1 (Continued)

No.	*Object*	*Inscription*	*Thumbnails*	*Translation*
43	Suspension bracket for five lamps	Obv. vertical rod: +ΑΓΙΟC Ο ΘƐΟC ΑΓΙΟC ΙCΧΥΡΟC /lateral rod: ΑΓΙΟC ΑΘΑΝΑΤΟC ƐΛƐΗCΟΝ ΗΜΑC.	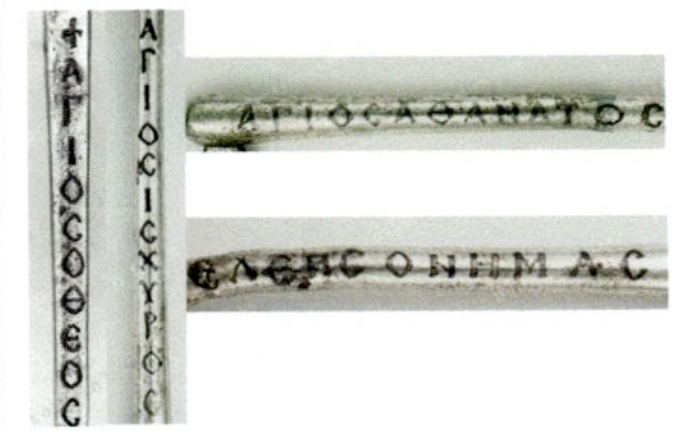	Obv: Holy God, holy mighty one, holy immortal one, have mercy on us
43	Suspension bracket for five lamps	Rev. vertical rod: + ΥΠƐΡ ƐΥΧΗC ΚΑΙ CωΤΗΡΙΑC ƐΥΤΥΧΙΑΝΟΥ /lateral rod: ƐΛΑΧΙCΤΟΥ ƐΠΙCΚΟΠΟΥ	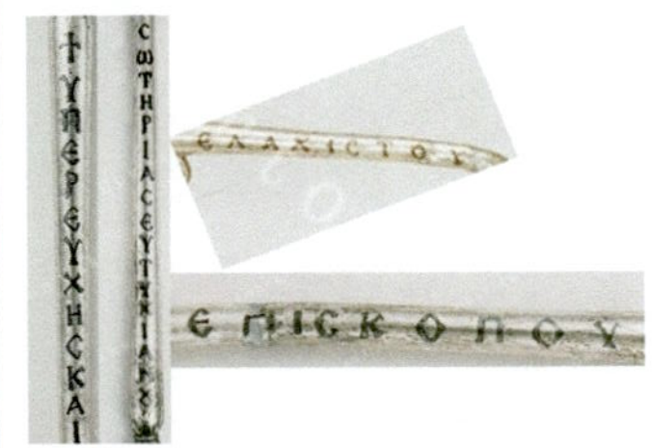	Rev: In fulfilment of a vow and for the salvation of Eutychianos, most humble bishop
45	Book cover	Front cover: ΥΠƐΡ ΜΝΗΜΗC Κ ΑΝΑΠΑΥCƐωC ΠΡΙΓΚΙΠΙΟΥ ΔΙΑΚΟΝΟΥ Κ ΣΤƐΦΑΝΗC Κ ΛƐΟΝΤΙΑC. Back cover: DO fragment: ΚΟΝωΝ … C … ΑΚΟΝ … Antalya Fragment: ΑΝΑΠΑΥCƐωC …		**Front cover**: For the memory and repose of Prinkipios, deacon, and Stephane and Leontia. **Back cover, DO fragment**: deacon Konon, **Antalya fragment**: for the repose of

47	Lampstand	ΑΝƐΝƐωΘΗ ΤΟ ƐΡΓΟΝ ΤΟΥΤΟ + ƐΠΙ ΘƐΟΔωΡΟΥ ΤΟΥ ΟCΙωΤΑΤΟΥ ƐΠΙCΚΟ..		This was renewed in the time of Theodore, most holy bishop
49	Candlestick	ƐΠΙ ΥΜΝΟΥ ΤΟΥ ΟCΙωΤΑΤΟΥ Ο..ΙCΚΟΣ ΚΑΤƐCΚƐΥΑCΘΗ		(At/for) the most holy hymn, this object was presented
51	Rim sheets for altar table	Front Panel: ΠΑΡΗΓΟΡΟC ƐΛΑΧ ƐΠΙCΚΟΠΟC ΥΠƐΡ ΜΝΗΜΗC Κ ΑΝΑΠΑΥCƐωC ΤωΝ ΑΥΤΟΥ ΓΟΝΑΙωΝ Κ.. Α[ΔƐ]ΛΦωΝ Κ ΑΝƐΨΙωΝ Κ ΝΙΚΟΛΑΟΥ CƐ (end of the front panel). Right edge: CƐΒΗΡΟΥ ΚΑΙ ΑΠΦΙΑΝΟΥ ΑΝΑΓΝ Χω Τω ΑΛΙΘƐΙΝω ΘƐω ΠΡΟCΦƐΡƐΙ		Paregoros, most humble bishop, offers this to Christ the true God for the memory and repose of his parents, and brothers and their children, and Nicholas, Severus, and Apphianos, the lector\

(*Continued*)

Table 2.1 (Continued)

No.	*Object*	*Inscription*	*Thumbnails*	*Translation*
53	Inscribed plain sheet	ΖΑΧΑΡΙΑC ЄΛΑΧs ΠΡЄCBS ЄΚΑΡΠΟΦΟΡΗCЄΝ		Zacharias, most humble priest, offered (this), brought forth fruit
54	Inscribed plain sheet	ΠΑΡΗΓΟΡΟC ЄΛΑΧS ЄΠΙCKOS ЄΚΑΡΠΟΦΟΡΗCЄΝ		Paregoros, most humble bishop, offered (this), brought forth fruit

3 Silver Stamps on the Sion Treasure

In total, twenty-five of the fifty-seven vessels in the Sion Treasure carry silver stamps: one of them is in a private collection (Digby-Jones) in London, eight of them are held in Antalya Museum, and the others in the Dumbarton Oaks collection (for details see Table 3.1).[1] All twenty-five were given to the monastery by bishop Eutychianos (nos 1, 7–20, 28, 33–38 and 41). Each generally includes five stamps. Some (nos 13, 14, 15, 17, 18 and 39) have six stamps as a result of the same stamp being applied twice; others have only one or four surviving stamps, either as a result of the object's fragmentary state, or because the stamps were deformed.[2] The five stamps were applied in five different shapes: round, hexagonal, square, long (actually oblong but called 'long' by Dodd) and cruciform.[3] Round, hexagonal, square, long stamps contain a bust or a monogram of Justinian I, surrounded by the name and the long and cruciform stamps bear cross-shaped monograms of various other individuals. However, the stamps of one standing lamp (no. 34) are completely different from all the others. It carries two stamps, one rectangular and the other a rosette (Figure 3.1).

The stamps on the Sion Treasure were first examined by Erika Cruickshank Dodd. She could not make public her full work on the Sion Treasure's silver stamps because she was not allowed to publish the Antalya vessels although she was able to view them. Dodd explained that there was conflict between the Antalya Museum and Dumbarton Oaks over the repatriation of the Sion Treasure. Despite having an agreement with Nezih Fıratlı (director of the

1 Part of this chapter was also published as A. Ari, 'Byzantine control stamps applied on the silver objects from the Sion Treasure', *Nevşehir Hacı Bektaş Veli Üniversitesi SBE Dergisi*, 12.1 (2022), 34–55.

2 Table 3.1 provides detailed information about all of the stamps. In general terms, the content of the stamps on the Sion Treasure objects is listed further. Some stamps on nos 16 and 17 are missing, but some of the surviving stamps are applied twice on this object. If the other stamps were not missing, there would be six stamps on these objects.

3 Especially the stamps on paten (no. 1), polycandela (nos 9, 15, 16, 17 and 18), amphora (no. 28), standing lamp (no. 33), openwork lamps (nos 35–41). Dodd, *Byzantine Silver Stamps* (Washington, DC, 1961), 6.

DOI: 10.4324/9781003345503-4

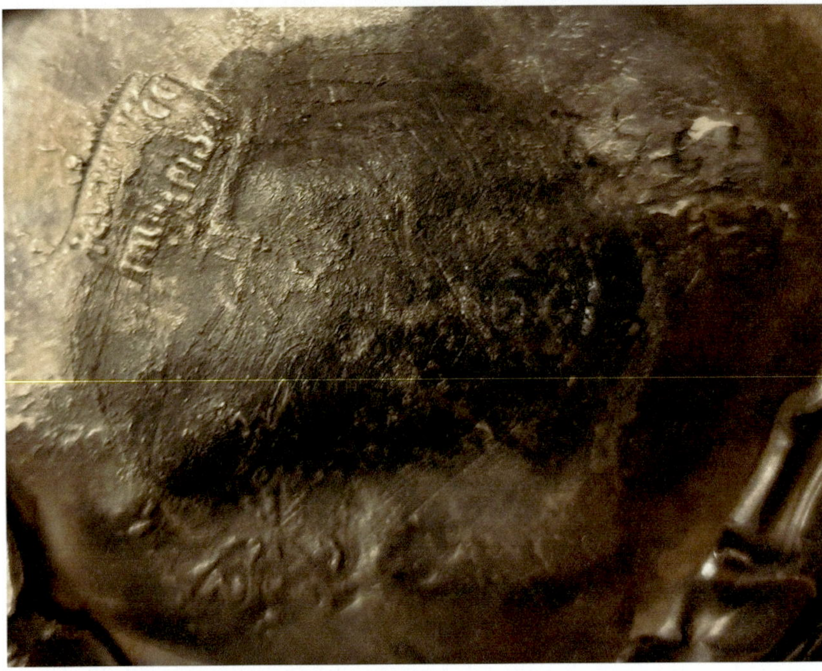

Figure 3.1 Irregular or non-imperial stamps applied on standing lamp (no. 34). Antalya Museum, Turkey (1042).

Source: Photograph by the author.

Istanbul Archaeology Museum) to publish everything, Antalya Museum refused to allow a scholar from Dumbarton Oaks to publish the Sion objects in the Antalya Museum.[4] Consequently, Dodd produced two papers discussing the possible workshop origins of the objects, which mentioned the stamps but contained no detailed information.[5] These papers present important material about the appearance of the stamps, and the information they provide about the date of the Treasure, and its circulation. However, they do not give detailed information about the names on the stamps and the information that we can gain from each stamp.[6] I have had the opportunity to examine the stamps in both collections, and I will present them both together here in this section.

4 E.C. Dodd, 'The question of workshop: evidence of the stamps on the Sion Treasure', in S.A.Boyd and M.M.Mango (ed.), *Ecclesiastical Silver Plate in Sixth-Century Byzantium* (Washington, DC, 1992), 57.

5 Dodd, 'The question of workshop', 57–64; Dodd, 'The location of silver stamping: evidence from newly discovered stamps', in *Ecclesiastical Silver Plate*, ed. Boyd and Mango, 217–24.

6 Dodd, 'The question of workshop', 57–64; Dodd, 'The location of silver stamping', 217–24.

Since the stamps on Sion silver vessels, except for the ones on the lampstand no. 34, include the bust and monogram of the reigning emperor and the names and monograms of officials working under the emperor, these stamps can be defined as imperial stamps.[7] The basic format for imperial silver stamps is that the round stamps bear the bust and name of the reigning emperor; the hexagonal and square stamps contain the monogram and name of the reigning emperor; the long stamps have the bust of the reigning emperor, cross monogram and the name; and the cruciform stamps bear the cross monogram and name of the individual.[8] This is also the case with the Sion silver.

The additional names on the stamps were generally common personal names or a title. These names belong to officials who responsible for applying stamps. These official names suggest how the system worked and how many officials were responsible for stamping silver in the name of the emperor. In the Sion silver, where there are five stamps, four or five different names are used, suggesting that perhaps up to five officials worked in the stamping process, a designated group representing imperial authority. Possibly each individual was responsible for applying the stamp on which his name was inscribed. As it can be seen in Table 3.1 in this chapter and the list of inscribed names in *Byzantine Silver Stamps* published by Dodd, some names can be seen in two different stamps, suggesting that one individual might have been responsible for more than one stamp. But this is not the case for every vessel, because on some objects (no. 19) there are five different names inscribed on five stamps.[9]

The cross monograms which appear on long and cruciform stamps are different from those belonging to the emperor.[10] On long stamps, we see these monograms with the bust of the emperor, while on the cruciform stamps we see only the monogram. The cross monograms are also helpful for understanding how the control of silver especially stamping silver worked. According to Dodd, these secondary monograms were those of someone whose position were higher than the other officials whose names were inscribed on the stamps. They indicate that the long and the cruciform stamps were applied under the authority of the officials whose monograms appear on them, presumably one of the senior fiscal officials responsible for the administration of silver.[11] Dodd makes this argument by relying on the fact that since these monograms were not the monograms of emperors, then the monograms might have belonged to the senior official known as the *Comes Sacrarum Largitionum*. Indeed, the names in monograms in long and cross stamps correspond to the names of the *Comites Sacrarum Largitionum* published by Dodd.[12] It seems highly probable that stamping silver

7 Dodd, *Byzantine Silver Stamps*, 8–15.
8 Dodd, *Byzantine Silver Stamps*, 8–15.
9 Dodd, *Byzantine Silver Stamps*, 17 and table IV.
10 Dodd, *Byzantine Silver Stamps*, 25–7 and 20, where she defines them as 'secondary' stamps.
11 Dodd, *Byzantine Silver Stamps*, 27–8.
12 Dodd, *Byzantine Silver Stamps*, Table V.

was controlled by the authority of the *Comes Sacrarum Largitionum*, who controlled mines, state mills and dye works and materials such as silver and gold for the purpose of taxation.[13] The emergence of this role dates back to the fourth century CE and continued into the seventh century until it was replaced by the position of *Sakellarios*.[14] The *comes* was a role in the imperial gift. The list of the different *Comites Sacrarum Largitionum* indicates that there was no fixed term for the role. During the reign of emperor Justinian I, there were five different *Comites*: Elias in 528 and 529; Starategius between 533 and 538; Petrus between 539 and 542; and Iohannes in 546 for one year before being replaced by Petrus Barysimes. Petrus Barysimes was assigned the position twice and after Petrus Barysimes, it looks as if Julianus was the last *comes* of Justinian's reign, since with emperor Justin II (565–578), Magnus was assigned the position.[15]

As for the standing lamp (no. 34) with totally different stamps, it may well be that these stamps were non-imperial or irregular. Other such irregular stamps on other silver vessels include rectangular stamps with inscriptions, rosette stamps and circular stamps bearing the figure of Christ. Some inscriptions on the rectangular stamps mention a place of stamping – Carthage and Antioch – but sadly this is not the case for the Sion lamp.[16] Therefore, it is plausible to say that twenty-four objects were stamped with imperial stamps and one was stamped with irregular stamps. Now I am going to present the imperial stamps applied on the twenty-four vessels from the Sion treasure.

The Stamps on Sion Silverware

Round Stamps are used on twenty of the twenty-four stamped vessels. They do not survive on four (nos 1, 16, 35, 36) and on two of the remaining twenty, the names are illegible and the bust of emperor is not clear (nos 9 and 18). On a polycandelon (no. 15) and an openwork lamp (no. 39), this stamp was applied twice.

The round stamps on the Sion silver all consist of a bust of Justinian I, and the name of an official. The bust of the emperor is nimbed, beardless, wearing a chlamys with pendants. It is identified by Dodd as Type I and as used during the reigns of Anastasius I (491–518), Justinian I (527–565) and Justin II (565–578).[17]

13 J.P.C. Kent, 'The Comes Sacrarum Largitionum', in Dodd, *Byzantine Silver Stamps*, 35–46; M.F. Hendy, 'The administration of mints and treasuries, fourth to seventh centuries, with an appendix on the production of silver plate', in M.F. Hendy (ed.), *The Economy, Fiscal Administration and Coinage of Byzantium* (Northampton, 1989), 1–18; A. Cutler and A. Kazhdan, 'Comes Sacrarum Largitionum' in *ODB*, vol. 1, 486; A.H.M. Jones, *Later Roman Empire 284–602: A Social, Economic, and Administrative Survey*, 2nd edn, 3 vols (Norman, 1986), vol. 1, 427–38.

14 Kent, 'The Comes Sacrarum Largitionum', 37.

15 Dodd, *Byzantine Silver Stamps*, table V.

16 Dodd, *Byzantine Silver Stamps*, nos 96 and 100; Dodd, 'The question of workshop', 61.

17 Dodd, *Byzantine Silver Stamps*, table I.

Hexagonal stamps are found on twenty of the twenty-four vessels. They contain the monogram of Justinian, and an inscribed name. The hexagonal stamps on four vessels (nos. 16, 17, 35 and 36) have not survived. On six of the twenty hexagonal stamps the names are illegible (nos 9, 15, 28, 33, 39 and 55). On one openwork lamp (no. 39), the hexagonal stamp was applied twice.

Square stamps are visible on twenty-one of the twenty-four. They bear the monogram of emperor Justinian, and an inscribed name. The square stamps on three vessels (nos 16, 35 and 36) have not survived and the square stamp on one lamp (no. 40) is completely illegible. On four of the surviving square stamps (nos 1, 20, 33, 41) the monogram of Justinian I is legible but inscribed names are illegible. On one polycandelon (no. 13), this stamp was applied twice, one of which was cut in half during decoration.

The long stamps are found on nineteen of the Sion vessels. Five (nos 16, 35, 36, 39, 40) lack it. The stamp bears the bust of emperor Justinian, the secondary monogram of the senior official of finance (the Comes Sacrarum Largitionum), and an inscribed name. The busts, secondary monogram and inscription on long stamps applied on two vessels (nos 9, 15), are obscure, whilst the secondary monograms on three (nos 17, 20, 33) and the names on three (nos 1, 20, 33) are illegible, though the busts on these stamps can be recognised.

The cruciform stamps are used on twenty-two of the twenty-four. They carry the monogram of a chief finance officer (secondary monogram), and a name. The cruciform stamps on two vessels (nos 39 and 40) have not survived. The secondary monograms on five (nos 28, 33, 35, 36 and 41) and the name on one (no. 41) are illegible. On three polycandela (nos 14, 17 and 18) this stamp was applied twice and one of them was cut in half during decoration.

Eight of the twelve polycandela (nos 7–14: three cruciform polycandela (nos 7–9), three circular polycandela (nos 10–12) and two rectangular polycandela with tri-lobed end pieces (nos 13–14)) have the same imperial control stamps. The names and secondary monograms are identical. On the round stamp, there is a bust of Justinian surrounded by an inscribed name: IωAN-NOV (Ioannou). On the hexagonal stamp, there is monogram of Justinian and the name: ITA –ΛOV (Italou). On the square stamp, there is monogram of Justinian and the name: ΔωPω- ΘEOV (Dorotheou). On the long stamp, there is a bust of Justinian – the same as on the round stamp – and the secondary monogram of a senior official and an inscribed name: IωAN-NOV (Ioannou). The letters on the monogram read; I-ω-A-N-OV which can also be read as Ioannou. On the cruciform stamp, there is a monogram of Iohannes and the name: ΠAVΛOV (Paulou) (Figure 3.2). This suggests that the silver for these eight polycandela were stamped under the supervision of Iohannes and might have been stamped at the same time or within a short amount of time.

The other four polycandela (nos 15–18) have the same imperial control stamps. However, no. 16 has only the cruciform stamp, since it is in a fragmentary condition. It seems reasonable to presume that the lost stamps

Figure 3.2 Imperial stamps applied on circular polycandelon (no. 10). Antalya Museum, Turkey (1053).

Source: Photograph by the author.

would match the stamps on the other three polycandela, since the cruciform stamp is identical to the others. The same applies to the polycandelon (no. 17) on which the hexagonal stamp is missing. When the stamps on these polycandela are examined, the round stamps have a bust of Justinian surrounded by an inscribed name: ΛΕΟΝ – ΤΙΟV (Leontiou), the hexagonal stamps have a monogram of Justinian surrounded by the name: ΙΤΑ –ΛΟV (Italou), and the square stamps have Justinian's monogram and the name: EVCE – TEIC (Euseteis). On the long stamps, there is a bust of Justinian, the same type as on the round stamps, a monogram of the senior official, reading A-Δ-E-OV, Adeou (Adeos) and a name: ΔΙΟΜ – ΙΔΟV (Diomidou). The cruciform stamps have the monogram of Adeos and the name EVΦPONIOV (Euphroniou) (Figure 3.3). This means that the silver for these polycandela were stamped under the supervision of Adeos.

Figure 3.3 Imperial stamps applied on rectangular polycandelon (no. 17). Dumbarton Oaks, Byzantine Collection, Washington, DC (DO.BZ.65.1.7).

Source: Photograph by Dumbarton Oaks, Byzantine Collection, Washington, DC.

The paten in Antalya Museum (no. 1) has four imperial stamps, with the names and secondary monograms close to the ones on the four polycandela with semi-circular end pieces (nos 15–18). The round stamp is missing. Here, the Hexagonal stamp has the monogram of Justinian surrounded by the name ΛΕΟΝ – ΤΙΟV (Leontiou). On the square stamp, there is the monogram of Justinian but the official's name is illegible. The long stamp bears the bust of Justinian, again the same type as the bust on the round stamps on other vessels, the monogram of a senior official, A-Δ-E-OV Adeou, and an illegible name. The cruciform stamp has Adeos's monogram and the name EVΓENIOV (Eugeniou).

The censer in Antalya Museum (no. 19) has five imperial stamps, which fit the usual pattern though with some different names. On the round stamp, there is a bust of Justinian surrounded by the name ΛΕΟΝ – ΤΙΟV (Leontiou); the hexagonal stamp has Justinian's monogram surrounded by the name XPICTO-ΦOPOV (Christoforou); the square stamp has a monogram of Justinian and the name: EVCE – TEIC (Euseteis); the long stamp carries the usual bust of Justinian, the monogram of the senior official Adeos and the name: ΔΙΟΜ – ΙΔΟV (Diomidou). Finally, the cruciform stamp has Adeos's monogram and the name EVΦPONIOV (Euphroniou) (Figure 3.4).

The stamps on the Antalya censer were repeated on the amphora in the Dumbarton Oaks Collection (no. 28), also stamped under the supervision of Adeos. Here the inscribed name on the hexagonal stamp is illegible. The same stamps also can be seen on the bowl (no. 55) from the Dumbarton Oaks

Figure 3.4 Imperial stamps applied on circular censer (no. 19). Antalya Museum, Turkey (1019).

Source: Photograph by the author.

collection, including the names ΛEON – TIOV (Leontiou) on the round stamp, and EVCE – TEIC (Euseteis) on the square stamp. The long and cruciform stamps again carry the monogram of Adeos. The additional names on the long and cruciform stamps are the same as those on the censer (no. 19), ΔIOM – IΔOV (Diomidou) and EVΦPONIOV (Euphroniou) (Figure 3.5). This indicates that these four objects were also stamped under the supervision of Adeos.

Six of the eight openwork lamps in the Sion treasure (nos 35, 36, 38, 39, 40 and 41) were stamped. On only two of the eight openwork lamps secondary monograms are legible. The stamps suggest that the silver for the openwork lamps was stamped under the supervision of two different officials, perhaps at two different times. The one in the Digby Jones Collection (no. 38) bears the

Figure 3.5 Imperial stamps applied on a bowl (no. 55). Dumbarton Oaks, Byzantine Collection, Washington, DC (DO. BZ.63.36.24).

Source: Photograph by Dumbarton Oaks, Byzantine Collection, Washington, DC.

monogram of Iohannes, which indicates the silver for this object was stamped under the supervision of the *Comes Sacrarum Largitionum* Iohannes.[18] The bust and monograms of Justinian and inscribed names are identical to those applied on the polycandela with the monogram of Iohannes (nos 7–14: three cruciform polycandela (nos 7–9), three circular polycandela (nos 10–12) and two rectangular polycandela with tri-lobed end pieces (nos. 13–14)). The silver of the openwork lamp (no. 41) was stamped by Adeos and its stamps match those on the polycandela (nos 15–18), one paten (no. 1), one censer (no. 19), one amphora (no. 28) and a bowl (no. 55). The other two openwork lamps (nos 35 and 36) have only one cruciform stamp surviving on each but the monograms on these stamps are illegible. The stamps bearing the secondary monograms on two lamps (nos 39 and 40) are not survived. But these two lamps (nos 39 and 40) have the name ΛΕΟΝ – ΤΙΟV on the round stamp and ΙΤΑ –ΛΟV on hexagonal stamps. On the only surviving cruciform stamps, visible on two lamps (nos 35 and 36) the inscribed name ΕVΦΡΟΝΙΟV

18 The information on the stamps applied on this object and summarised in Table 3.1 gained from Dodd, 'The question of workshop', 61.

survives. Because all of these lamps carry the same names as the silver stamped under the supervision of Adeos, we can assume that they too were stamped under Adeos. Therefore, it is plausible to say that lamp (no. 38) was stamped under the supervision of Iohannes and other five openwork lamps were stamped under supervision of Adeos.

The monograms on the square, long and cruciform stamps on the censer (no. 20) and standing lamp (no. 33) in the Dumbarton Oaks Collection are also illegible. The round stamp on the censer bears the bust of Justinian surrounded by the name XPICTO- ΦOPOV, also the name on the hexagonal stamp of the Antalya Museum censer (no. 19). On the hexagonal stamp, the name is ITA –ΛOV, also used on the hexagonal stamps of all the polycandela whether stamped under the supervision of Iohannes or Adeos. The cruciform stamp on the DO censer and lamp has a new name, CEPΓIOV (Sergiou) (Figures 3.6–3.7). However, the stamps on a plate with a relief of Venus in the Tent of Anchises from the Hermitage Museum (acc. no. W.350) and on a reliquary also in the Hermitage bear the inscribed name CEPΓIOV (Sergiou) associated with the monogram of Julianus.[19] Therefore, it is plausible that the silver for these two vessels in the Sion Treasure were stamped under the supervision of Julianus.

Figure 3.6 Imperial stamps applied on hexagonal censer (no. 20). Dumbarton Oaks, Byzantine Collection, Washington, DC (DO.BZ.65.1.5).

Source: Photograph by Dumbarton Oaks, Byzantine Collection, Washington, DC.

19 Dodd, *Byzantine Silver Stamps*, table IV, 16–17b.

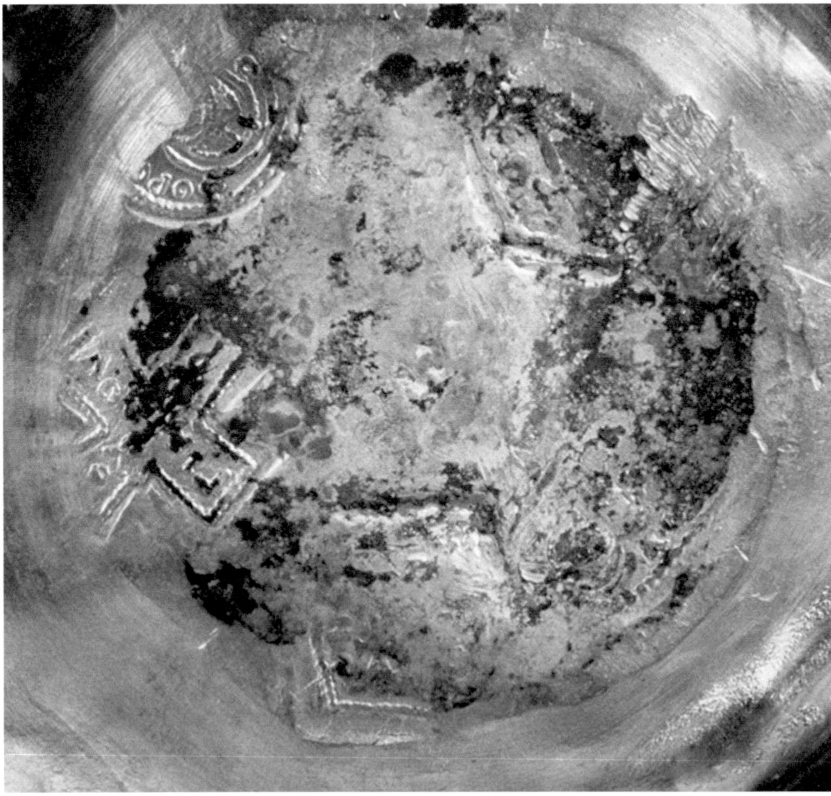

Figure 3.7 Imperial stamps applied on standing lamp (no. 33). Dumbarton Oaks, Byzantine Collection, Washington, DC (DO.BZ.63.36.17).

Source: Photograph by Dumbarton Oaks, Byzantine Collection, Washington, DC.

When the monograms of the senior imperial officials on the Sion silver are examined, it is clear that three different *Comites Sacrarum Largitionum* supervised the control of the metal, Iohannes, Adeos and Julianus. This implies that the silver was not all stamped at the same time. Interestingly, the names of the officials working under the *Comes Sacrarum Largitionum* are not all the same: stamps of the same *comes* can have different names associated with them, indicating that these officials could change.[20]

The bust and monograms of Justinian indicate a date in the sixth century. The names of the *Comites Sacrarum Largitionum* offer a way of refining this.[21] As I already mentioned, we know of five men acting as *Comes* in the reign of

20 Dodd, *Byzantine Silver Stamps*, 27–35.
21 Dodd, *Byzantine Silver Stamps*, 15, table V; Kent, 'The Comes Sacrarum Largitionum', 34–5.

Justinian: Elias (528–529), Strategius (533–538), Petrus Barysimes (539–542), Iohannes of Palestine (546), Petrus Barysimes (547–550) and Julianus (?). But there are gaps and missing names here. There are no names listed between 529 and 533 and between 550 and 565 when the objects from the Sion treasure were dated. Adeos, who has his monogram on stamps on the Sion silver does not appear in this list. We know of an Adeos who was a Syrian in control of shipping in Constantinople and Praetorian Prefect in 551.[22] This suggests he could have been *comes* sometime after 550. Presumably, the Iohannes on the Sion stamps was Iohannes of Palestine, *CSL* in perhaps 546 and it is not certain if he was the *comes* again after 560 – making it impossible to be sure whether he or another Iohannes stamped the Sion silver.[23] We also do not know for certain when Julianus was *comes*, though it seems to have been after 550.

Some of the inscribed names of officials including Iohannes, Italos and Dorotheos appear on stamps from the end of the reign of Justinian I and beginning of the reign of Justin II. At Sion, these names are on the polycandela (nos 7–14) and the objects from the Hermitage Museum which are dated to the later reign of Justinian, but they are also found on the Riha paten and flabellum, and the Stuma flabellum, dated to the beginning of the reign of emperor Justin II.[24] This suggests that the silver stamped with these names belongs to the end of Justinian I's reign.[25] Since these officials worked under Iohannes (as appears in monograms), when he was *comes* in Justinian I's reign and he left when Justinian's reign ended, but these officials with same names which were found also on stamps applied during the reign of Justin II continued working under another *comes,* since on the Riha paten and flabellum, and the Stuma flabellum, the stamps bear the monograms of Theodoros (ΘΕΟΔΟΡΟΥ) indicating that he was comes in the beginning of the reign of Justin II. This might suggest that – if we believe that the officials whose names appears on both Sion polycandela and Riha and Stuma vessels are same individuals – Iohannes was the last *comes* in Justinian's reign or he was the *comes* just before the end of Justinian's reign. However, it is not certain if he was Iohannes of Palestine or someone else. As I mentioned earlier, Iohannes of Palestine was *comes* in 546. The objects which were stamped under the supervision of Iohannis cannot be dated to 546 because they bear different inscribed names and types of emperor bust from the stamps dated around 540–550.[26]

22 Procopius, *Ἀπόκρυφη Ἱστορία (Historia Arcana)*, 25, ed. B.G. Niebuhr, *Procopius Vol. 3,* CSHB, 42 (Bonn, 1838), 139, tr. H.B. Dewing, *Procopius vol 6: Anecdota or Secret History,* Loeb Classical Library, 290 (London and Cambridge, MA, 1935), 295; also cited in Dodd, 'The question of workshop', 59, note 16.

23 Dodd, 'The question of workshop', 59.

24 Dodd, *Byzantine Silver Stamps*, 85–9, nos 16–18.

25 Dodd, 'The question of workshop', 59; D. Feissel, 'Le Préfet de Constantinople, les poids étalons et L'estampillage de l'argenterie au VIe et au VIIe siècle', *RN*, 28 (1986), 119–42.

26 Dodd, *Byzantine Silver Stamps*, 65–81 and tables I and IV.

Dodd dated the silver stamped by Julianus before the silver of Adeos.[27] This would make the silver stamped by Julianus the first in the Treasure. This silver was used for a censer (no. 20) and a standing lamp (no. 33) in the Dumbarton Oaks collection. This was followed by the stamps applied under the supervision of Adeos. This silver was used to make four polycandela with semi-circular end pieces (nos 15–18), a censer in Antalya Museum (no. 19), the amphora (no. 28), a paten (no. 1), three openwork

Figure 3.8 Hexagonal stamp cut in half during the making of the monogram of Eutychianos on the rectangular polycandelon (no. 13). Dumbarton Oaks, Byzantine Collection, Washington, DC.

Source: Photograph by the author.

27 Dodd, *Byzantine Silver Stamps*, table III.

lamps (nos 39, 40 and 41) and a bowl (no. 55). The latest stamps were the ones applied under the supervision of Iohannes which were applied on the silver used for eight polycandela (nos 7–14) and an openwork lamp (no. 38).[28]

How close the date of the stamping of the silver and the making of the vessels were is debatable. The stamps alone do not tell us. They were applied to the silver before it was shaped or cut for decoration. This is clear from the fact that some of the stamps were cut in half during their decoration (nos 13 and 14), or that rivets were put through stamps (no. 18), or that some of the stamps were burnished (nos 10 and 11) (Figure 3.8). It is also intriguing that some stamps were applied twice. Possibly the silver sheets were stamped more than once. The same can be seen in the Riha flabellum where part of the cruciform stamp was erased during decoration, as was the bust of the emperor on the long stamp when a hole was made in the handle.[29]

The Purpose and Places of Stamping

Imperial silver stamps were used from the reign of Anastasius I (CE 491–518) to Constans II (CE 641–668). Silver stamped in this way, with the names of officials and emperor, was authorised by the empire: effectively, these stamps were the hallmarks demonstrating the control of the state over valuable materials.[30] Further, Marlia Mundell Mango suggested that stamps on a piece of silver indicate that it was not made for private sale but for imperial sale.[31] If so, then the silver used in the Sion Treasure was authorised and sold by the state.

Unlike coins, silver stamps do not give any information on where they were applied. It is possible that silver was only imperially stamped in Constantinople. This is where the *Comes Sacrarum Largitionum* and his officials were based. In this way, the stamps with the names and monograms of the officials represented imperial authority in the capital itself.[32] The silver was then sold directly to silversmiths or patrons. However, Marlia Mundell Mango came to a different conclusion in her examination of the stamps applied to the silver objects in the Kaper Koraon Treasure.[33] She argued that not all imperial stamps were applied in Constantinople: it was a long journey

28 Dodd, 'The question of workshop', 59.
29 Dodd, *Byzantine Silver Stamps*, 1–3.
30 Dodd, *Byzantine Silver Stamps*, 5–6.
31 M.M. Mango, 'The purpose and places of Byzantine silver stamping', in *Ecclesiastical Silver Plate*, ed. Boyd and Mango, 214. She also argued that when silver was not used for coinage between 400 and 615, the stamped silver owned by the state was exchanged for solidi.
32 Dodd, *Byzantine Silver Stamps*, 23.
33 M.M. Mango, *Silver from Early Byzantium: The Kaper Koraon and Related Treasures* (Baltimore, MD, 1986), 6–15.

from Syria to Constantinople just to buy stamped silver. Perhaps stamps were applied in other centres at the same time, as was the case with the making of coins.[34] In this suggestion, dies bearing the name of relevant officials must have been circulated within the empire, perhaps to certain selected centres, as was the case with mints, though, unlike the minting of coins, the name of these centres was not included. The unknown here is how often the officials changed and so how often the dies might need replacing.[35] We cannot be certain either way.

It has often been assumed that the stamps guaranteed the purity of the silver, that, for example, the stamped silver in the Sion Treasure was of higher quality – in terms of raw materials and indeed also of decoration – than the unstamped. So, for example, Dodd argued that the silver in the stamped paten donated by Eutychianos (no. 1), was purer than the silver in the unstamped paten which was donated 'for the memory of Maria' (no. 6).[36] However, a technical examination reveals that Maria's unstamped paten (no. 6) weighs 8,000 grams and whilst Eutychianos's weighs 4,300 grams (no. 1), whilst the silver content of both is almost identical. Approximately 87% of both patens are made of silver, the remaining 10% being made of iron, gold and copper related to ores and to increase the hardness of silver. Both objects were equally good in terms of the quality of the silver used.[37] Rather, it seems likely that the stamps were an authorisation of the release of state silver.[38]

More widely, the Antalya vessels have a silver content between 87% and 89% and the Dumbarton Oaks ones one of 87–99%.[39] Hendy suggested that anything with a silver content higher than 85% should be seen as pure silver.[40] The rest of the metal is iron, gold, copper and mercury, present because of the cupellation process through which silver was extracted from lead.[41] Copper was also added to silver to make it harder and durable before shaping and working on the object.[42] Mercury on the gilded surfaces results from the way

34 Mango, 'The purpose and places of Byzantine silver stamping', 210–12; Mango, 'Tracking Byzantine silver and copper metalware, 4th–12th Centuries', in M.M. Mango (ed.), *Byzantine Trade, 4th–12th Centuries: The Archaeology of Local, Regional and International Exchange*, SPBS, 14 (Farnham, 2009), 221–36.

35 Dodd, 'The location of silver stamping', 222.

36 Dodd, 'The question of workshop', 60. Also see J.W. Nesbitt, 'Some observations on Byzantine control stamps', in *Ecclesiastical Silver Plate*, ed. Boyd and Mango, 225–7.

37 P. Meyers, 'Elemental compositions of the Sion Treasure and other Byzantine silver objects', in *Ecclesiastical Silver Plate*, ed. Boyd and Mango,169–77.

38 Mango, 'The purpose and places of Byzantine silver stamping', 215.

39 Meyers, 'Elemental compositions', table I.

40 Hendy, 'The administration of mints and treasuries', 13.

41 Meyers, 'Elemental compositions', 171–5; K.A. Yener, 'Byzantine silver mines: an archaeometallurgy project in Turkey', in *Ecclesiastical Silver Plate*, ed. Boyd and Mango, 157.

42 C.E. Snow, 'From ingot to object: fabrication techniques used in the manufacture of the Hama Silver', in *Ecclesiastical Silver Plate*, ed. Boyd and Mango, 198.

in which the silver was gilded, amalgamating mercury and gold into a sort of paste to be brushed onto the silver before vaporising the mercury off.[43]

The stamps on Sion objects were not about guaranteeing the purity of silver. They indicated that the metal was controlled by officials who worked under the emperor. This issue about the authorisation of stamped silver and its circulation is what I will now move to consider.

43 R. Newman and H. Lie, 'The technical examination and conservation of objects in the Sion Treasure', in *Ecclesiastical Silver Plate*, ed. Boyd and Mango, 81.

Table 3.1 Stamps on Sion Objects

No.	*Object*	*Round*	*Hexagonal*	*Square*	*Long*	*Cruciform*
1	Paten ANT.1020	Not surviving	Monogram of Justinian I. Inscribed name: ΛΕΟΝ – ΤΙΟV (Leontiou)	Monogram of Justinian I. Inscription is illegible	Bust of emperor Justinian I. Inscription is illegible. Cruciform monogram of official Adeos: A- Δ-E-OV (Addeou)	Cruciform monogram of official Adeos: A-Δ-E-OV (Addeou). Inscribed name: EVΓENIOV (Eugeniou)
7	Polycandelon (Cruciform) ANT. 1051	Bust of Justinian I. Inscribed name: IωAN- NOV (Ioannou)	Monogram of Justinian I. Inscribed name: ITA –ΛOV (Italou)	Monogram of Justinian I. Inscribed name: ΔωPω- ΘEOV (Dorotheou)	Bust of emperor Justinian I. Cruciform monogram of official Iohannes (I-ω-A- N-OV). Inscribed name: IωAN-NOV (Ioannou)	Cruciform monogram of official Iohannes (I-ω-A-N-OV). Inscribed name: ΠAVΛOV (Paulou)
8	Polycandelon (Cruciform) ANT. 1052	Bust of Justinian I. Inscribed name: IωAN- NOV (Ioannou)	Monogram of Justinian I. Inscribed name: ITA –ΛOV (Italou)	Monogram of Justinian I. Inscribed name: ΔωPω- ΘEOV (Dorotheou)	Bust of emperor Justinian I. Cruciform monogram of official Iohannes (I-ω-A- N-OV). Inscribed name: IωAN- NOV (Ioannou)	Cruciform monogram of official Iohannes (I-ω-A-N-OV). Inscribed name: ΠAVΛOV (Paulou)
9	Polycandelon (Cruciform) DO. BZ. 65.1.1	Illegible	Monogram of Justinian I. Inscription is illegible	Monogram of Justinian I. Inscribed name: ΔωPω- ωEOV (Dorotheou)	Illegible	Cruciform monogram of official Iohannes (I-ω-A-N-OV). Inscribed name: ΠAVΛOV (Paulou)
10	Polycandelon (Circular) ANT. 1053	Bust of Justinian I. Inscribed name: IωAN- NOV (Ioannou)	Monogram of Justinian I. Inscribed name: ITA –ΛOV (Italou)	Monogram of Justinian I. Inscribed name: ΔωPω- ΘEOV (Dorotheou)	Bust of emperor Justinian I. Cruciform monogram of official Iohannes (I-ω-A-N-OV). Inscribed name: IωAN-NOV (Ioannou)	Cruciform monogram of official Iohannes (I-ω-A-N-OV). Inscribed name: ΠAVΛOV (Paulou)

(*Continued*)

Table 3.1 (Continued)

No.	*Object*	*Round*	*Hexagonal*	*Square*	*Long*	*Cruciform*
11	Polycandelon (Circular) ANT. 1054	Bust of Justinian I. Inscribed name: IωAN- NOV (Ioannou)	Monogram of Justinian I. Inscribed name: ITA –ΛOV (Italou)	Monogram of Justinian I. Inscribed name: ΔωPω- ΘEOV (Dorotheou)	Bust of emperor Justinian I. Cruciform monogram of official Iohannes (I-ω-A-N-OV). Inscribed name: IωAN-NOV (Ioannou)	Cruciform monogram of official Iohannes (I-ω-A-N-OV). Inscribed name: ΠAVΛOV (Paulou)
12	Polycandelon (Circular) DO. BZ. 63.36.4	Bust of Justinian I. Inscribed name: IωAN- NOV (Ioannou)	Monogram of Justinian I. Inscribed name: ITA –ΛOV (Italou)	Monogram of Justinian I. Inscribed name: ΔωPω- ΘEOV (Dorotheou)	Bust of emperor Justinian I. Cruciform monogram of Iohannes (official) I-ω-A-N-OV. Inscribed name: IωAN-NOV (Ioannou)	Cruciform monogram of Iohannes (official) I-ω-A-N-OV. Inscribed name: ΠAVΛOV (Paulou)
13	Polycandelon (Rectangular, Tri-lobed end pieces) DO. BZ. 63.36.5	Bust of Justinian I. Inscribed name: IωAN- NOV (Ioannou)	Monogram of Justinian I. Inscribed name: ITA –ΛOV (Italou)	Monogram of Justinian I. Inscribed name: ΔωPω- ΘEOV (Dorotheou). Applied twice	Bust of emperor Justinian I. Cruciform monogram of official Iohannes (I-ω-A- N-OV). Inscribed name: IωAN- NOV (Ioannou)	Cruciform monogram of official Iohannes (I-ω-A-N-OV). Inscribed name: ΠAVΛOV (Paulou)
14	Polycandelon (Rectangular, Tri-lobed end pieces) DO. BZ63.36.6/ ANT 1033- 31–28	Bust of Justinian I. Inscribed name: IωAN- NOV (Ioannou)	Monogram of Justinian I. Inscribed name: ITA –ΛOV (Italou)	Monogram of Justinian I. Inscribed name: ΔωPω- ΘEOV (Dorotheou)	Bust of emperor Justinian I. Cruciform monogram of official Iohannes (I-ω-A- N-OV). Inscribed name: IωAN-NOV (Ioannou)	Cruciform monogram of official Iohannes (I-ω-A-N-OV). Inscribed name: ΠAVΛOV (Paulou). Applied twice, one was cut in half during decoration
15	Polycandelon (Rectangular, semi-circular end pieces and paired dolphins) DO. BZ. 63.36.7-BZ.79.14.4	Bust of Justinian I. Inscribed name: ΛEON – TIOV (Leontiou). Applied twice	Monogram of Justinian I. Inscription is illegible	Monogram of Justinian I. Inscribed name: 'EV … ..'	Illegible	Cut in half during decoration. Cruciform monogram of official Adeos (A- Δ-E-OU). Inscribed name: EVΦPONIOV (Euphroniou)

16	Polycandelon (Rectangular, semi-circular end pieces with paired dolphins decoration) DO.BZ.65.1.8	Not surviving	Not surviving	Not surviving	Not surviving	Cruciform monogram of official Adeos (A- Δ-E-OU). Inscribed name: EVΦPONIOV (Euphroniou). Cut in half during decoration
17	Polycandelon (Rectangular, semi-circular end pieces and foliate design decoration) DO. BZ. 65.1.7-ANT.1030	Bust of Justinian I. Inscribed name: ΛEON – TIOV (Leontiou)	Not surviving	Monogram of Justinian I. Inscribed name: EVCE – TEIC (Euseteis)	Bust of emperor Justinian I. Monogram is illegible. Inscribed name: ΔIOM - IΔOV (Diomidou)	Cruciform monogram of official Adeos (A- Δ-E-OU). Inscribed name: EVΦPONIOV (Euphroniou). Applied twice, one was cut in half during decoration
18	Polycandelon (Rectangular, Semi-circular end pieces and foliate design decoration) ANT. 2018/74-DO.BZ.79.14.1	Illegible	Monogram of Justinian I. Inscribed name: ITA –ΛOV (Italou)	Monogram of Justinian I. Inscribed name: EVCE – TEIC (Euseteis)	Bust of the emperor Justinian I. Cruciform monogram of official Adeos (A- Δ-E-OU). Inscribed name: ΔIOM - IΔOV (Diomidou)	Cruciform monogram of official Adeos (A- Δ-E-OU). Inscribed name: EVΦPONIOV (Euphroniou). Applied twice
19	Censer ANT. 1019	Bust of Justinian I. Inscribed name: ΛEON – TIOV (Leontiou)	Monogram of Justinian I. Inscribed name: XPICTO-ΦOPOV (Christophorou)	Monogram of Justinian I. Inscribed name: EVCE – TEIC (Euseteis)	Bust of Justinian I. Cruciform monogram of official Adeos (A- Δ-E-OU). Inscribed name: ΔIOM - IΔOV (Diomidou)	Cruciform monogram of official Adeos (A- Δ-E-OU). Inscribed name: EVΦPONIOV (Euphroniou)
20	Censer DO.BZ.65.1.5	Bust of Justinian I. Inscribed name: XPICTO-ΦOPOV (Christoforou)	Monogram of Justinian I. Inscribed name: ITA –ΛOV (Italou)	Monogram of Justinian I. Inscription is illegible	Bust of emperor Justinian I. Monogram and inscription are illegible	Monogram of the official is illegible. Inscribed name: CEPΓIOV (Sergiou)

(*Continued*)

Table 3.1 (Continued)

No.	*Object*	*Round*	*Hexagonal*	*Square*	*Long*	*Cruciform*
28	Amphora DO.BZ. 65. 1.4	Bust of Justinian I. Inscribed name: ΛEON –TIOV (Leontiou)	Monogram of Justinian I. Inscribed name: Illegible	Monogram of Justinian I. Inscribed name: EVCE – TEIC (Euseteis)	Bust of emperor Justinian I. Cruciform monogram of official Adeos (A- Δ-E-OU). Inscribed name: ΔIOM - IΔOV (Diomidou)	Monogram of the official is illegible. Inscribed name: EVΦPONIOV (Euphroniou)
33	Standing lamp DO. BZ. 63. 36. 17	Bust of Justinian I. Inscribed name: XPICTO- ΦOPOV (Christoforou)	Monogram of Justinian I. Inscription is illegible	Monogram of Justinian I. Inscription is illegible	Bust of Justinian I. Monogram and inscription are illegible	Monogram of the official is illegible. Inscribed name: CEPΓIOV (Sergiou)
35	Openwork lamp BZ. DO. 63.36.25/21	Not surviving	Not surviving	Not surviving	Not surviving	Monogram of the official is illegible. Inscribed name: EVΦPONIOV (Euphroniou)
36	Openwork lamp DO. BZ. 63.36.25a/ 65.1.14	Not surviving	Not surviving	Not surviving	Not surviving	Monogram of the official is illegible. Inscribed name: EVΦPONIOV (Euphroniou)
38	Openwork lamp London Digby Jones Collection	Bust of Justinian I.	Monogram of Justinian I.	Monogram of Justinian I.	Bust of emperor Justinian I. Cruciform monogram of official Iohannes (I-ω-A-N-OV)	Cruciform monogram of official Iohannes (I-ω-A-N-OV)
39	Openwork lamp DO. BZ. 65.1.19 a-c/79.11/63.36.22	Bust of Justinian I. Inscribed name: ΛEON – TIOV (Leontiou). Applied twice	Monogram of Justinian I. Inscription is illegible. Applied twice	Monogram of Justinian I. Inscribed name: ΛEON – TIOV (Leontiou)	Not surviving	Not surviving

40	Openwork lamp DO. BZ. 79.10/ 63.36.23- 32	Bust of Justinian I. Inscribed anme: ΛEON – TIOV (Leontiou)	Monogram of Justinian I. Inscribed name: ITA–ΛOV (Italou)	Illegible	Not surviving	Not surviving
41	Openwork lamp DO. BZ. 65. 1. 12	Bust of Justinian I. Inscribed name: ΛEON – TIOV (Leontiou)	Monogram of Justinian I. Inscribed name: ITA –ΛOV (Italou)	Monogram of Justinian I. Inscription is illegible	Bust of emperor Justinian I. Cruciform monogram of official Adeos (A-Δ-E-OU). Inscribed name: ΔIOM -IΔOV (Diomidou)	Illegible
55	Bowl DO. BZ. 63. 36. 24	Bust of Justinian I. Inscribed name: ΛEON–TIOV (Leontiou)	Monogram of Justinian I. Inscription is illegible	Monogram of Justinian I. Inscribed name: EVCE – TEIC (Euseteis)	Bust of emperor Justinian I. Cruciform monogram of official Adeos (A-Δ-E-OU). Inscribed name: ΔIOM -IΔOV (Diomidou)	Cruciform monogram of official Adeos (A-Δ-E-OU). Inscribed name: EVΦPONIOV (Euphroniou)
Irregular Stamps						
No.	Object	Rectangular	Rosette			
34	Standing lamp ANT. 1050–1042	Inscription is illegible	No inscription			

4 Questions of Circulation, Production and Cost of the Sion Treasure

The Circulation of the Sion Treasure

There is no written evidence to indicate where the silver used in the Sion Treasure came from, nor where the silver vessels were made and sold. Nor do the elemental compositions give any clues as to where the silver was mined. However, it is worth considering how silver in general circulated as both a raw material and a finished object in the early Byzantine period as this will give some indications about how the Sion silver might have travelled within the Byzantine world.

Recent archaeological analysis shows that in the early Byzantine period, silver was mined in Greece, Anatolia and Eastern Mediterranean. Lead isotope analysis – which has been made on samples from the twenty-five silver vessels and coins from the reign of Heraclius and eighteen other vessels dated to 542–641 by relying on the stamps – points to silver mining in sixth- and seventh-century Byzantine Anatolia, especially in Bolkardag valley in the Taurus Mountains and in the Black Sea region.[1] The silver ore was combined with copper and lead; once mined, it was smelted to make it purer and to remove the lead and copper. The silver was then alloyed with copper and gold to make it harder so that it was ready to shape.[2] The silver exploited from the Black Sea, as Marlia Mango argues, relying on the inscriptions on coins made from silver mined in the Black Sea, was possibly manufactured in Constantinople and the

1 For Anatolia, see K.A. Yener, 'Byzantine silver mines: an archaeometallurgy project in Turkey', in S.A. Boyd and M.M. Mango (ed.), *Ecclesiastical Silver Plate in Sixth-Century Byzantium* (Washington, DC, 1992), 155–67. For examples in Greece, see J.C. Edmondson, 'Mining in the later Roman empire and beyond: continuity or disruption?', *JRS*, 79 (1989), 84–102. Also see M.M. Mango, 'Tracking Byzantine silver and copper metalware, 4th–12th Centuries', in M.M. Mango (ed.), *Byzantine Trade, 4th–12th Centuries: The Archaeology of Local, Regional and International Exchange,* SPBS, 14 (Farnham, 2009), 222.

2 R. Newman and H. Lie, 'The technical examination and conservation of objects in the Sion Treasure', in Ecclesiastical *Silver Plate,* ed. Boyd and Mango 78; C.E. Snow, 'From ingot to object: fabrication techniques used in the manufacture of the Hama Silver', in *Ecclesiastical Silver Plate,* ed. Boyd and Mango, 197.

DOI: 10.4324/9781003345503-5

silver exploited from the Taurus Mountains might have been manufactured locally.[3] As she demonstrated elsewhere, objects which were manufactured from Taurus silver, were stamped locally (with non-imperial stamps) in Tarsus and Antioch.[4] This proves that silver was manufactured in both Constantinople and in other areas of the empire.

It is generally accepted that the mined silver circulated in the Byzantine empire in two different way: one was the state-controlled cycle and the other a private cycle.[5] Silver in the state-controlled cycle was stamped and in the private cycle, as Hendy argues, miners had to pay to the Largitiones an annual 'quantum' from their income.[6] In both cases the state had control over silver, one directly the other indirectly.

In the case of the Sion Treasure, there is a question as to whether the stamped silver was bought by silversmiths and decorated in local workshops, or bought directly by the donor – Eutychianos (the only donor named on the stamped vessels). There is also a question about whether the stamped vessels were made in state workshops in Constantinople or, as suggested, in other places and sold to the public.[7] The presence of the imperial stamps – since they were guaranteeing state control over this luxury material – has led to the assumption that the stamped Sion silverware was stamped and crafted in Constantinople, in state workshops controlled by the Comes Sacrarum Largitionum and sold to the public.[8] The other argument is that state workshops were not only in Constantinople, but also in dioceses where there were the offices of *Sacrara Largitiones* who controlled and produced silver.[9] But if we assume that the *Sacrara Largitiones* manufactured silver it means that stamped silver was only supplied by the state to donors and did not reach the hands of silversmiths. There is a further unexplored issue here: was stamped silver manufactured as desired objects and sold to donors directly by state workshops controlled by the Comes Sacrarum Largitionum? Or did stamped silver get sold to silversmiths as silver sheets and was manufactured by them and sold to donors? Or, as has been suggested, was the stamped silver cut into basic shapes by the officials of

3 Mango, 'Tracking Byzantine silver', 222.

4 M.M. Mango, 'The purpose and places of Byzantine silver stamping', in *Ecclesiastical Silver Plate,* ed. Boyd and Mango, 207.

5 Jones, *Later Roman Empire 284–602: A Social, Economic, and Administrative Survey*, 3 vols (Oxford, 1964), vol. 2, 838–39. Also see M.F. Hendy, 'The administration of mints and treasuries, fourth to seventh centuries, with an appendix on the production of silver plate', in M.F. Hendy (ed.), *The Economy, Fiscal Administration and Coinage of Byzantium* (Northampton, 1989), 17; K. Matschke, 'Mining' in A.E. Laiou (ed.), *The Economic History of Byzantium: From the Seventh through the Fifteenth Century,* 3 vols, DOS, 39 (Washington, DC, 2002), vol. 1, 115; Edmondson, 'Mining in the later Roman empire and beyond', 84–5.

6 Hendy, 'The administration of mints and treasuries', 17.

7 Mango, 'The purpose and places of Byzantine silver stamping', 207–11.

8 E.C. Dodd, 'The question of workshop: evidence of the stamps on the Sion Treasure', in *Ecclesiastical Silver Plate,* ed. Boyd and Mango, 217.

9 For this argument see Mango, 'The purpose and places of Byzantine silver stamping', 203–7.

the Comes Sacrarum Largitionum – and sold on to be worked further by silversmiths?[10] It seems unlikely that the state bothered with shaping and decorating silver before selling it; more plausible is that silversmiths acquired silver in the form of sheets and shaped and decorated these in their workshops. Indeed, it was the main aim for the state to turn the silver into gold coins, not manufacturing desired objects by individuals.[11] What this means is that although it is possible that Eutychianos bought his stamped silver (as sheets or objects) in Constantinople or from other places where state workshops stamped silver, it is also possible that he acquired it locally, but that the objects reached their final shape in the hands of silversmiths not in state workshops.

In this context, it needs to be remembered that there are unstamped vessels in the Sion Treasure very similar to those made from stamped silver. For example, there are two identical patens presented by Eutychianos: a stamped one, kept in the Antalya Museum (no. 1); and an unstamped paten in the Dumbarton Oaks Museum (no. 3) (Figures 1.1 and 1.2). It is possible that the unstamped paten was made as a copy of the stamped paten – but does this assume that they were made in the same workshop? And if so, was that state workshop in Constantinople or somewhere else? Or was the stamped paten exported from a state workshop in its basic shape and decorated together with the unstamped paten in a local workshop? Or perhaps Eutychianos procured the stamped paten from a state workshop in Constantinople or somewhere else and took it to the local workshop where it was copied by the silversmith.[12] There is also another possibility that Eutychianos bought both of these patens locally from a silversmith who had already obtained the stamped silver paten from a state workshop and the other from private mines possibly near Lycia. All of these are plausible scenarios, but each tells a slightly different story about how we think silver might have travelled in Byzantium.

The narratives also depend on narratives about Eutychianos. They imply that he was wealthy enough to go to Constantinople or perhaps that he travelled there in his role as a bishop.[13] They also suggest that silver vessels from Constantinople were more valued by the Byzantines as objects than those made locally – and this is an assumption based on models of centre and periphery that need challenging. And they overlook questions around local access to silver: could localised workshops outside Constantinople acquire stamped silver from the state? As I argued, they could. There were metal workshops in Lycia, and the excavation of tools for making silver and

10 Dodd, 'The question of workshop', 62.

11 Mango, 'Tracking Byzantine silver and copper metalware', 223.

12 Dodd, 'The question of workshop', 60.

13 For the wealthy and elite status of bishops, see C. Rapp, 'The elite status of bishops in late antiquity in ecclesiastical, spiritual and social context', *Arethusa*, 33.3 (2000), 377–99; Rapp, 'Bishops in late antiquity: a new social and urban elite?', in J. Haldon and L.I. Conrad (ed.), *The Byzantine and Early Islamic Near East: Elites Old and New in the Byzantine and Early Islamic Near East* (Princeton, 2004), 149–78.

decorating metal objects suggest that there were also silversmiths in this area, so why should not Eutychianos have looked locally?[14] Just as it was a long journey from Syria to Constantinople to buy stamped silver, so too was it from Lycia to Constantinople.[15]

What about the majority of objects in the Treasure which were not stamped? Only twenty-five of fifty-seven objects in the Sion Treasure were made from stamped silver (one is stamped with non-imperial stamps, no. 34); the remaining thirty-two are fashioned from unstamped silver. In terms of quality of silver, it is worth reiterating that there is no difference between the unstamped and stamped vessels in the Sion Treasure. Other silver treasures are also a mix of stamped and unstamped silver, for example, the Kaper Koraon Treasure. This suggests that silver was not necessarily or automatically authorised by the state. It also means that silversmiths had access to and used both stamped and unstamped silver. The unstamped silver in the Sion Treasure might have been acquired directly by silversmiths from private miners who were close to Lycia. Even though there were no silver sources in Lycia, the silversmith might have bought his silver from closer mines, such as those in the Taurus Mountains. During the Byzantine empire there were important mines of silver in the Taurus mountains which are close to Lycia.[16] It is also possible that Eutychianos or the other donors might have owned some silver and brought that to a silversmith to be made into the required vessel. The stories indicate that donors also brought their silver or gold to silversmiths and goldsmiths to be manufactured. In a story from the *Life* of St Sabas, we are told that a silversmith in Jerusalem reported his shop burgled, with approximately 100 Roman pounds of silver stolen. When the silversmith spoke to St Sabas, he also explained that much of the silver was not his own property.[17] This story illustrates that not only did silversmiths buy their own materials, but that some of the silver to be worked was brought in by others, presumably patrons. This is supported by a story told by John Moschos in which we see that donors could also obtain even gold. The story mentions that a patrician commissioning a gold cross from a goldsmith brought his own gold and other materials.[18]

14 A. Oransay, 'Arykanda Antik Kenti'nde 1971–2002 kazı sezonlarında ele geçen madeni buluntular ve madencilik faaliyetleri' (Unpublished PhD Diss., Ankara University, 2006), 19–25.

15 M.M. Mango, *Silver from Early Byzantium: The Kaper Koraon and Related Treasures* (Baltimore, MD, 1986), 6–15; Mango, 'The purpose and places of Byzantine silver stamping', 203.

16 Yener, 'Byzantine silver mines', 155–67.

17 Cyril of Scythopolis, *Βίος Τοῦ Ὁσίου Πατρὸς Ἡμῶν Σάββα*, c. 78, ed. E. Schwartz, *Kyrillos von Skythopolis*, TU, 49.2 (Leipzig, 1939), 185, tr. R.M. Price, *Cyril of Scythopolis: Lives of the Monks of Palestine* (Kalamazoo, MI, 1991), 193.

18 John Moschos, *Pratum Spirituale*, c. 200, PG 87(3): 3087, tr. J. Wortley, *The Spiritual Meadow (Pratum Spirituale) by John Moschos* (Kalamazoo, MI, 1992), 178.

The Production of the Sion Treasure

Most of the objects in the Sion Treasure were made from a single sheet of silver. Vessels with feet and hoops had these joined by silver soldering after they had been shaped. Some items, including the circular censer and patens, were produced by working on a lathe. The silver sheets were shaped, compressed and stretched by hammer to make the desired object, which was then decorated. The feet were silver soldered to the chalices and silver soldering was also used for the holes for chains in the polycandela and censers. Inscriptions were engraved and nielloed. Relief techniques were used on the patens and censers. After decoration, gilding was used on some pieces.[19]

I put this summarised information here to start discussion on how far the evidence about the production, stamps and elemental compositions can help us to establish the workshops where these objects were produced or to begin making assumptions about the workshops. It is almost impossible to know whether resemblances in the decoration, inscription and even the stamps mean that the objects were produced in the same workshop, any more than whether the differences indicate that they were produced in different workshops. Either view makes unfounded assumptions about the levels of skill possessed by silversmiths in this period.

Looking at the patens in more detail, all have individual decoration, styles and measurements, from which assumptions have been made about their production. The three patens (nos 1, 2 and 3) which bear the name of Eutychianos are similar in appearance, with Christogram, niello borders and inscription and bands of decoration. They are also different. The paten in Antalya (no. 1) has an eight-armed Christogram, and a cusped border decorated with repoussé leaves, whereas the Geneva and Dumbarton Oaks patens (nos 3 and 4) have six-armed Christograms, and borders decorated with leaves and Sasanian palmettes. The number of concavities filled by the leaves also differs: the Antalya paten has twenty-nine, while the Geneva and Dumbarton Oaks patens have twenty-six and twenty-four, respectively. There are also differences in the style of the Christograms, and in the inscriptions. The Christogram on the Geneva paten is the smallest, and has a basic design, while the patens in Antalya and Dumbarton Oaks have larger Christograms, with elegant serifs, and are smooth in style (Figures 1.1 –1.3).

Based on these differences, Susan Boyd suggested that these objects were the product of two different craftsmen, and might have been produced in two different workshops.[20] She also suggested that the similarities between the form of these objects indicated mass production, with for example cusped

19 Newman and Lie, 'The technical examination', 78; Snow, 'From ingot to object', 198–9.

20 S.A. Boyd, 'A "metropolitan" treasure from a church in the provinces: an introduction to the study of the Sion Treasure', in *Ecclesiastical Silver Plate,* ed. Boyd and Mango, 14–15.

border patens made to a certain point, and then later decorated and finished at different workshops. Boyd thought that the stamped Antalya paten was produced in Constantinople, whilst the two other unstamped patens were made (or even copied) locally in Lycia.[21] This is plausible but it is not the only possible explanation. Why were they mass produced as cusped border dishes in one workshop and decorated in another? We cannot say that they were mass produced as they are different in diameter. Possibly, as I discussed earlier, they were sold to the silversmith as silver sheets and manufactured and decorated in the same workshop. Otherwise, there would be a large number of workshops which produce silver, for example one shaped it up to a certain point and another decorated it and a third inscribed it. Why did this process not occur in a single workshop? It is more plausible to say that the patens were produced in the same workshop by one craftsman who decided to decorate them differently; or alternatively they could have been made by two or three craftsmen in the same workshop. And this workshop acquired stamped silver in the form of sheets and others possibly in the form of bullion.

Similar assumptions are made about the other three patens. The two in Dumbarton Oaks (nos 4 and 5), which were donated in memory of Angeleouos and John, respectively, are identical in shape and decoration. It has been presumed that they were produced at the same workshop, at the same time.[22] In contrast, the differences in terms of its lettering and decoration in the paten in Antalya Museum (no. 6), donated in memory of Maria, have led to the suggestion that it was made in a different workshop. We need to recognise these as assumptions and explore the ideas about the workshops, and the conditions and circumstances behind the production of the objects that they imply. For example: how many craftsmen might have been in one workshop? Did they always produce work that looked the same? Were assistants involved in the production and decoration of silver vessels? Since little is known about workshop culture in the sixth century, it is hard to answer these questions, and we must recognise that only a very small amount of silverware from the period survives now. But the different answers that can be given underline the possibilities. These vessels may have been produced and decorated by different craftsmen in the same or different workshops – the implication being that individual craft workers produced objects so stylistically definitive that we can detect their hands now, but that they lacked the skill to produce work in any other style. Alternatively, perhaps, one craftsman decorated these objects and made them different according to his taste or he decided on the decoration and manufacture according to the materials he had – suggesting that craft workers could work their materials in a variety of ways and techniques and with different decorative forms.

21 Boyd, 'A "metropolitan" treasure', 15.
22 Boyd, 'A "metropolitan" treasure', 15–16.

The same ideas and assumptions apply to other pieces in the Sion Treasure. There are three different forms of polycandela, but all twelve polycandela were the gift of the same donor. The three circular polycandela (nos 7–9, Figures 1.6–1.8) are identical in shape, decoration and stamps but are different from the three cross-shaped ones (nos 10–12, Figures 1.9–1.11), though these three are identical. Unlike the circular and cross-shaped polycandela, the six rectangular polycandela (nos 13–18) all differ from each other in terms of their form, decoration and stamps but they all bear the same inscription. The pair of polycandela with tri-lobed end pieces (nos 13 and 14, Figures 1.12 and 1.13) have identical decoration with paired dolphins, flanking holes and the monogram of the donor and are also identical in form, inscription and stamps to each other. Even the names of the officials on stamps are identical. However, the other four rectangular polycandela (nos 15–18), although they have inscriptions identical to the other two polycandela, differ in terms of stamps and form. Two of the four rectangular polycandela with semi-circular end pieces have decoration (nos 15 and 16, Figures 1.14 and 1.15) identical to the other two polycandela with tri-lobed end pieces, while the other two have foliate design decoration (nos 17 and 18, Figures 1.16 and 1.17a–1.17b). However, the stamps on these four polycandela with semi-circular end pieces are identical, and all the rectangular polycandela have the same inscription.

If we rely on their stamps, we might argue that the silver for three circular, three cross-shaped and two rectangular polycandelon with tri-lobed end pieces was stamped under the same officials in state workshops and worked there – or sold to a silversmith in Lycia as stamped silver sheets. The other four polycandela with semi-circular end pieces could have been stamped at a different time, since the names of the officials on the stamps are completely different. But this does not prove that these polycandela were decorated, inscribed and given to the church at different times. It may be that the silversmith bought the stamped silver at different times and decorated and inscribed them all together. Nor do the differences of decoration confirm that the polycandela were produced in different times or by different workshops. The six rectangular polycandela have identical inscriptions but different forms, decoration and stamps: this might suggest that the silver was bought, shaped and decorated at different times but inscribed all together when purchased, a model implying that some silver could be picked up off the shelf rather than deliberately commissioned. Equally, the polycandela could have been shaped, decorated and inscribed in the same workshop at the same time, since there might have been more than one silversmith in the same workshop. This may also be true for the circular, cross-shaped and two rectangular polycandela with tri-lobed end pieces.

All of this opens a variety of possible scenarios. Perhaps the silver was stamped as sheets by the Comes Sacrarum Largitionum and sold as such. When the silversmith received an order for polycandela, if there was not enough silver in his shop, he (or the patron) acquired silver from Constantinople or the local stamping office. The workshop master then had the silver shaped and decorated, balancing the number of vessels required, the amount of silver and the number of workers and skill of his workshop. This explains why vessels were decorated differently and share different inscriptions although they have the same stamps. The four polycandela (nos 15–18) with semi-circular end pieces have different stamps from the others, but the same inscription, perhaps because the silver was bought by the silversmith at a different time from the silver for the remaining eight. And when Eutychianos ordered his polycandela they might have been decorated and inscribed at the same time. In terms of the differences between the circular, cross-shaped and rectangular polycandela in design, inscription and decoration, this was perhaps the choice of the donor.

Another implicit conjecture in these discussions is the unthinking attribution of quality to Constantinople. Dodd compared the stamped paten in Antalya given by Eutychianos (no. 1) and the unstamped paten given for the memory of Maria (no. 6) and suggested that the stamped one was decorated so elegantly that it must have come from Constantinople (Figures 1.1 and 1.5). The unstamped paten is decorated 'only' with a gilded cross, and so is deemed of 'lesser quality' and made in a local workshop.[23] But can we really say this, only by looking at the decoration? There is no difference between the two in terms of the purity of the silver metal used. And the paten given for the memory of Maria weighs 1600 grams more than the stamped paten given by Eutychianos, and is bigger (its diameter is 77.5; the other paten's diameter is 61 cm). It is also worth noting a paten preserved in the Istanbul Archaeological Museum from the village of Stuma. This is stamped with five imperial stamps but has very similar decoration to the paten given for the memory of Maria with a cross in its centre and inscription surrounding the rim.[24]

Moreover, the decoration is only one element in the 'quality' of the vessel – and perhaps not the most important. One little-explored issue here is whether it was weight or decoration that really mattered. There are plenty of examples to indicate that silver objects were most valued in terms of their weight and monetary value – their ability to be melted down and transformed into something else, money if needed.[25] Justinian allowed the monasteries to melt down their silver and use them in the time of financial difficulties.[26] Silver from churches was melted down in the reign of Heraklios to ransom prisoners

23 Dodd, 'The question of workshop', 60.

24 Mango, *Silver from Early Byzantium*, 171–4.

25 A. Eastmond, 'Consular diptychs, rhetoric and the languages of art in sixth-century Constantinople', *ArtH*, 33.5 (2010), 747.

26 Justinian, *Novellae Constitutiones*, CXX. 10, tr. S.P. Scott, *The Civil Law*, 17 vols (Cincinnati, 1932), vol. 17, 77; cited in Boyd, 'A "metropolitan" treasure', 7; M.M. Mango, 'The monetary value of silver revetments and objects', in *Ecclesiastical Silver Plate*, ed. Boyd and Mango, 135.

of war.[27] John Moschos tells a story in which the weight of gold appears to be of more importance than the decoration. A patrician brought gold for the making of a cross; the young goldsmith charged with the manufacture added to it the amount he would have earned for making the cross. When the patrician discovered his cross weighed more than the gold he gave, he accused the craftsman of tampering with the gold.[28] It is a story that underlines the importance of the weight of a gift. Gifts are often referred to in terms of their weight not appearance. A letter from Quintus Aurelius Symmachus to Areobindus in the sixth century accompanied an ivory diptych and a small silver bowl 'weighing two pounds', implying that the weight mattered.[29] Eastmond states that the silver objects were ranked by their weights and their monetary value and at the head of this ranking is the Missorium of Theodosius which was made for the tenth anniversary of the reign of the emperor in CE 380. The donor of this gift was the emperor and in terms of its weight, it was made of quite valuable material. It weighs 50 Roman pounds. equivalent to 16.13 kilograms.[30] This object was also valuable for its recipient since they might want to reuse it. In this context, when it comes to the two patens (nos 1 and 2) in the Sion Treasure, the one given for the memory of Maria weighs more than the one given by Eutychianos (no. 1), making it more valuable in terms of its materials.

The weight of the Sion silver allows calculations to be made about its cost, although it is impossible to predict how much the decoration and gilding of the vessels increased their value.[31] Additionally, some of the objects are incomplete, making it difficult to find their exact weights. The weight of the silver pieces from the Sion Treasure, as it survives and including fragments and nails, is approximately 125,934.9 grams or 125.9349 kilogrammes in today's measurements. This equals 384.924 Roman pounds in the sixth century.[32] The sixth-century *Ecclesiastical History* of John of Ephesus said that for one pound of silver one had to pay 4 solidi and for one pound of gold, 72 solidi.[33] The number

(footnote continued)

27 Theophanes, *Χρονογραφία*, ed. C. de Boor, *Theophanis Chronographia*, 1 (Leipzig, 1883), 303, tr. C. Mango and R. Scott, *The Chronicle of Theophanes Confessor* (Oxford, 1997), 435, cited in M.F. Hendy, *Studies in the Byzantine Monetary Economy 300–1450* (Cambridge, 1985), 495.

28 John Moschos, c. 200, PG 87: 3087, tr. Wortley, *The Spiritual Meadow*, 178.

29 Quintus Aurelius Symmachus, *Lettres III (livres VI–VIII)*, ed. tr. J.P. Callu, (Paris, 1995), vol. 7, 76, cited in Eastmond, 'Consular diptychs', 745.

30 Eastmond, 'Consular diptychs', 747.

31 Mango, 'The monetary value of silver revetments', 123–36.

32 Eastmond, 'Consular diptychs', 747, n. 16.

33 John of Ephesus, *Historiae Ecclesiasticae* III, 11–12, ed. and Lat. tr. E.W. Brooks, *Iohannis Ephesini, Historiae Ecclesiasticae Pars Tertia*, CSCO, Scriptores Syri, 55 (Louvain, 1936), 101, tr. R.P. Smith, *The Third Part of the Ecclesiastical History of John Bishop of Ephesus* (Oxford, 1860), 186–7. For the costs of silver and gold as solidi, also see Hendy, *Studies in the Byzantine Monetary Economy*, 165; Mango, 'The monetary value of silver revetments and objects', 124.

of grams in a Roman pound varied between 313 and 322 in the sixth and seventh centuries but is often taken as 327.45 grams to one Roman pound.[34] There has been some debate about this and a more recent equivalence widely accepted is that of 327.168 grams to the Roman pound.[35] This is what I shall use here. So, if 72 solidi equated to one Roman pound of gold, this means one solidus was approximately 4.5 grams of gold. So 4 solidi (18 grams of gold) bought 327.168 grams of silver. Consequently, the approximate cost of the objects in the Sion treasure is 1539.69 solidi/6928.63 grams gold.

It is also possible to calculate the weight in silver given by each donor. Table 4.1 shows the number of objects that were given by each donor, their total weight and potential costs.

Bishop Eutychianos donated the most silver. His gifts consisted of three patens, twelve polycandela, two censers, two amphorae, four standing lamps, eight openwork lamps and one suspension bracket for five lamps. In total, Eutychianos donated at least 62,216 grams, or 62.216 kilograms (approximately 190.16 Roman pounds) of silver to the monastery of Sion, presumably on several separate occasions. This weight of silver equates to perhaps 760 solidi/3420 grams gold. Some of the surviving silver is folded, flattened and crushed and consequently, it is difficult to estimate the exact weights of the original objects – it was probably more than the weight recorded. In the Kaper Koraon Treasure, one of the donors, named Megas, gifted silver worth 75 solidi and a paten of bishop Paternus cost 80 solidi.[36]

The name Paregoros is found on the rim sheeting of the altar table revetments (nos 51 and 52) as well as on the inscribed plain sheet (no. 54). If all the silver for the altar table was given by Paregoros, then the altar table revetments including the plain sheet weigh 27,859 grams/ 27.859 kilograms/ 85 Roman pounds, for which he could have paid approximately 340 solidi/1500 grams of gold. The priest Zacharias donated one plain sheet with cross (no. 53) weighing 3,164 grams/3.164 kilograms/ 9 Roman pounds, and by the conversion rate, costing perhaps 38 solidi/ 171 grams gold.

Using the same conversion rate, the paten (no. 6), given 'for the memory of Maria', cost 97 solidi /436.5 grams gold; the paten (no. 4) 'for the memory of Angeleuos Roufinos' 55 solidi/247.5 grams gold; the paten (no. 5) given 'for the memory of John' perhaps 51 solidi/229.5 grams gold. The book cover given 'for the memory of deacon Prinkipios, Stephane, Leontia and deacon Konon', cost approximately 3.8 solidi/17.1 grams gold. The openwork lamps given 'for the memory of Eutychianos' and Himeria (nos 39 and 40) each cost approximately 6 solidi/27 grams gold.

34 Mango, 'The monetary value of silver revetments and objects', 124, n. 16.

35 Eastmond, 'Consular diptychs', 747, n. 16.

36 Mango, 'The monetary value of silver revetments and objects', 133.

The chalices were not included in the table because they do not bear the name of their donors. Their total weight is approximately 3,553 grams/ 3.553 kilograms/ 10.8 Roman pounds. This is the equivalent of approximately 44 solidi worth of silver (198 grams gold). The other uninscribed vessels weigh approximately 7,197 grams, 7.197 kilograms/22 Roman pounds, which equates to 88 solidi/396 grams gold.

Eutychianos spent the most. However, it is hard to know what proportion of his wealth this may have represented and whether these were exceptional or normal gifts. Bishops earned their incomes from church endowments and they were responsible for the finance of the churches, but there is no evidence of how much the bishops of Sion monastery earned or received from their congregation in a year.[37] Theodore of Sykeon received a solidus a day, totalling 365 solidi a year.[38] Eutychianos's total donations, of approximately 760 solidi, are almost the equivalent of two years' salary for Theodore of Sykeon. However, Eutychianos's donations might not have been made at the same time but spread out over many years. Comparing the salaries of imperial officials from the time of Justinian, it becomes clear that the amount spent by Eutychianos would not be exceptional for high-ranking persons, but would be a significant donation for the middle and lower classes. For example, the advisers to the Prefect of Africa were paid 1440 solidi a year, his secretary was paid 504 solidi a year and his officers were paid 10 solidi a year. His soldiers earned 9 solidi a year.[39]

Imperial gifts of precious metal to churches are, of course, much bigger. Justinian's silver donated to Hagia Sophia has been estimated to weigh approximately 40,000 Roman pounds, perhaps some 160,000 solidi.[40] The *Liber Pontificalis* provides some figures for gifts to churches in Rome. The Lateran Church, for example, received 17,725 Roman pounds of silver over the centuries, mostly from Constantine.[41]

37 Rapp, 'The elite status of bishops in late antiquity', 380–3; Jones, *Later Roman Empire 284–602*, vol. 2, 894–904.

38 Averil Cameron et al., eds, *Late Antiquity: Empire and Successors, AD 425–600,* CAH, 14 (Cambridge, 2000), 741.

39 Hendy, *Studies in the Byzantine Monetary Economy*, 165.

40 Procopius, *Περι Κτισμάτων (De Aedificiis*), I.i.65, ed. tr. H.B. Dewing, *Procopius VII: Buildings,* Loeb Classical Library, 343 (Cambridge, MA, 1940), 29, tr. C. Mango, *The Art of the Byzantine Empire: 312–1453, Sources and Documents* (Toronto, 1986), 76; see also M.M. Mango, 'The monetary value of silver revetments and objects', 128.

41 *Le Liber Pontificalis*, 172–4, 233, 242–3, ed. L. Duchesne, (Paris, 1886); cited in Mango, 'The monetary value of silver revetments and objects', 134; B. Caseau, 'Objects in churches: the testimony of inventories', in L. Lavan et al. (ed.), *Objects in Context, Objects in Use: Material Spirituality in Late Antiquity* (Boston, 2007), 555.

Table 4.1 The Cost of the Sion Objects to Their Donors

Donor	*Objects*	*Total Weight*	*Potential Cost*
Bishop Eutychianos	Three patens (nos 1, 2 and 3), twelve polycandela (nos 7–18), two censers (nos 19 and 20), two amphorae (nos 28 and 29), four standing lamps (nos 31–34), five openwork lamps (nos 35–38 and 41), one suspension bracket (no. 43)	62,216 grams /190.16 Roman pounds	760 solidi/3,420 grams of gold
The priest Zacharias	One plain sheet (no. 53)	3,164 grams/9 Roman pounds	38 solidi/171 grams of gold
Bishop Paregoros	Altar table sheets (nos 51 and 52), one plain sheet (no. 54)	27,859 grams/85 Roman pounds	340 solidi/1500 grams of gold
For the memory of Maria	Paten (no. 6)	8000 grams/24.45 Roman pounds	97 solidi/436.5 grams of gold
For the memory of Angeleuos Roufinos	Paten (no. 4)	4,537 grams/13.8 Roman pounds	55 solidi/247.5 grams of gold
For the memory of John and his daughter	Paten (no. 5)	4,234 grams/12.9 Roman pounds	51 solidi//229.5 grams of gold
For the memory of deacon Prinkipios, Stephane, Leontia and deacon Konon	Book cover (no. 45)	317 grams/0.96 Roman pounds	3.8 solidi/17.1 grams of gold
For the memory of Eutychianos	Openwork lamp (no. 39)	566 grams/1.7 Roman pounds	6 solidi/27 grams of gold
For the memory of Himeria	Openwork lamp (no. 40)	565 grams/1.7 Roman pounds	6 solidi/27 grams of gold

5 The Lives and Biographies of the Sion Vessels

I move now to consider the Sion Treasure in a different way, going from issues of cost to those of value, and questions about the roles and functions of the Treasure. My aim is to trace the changing perceptions of, and values placed on, the Treasure throughout the course of its life. In this context, in order to add to our understanding of these objects and their use I shall use the concept of the 'biography of objects'.[1] Thinking about 'cultural biography' is a helpful tool in unpacking the ways in which the objects from the Sion Treasure were valued by their producers, donors, users and audiences. In the sixth century, the vessels from the Sion Treasure existed in three different frameworks: as commodities, as gifts, and as 'things to be used' inside a church. These varying situations mean that the makers, donors and users of the Treasure all perceived the silverware in different ways.

Three different, but interrelated, factors come together to affect the ways in which the silverware was thought about: human agency, material agency and context. Human agency covers the role of people in giving materials values and functions depending on their intentions, affected by their social, religious and educational background. 'Material agency' here is the idea that objects were able to fulfil the intentions of people when given those functions. The material properties of objects affect their use. A silver dish and a ceramic dish may have different functions and will certainly be perceived differently. A silver dish used on the dining table or in the Eucharist functions differently and is understood differently.[2]

1 A. Appadurai, 'Introduction: commodities and the politics of value', in A. Appadurai (ed.), *The Social Life of Things: Commodities in Cultural Perspective* (Cambridge, 1986), 3–63; I. Kopytoff, 'The cultural biography of things: commoditization as process', in *The Social Life of Things*, ed. Appadurai, 64–91.

2 J.M. Skibo and M.B. Schiffer, *People and Things: A Behavioral Approach to Material Culture* (New York, 2008); M.B. Schiffer, *Behavioral Archaeology: First Principles* (Salt Lake City, 1995); C. Knappett, *Thinking Through Material Culture: An Interdisciplinary Perspective* (Philadelphia, 2005); Knappett, 'The neglected networks of material agency: artefacts, pictures and texts', in C. Knappett and L. Malafouris (ed.), *Material Agency: Towards a Non-Anthropocentric Approach* (New York, 2008), 139; S.E. Van der Leeuw, 'Agency, Networks,

DOI: 10.4324/9781003345503-6

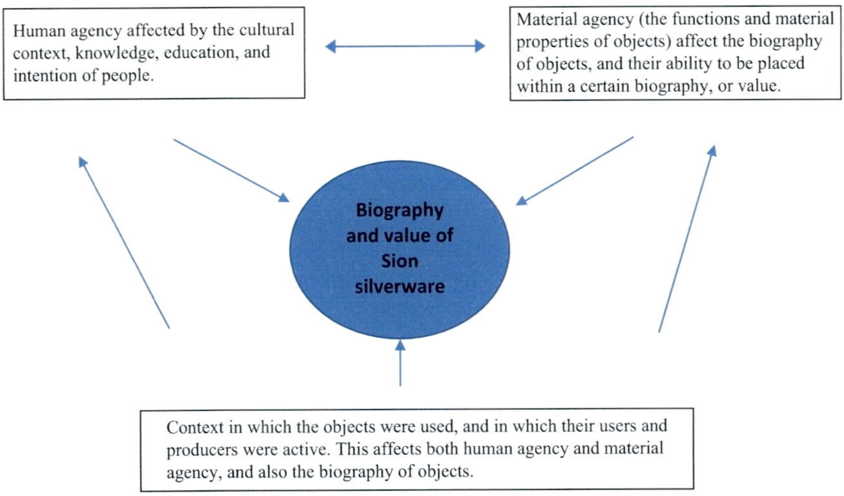

Diagram 5.1 Interrelationships between silverware, people and context.

In other words, objects themselves also affected people and 'made' people act in particular ways.[3] Indeed, human agency and material agency cannot be separated when examining the biography of objects: both the intentions of people and the materiality of the Sion vessels put into different uses affected their biography as commodities, gifts to God and objects used in religious contexts and have religious functions along with their primary functions such as holding the wine and lighting the church.[4]

The silverware in the Sion Treasure had lives, as people do, and through their life, these objects moved from one context to another, from their production to their being given to the church to their use within the church, and so from the hand of one person to the hand of another person. In these different contexts and hands of different people they had different life stories and gained new biographies.[5]

Past and Future', in *Material Agency,* ed. Knappett and Malafouris, 220; L. Malafouris, 'At the potter's wheel: an argument for material agency', in Material Agency, ed. Knappett and Malafouris, 22; C. Gosden, 'What do objects want?', *JAMT,* 12.3 (2005), 193–211; P. Bloom, 'Intention, history, and artifact concepts', *Cognition,* 60 (1996), 1–29; S. Küchler and T. Carroll, *A Return to the Object: Alfred Gell, Art, and Social Theory* (New York, 2021).

3 A. Gell, *Art and Agency: An Anthropological Theory* (Oxford, 1998), 16.

4 For how human agency and material agency affect each other see Knappett, 'The neglected networks of material agency', 139; Gosden, 'What do objects want?', 193–211; H. Morphy, 'Art as a mode of action: some problems with Gell's *Art and Agency*', *JMC,* 14.1 (2009), 6.

5 As Kopytoff argues, things have social lives and they move from one context to another context which gives them different biographies. See Kopytoff, 'The cultural biography of things', 74–6.

The first stage of life of the Sion objects starts with their production and circulation: as raw silver, a significant commodity in sixth-century Byzantium. Further, the Sion vessels were, in the first instance, created for the purpose of economic exchange, for sale, meaning they had a commercial value when they first entered circulation and production.[6] Donors used their wealth to obtain these objects, and the producer or seller earned some money through creating them and they were controlled by the state (stamped or unstamped ones) to collect taxes clarifies that these objects have exchangeability. This indicates that even though the silverware in the Sion Treasure was produced for sacred transactions, they were candidates to be commodities and had potential to be placed in the commodity phase.[7] The commodity phase in which the Sion silver were put was shaped by the Byzantine cultural and religious context which affected the intentions and the cognition of the producers and donors of the Sion vessels. The artists of the Sion Treasure knew what church silver looked like – what was appropriate to create as patens and chalices to meet the demands of donors.[8] Artists had to decide where to decorate or how to decorate the vessels according to their functions and the space available.[9] So in order to understand or evaluate the differences between shapes and decorations of certain objects such as patens (esp. nos 1–3) and polycandela (nos 13–18) which I have discussed earlier in Chapter 4, these external factors need to be considered, rather than using these differences to define the workshops of these objects.

Second, when the Sion vessels were sold to patrons, they gained another purpose; as gifts to God. They represented a willingness on the part of the donor to sacrifice their wealth. They requested salvation, protection and remembrance from God. The inscriptions on the Sion silverware tell us something about the expectations of the donors, in terms of what they believed donating the objects to churches as gifts to God would do for them.[10] The inscriptions perhaps served to underline the role of the silver

6 Appadurai, 'Introduction: commodities and the politics of value', 3.

7 As Appadurai argues 'commodity situation' is the stage in the life of a thing that has the potential to be a commodity, and he divided the definition of a commodity situation into three parts: first, the 'commodity phase of a thing'; second, the 'commodity candidacy of a thing'; and third, 'the commodity context in which things can be placed'. See Appadurai, 'Introduction: commodities and the politics of value', 13.

8 J. Robb, 'Beyond agency', *World Archaeology,* 42.4 (2010), 494; Robb, 'What do things want? Object design as a middle range theory of material culture', *Archaeological Papers of the American Anthropological Association,* 26.1 (2015), 167; for the prototype of objects and how these prototypes were considered by artists, also see M. O'Malley, 'Altarpieces and agency: the altarpiece of the Society of the Purification and its "invisible skein of relations"', *ArtH* 28.4 (2005), 417–41.

9 For these ideas and discussions see Leeuw, 'Agency, networks, past and future', 220; Malafouris, 'At the potter's wheel', 23; Schiffer, *People and Things*, 11; Knappett, *Thinking Through Material Culture*, 22; Knappett, 'The neglected networks of material agency', 139.

10 See Table 2.1 in Chapter 2.

vessels as gifts to God, carrying this message for as long as they remained in existence. This malleability and functionality of the objects and intentions of their donors to use them in this way put these vessels in another context where they gained new biography.

Finally, once inside the church, as well as carrying their donors' hopes, the Sion silver had another life – as functional ecclesiastical vessels with jobs to do. Inside the church, some of the vessels were used for Communion; some of the silver was lighting equipment, and some church revetments. Inside the church, different people – monks, priests, lay people, men, women – interacted with these objects with all of their senses, their imaginations and emotions. The form of the Sion objects, their function (which changed according to the context in which they were used), and their users' knowledge and psychology (which was influenced by the context in which they dwelt) changed perceptions of the silverware. What happened when people experienced the silver objects with their senses, by touching, smelling and kissing? What happened when people experienced these objects from afar? What happened when they read or did not read the inscriptions on the objects? And how can we access this? The experience of a person examining and touching the object in a museum is very different from that of a person touching and seeing the object in a church, which showcases the effect of environment and background knowledge. The patens and chalices could carry bread and wine to a dining table, but what made them different within the church was the importance of the wine and bread they carried and the worshippers' knowledge of this importance.

The Sion Silver Vessels as Commodities

As useful goods, the silver and the vessels made from silver were both in demand, and demand breeds demand. The more silver vessels were given to churches, the more valuable they became, and presumably, the greater the desire on the part of the patron to purchase something distinctive, thereby affecting the ways in which silver vessels were decorated. Just as the motives of patrons created the market for silver, so producers sought to create objects that would please their clients. There was a socially and culturally generated impulse here, which was not based on individual desires and needs but on cultural and religious forces which determined demand, need and utility.[11]

Unlike the silver vessels used in private houses, the Sion silverware was made specifically to be used in a church. The craftsmen were aware of this and worked the form of the Sion vessels to fit this context – they were deliberately made for specific purposes, and both maker and purchaser were aware of these purposes. The vessels needed to be functional religious objects – things in which the wine and bread for the Eucharist could be held; objects suitable for lighting

11 Appadurai, 'Introduction: commodities and the politics of value', 32.

a church. They also needed to be treasures suitable to be a fitting gift to God. There is a question here, which is impossible to answer, as to whether silver vessels were made only to commission or whether they were ever made to be bought 'off the shelf', either complete or with space to be personalised, for example by adding an inscription.

Byzantine culture created a system in which churches needed sacred vessels, and gift-giving to churches was seen as an appropriate social action. The vessels of the Sion Treasure show what sort of equipment was used inside a church. All churches required chalices and patens, as vessels to hold the bread and wine of the celebration of the Eucharist. As the *Vita* of St Pankratios tells us, St Peter sent Pankratios and a preacher named Marcian to the west to spread the gospel there, and 'provided them with the equipment needed for setting up a church', such as 'two sets of silver paten and chalice, two crosses made of cedar boards ...'[12] In addition, churches needed censers for burning incense, candlesticks or lampstands, polycandela and lamps for lighting the church, book covers to cover and protect the sacred books and altar table sheets to cover the altar table.

Silver was a good material for making items for lighting and for the Eucharist: it is a durable and shiny material which is resistant to corrosion caused by food and natural acids.[13] It is and was also cheaper than gold, which increased the number of donors able to afford it. It is clear from several sources indicating the usage of silver inside the churches that churches and monasteries wanted silver for the adornment of the church. St Demetrios explained that his shrine was decorated with silver. 'It is hexagonal in plan, having six columns and as many partitions, shaped out of carved, assayed silver. At the top it bears a silver sphere of no small size'.[14] John of Ephesus's *Ecclesiastical History* explains that the ciboria of churches in the capital were decorated with silver revetments. When the emperor Maurice started to restore his native town of Arabissus he ordered a search for skilful craftsmen, blacksmiths and builders, and the old church was taken down and a new church constructed: 'he sent himself a large and splendid set of church furniture of silver and gold, with beautiful vessels for the altar, and for the adornment of the building and large ciborium'.[15] The adorning of the church, especially the holy altar, was also important.

12 C. Mango, *The Art of the Byzantine Empire: 312–1453, Sources and Documents* (Toronto, 1986), 137–8.

13 C.E. Snow, 'From ingot to object: fabrication techniques used in the manufacture of the Hama Silver', in S. A. Boyd and M. M. Mango (ed.), *Ecclesiastical Silver Plate in Sixth-Century Byzantium* (Washington, DC, 1992), 197.

14 *Miracula S. Demetrii*, mir. 10, PG 116:1265, tr. Mango, *The Art of the Byzantine Empire*, 129.

15 John of Ephesus, *Historiae Ecclesiasticae*, V, 22, ed. and Lat.tr. E.W. Brooks, *Iohannis Ephesini, Historiae Ecclesiasticae Pars Tertia*, CSCO, Scriptores Syri, 55 (Louvain, 1936), 206–7, tr. R.P. Smith, *The Third Part of the Ecclesiastical History of John Bishop of Ephesus* (Oxford, 1860), 362.

These expectations helped create the market for ecclesiastical silver. St Jerome mentions in his letter to Nepotian (Letter 52), that wealthy Christians should 'augment churches, may adorn their walls when built with marbles, may procure massive columns, may deck the unconscious capitals with gold and precious ornaments, may cover church doors with silver and adorn the altars with gold and gems'.[16] Similarly, Severus of Antioch in a homily, speaking about the silver ciborium of the Martyrium of St Drosis, asked his congregants to offer what they could afford to construct an altar. He encouraged them by saying: if someone who possesses very little gives a pound of silver, what everyone gives would be perfect and will be the sufficient sum. He criticised wealthy people who gave nothing for lying in high beds and eating from silver dishes. 'But they are negligent and hesitate to give some of their objects'. He encourages them by advising them: 'stretch out your hand and give joyfully. You will obtain rich rewards and your family will be healthy, and after your departure from here below, you will be in the kingdom of heaven'.[17] In this context, it is understood that the rich should be willing to philanthropically sacrifice their wealth, which was given to them by God, to supply what was needed and help the church and receive rich rewards. All of these circumstances also had an effect on the market for silverware.

So many of the donors of the Sion treasure were clergy. They were bishop Eutychianos, who donated the largest amount of objects in the treasure, bishop Paregoros, the deacon Prinkipios, the priest Zacharias. The donations were undoubtedly fuelled by their positions and the work they engaged in during their daily life. Giving to God was perhaps almost part of the job, part of being a bishop and displaying piety.[18] In the *Laws* of Justinian it was said that the most important qualification for the clergy was piety and good reputation.[19] A bishop such as Eutychianos had religious obligations to fulfil – from the celebration of the liturgy to the furnishing of the church. Proper behaviour reinforced spiritual authority.[20] As the bishop of the Sion monastery, Eutychianos will have spent most of his time in the monastery, responsible for the administration of the church, probably the city, donations of the congregation, and education of the congregation especially teaching of the catechumens.[21] He knew how people

16 Jerome, *Letter 52*, tr. P. Schaff and H. Wace, *A Select Library of Nicene and Post-Nicene Fathers of the Christian Church*, s. 2, vol. 6 (New York, 1893), 94. Revised and edited citation in M.M. Mango, 'The monetary value of silver revetments and objects', in *Ecclesiastical Silver Plate*, ed. Boyd and Mango, 123.

17 Severus of Antioch, *Homiliae Cathedrales*, 100, ed. and Fr. tr. I. Guidi, *Les Homiliae Cathedrales de Sévère d'Antioche. Homelies XCIX à CIII*, PO 22 (Paris, 1930), 247–8.

18 C. Rapp, *Holy Bishops in Late Antiquity: The Nature of Christian Leadership in an Age of Transition* (London, 2005), 178–9.

19 Rapp, *Holy Bishops in Late Antiquity,* 179.

20 Rapp, *Holy Bishops in Late Antiquity,* 16, 23, 156.

21 Rapp, 'The elite status of bishops in late antiquity', *Arethusa*, 33.3 (2000), 379–99; Rapp, 'Bishops in late antiquity: a new social and urban elite?', in J. Haldon and L.I. Conrad (ed.),

expressed their faith, requested protection and salvation from God; indeed, he must have advised his congregation about matters like this.[22] Given his background and role in the church, Eutychianos surely considered the implications of his devotional and votive gifts of this silverware within the context of providing financial support to holy places. His actions fit into that model of behaviour of bishops apparent in Christian society in this period: as representatives of Christ in the world, bishops had responsibility for engaging in philanthropy.[23]

The Sion Treasure contains six large patens, seven chalices and more than twenty pieces of lighting equipment.[24] There is a question about whether all of this was needed. It is hard to say whether the quantity of silverware in the Sion Treasure is unusual because so little else survives. The Sion Treasure is the only example from Anatolia with so many vessels used in the monastery, even the nails used to attach the altar table sheets. However, when it is compared to the silver given to churches in Rome and Constantinople it seems very little. Imperial donations made to churches and cathedrals in Rome and Constantinople were considerably greater. Constantine gave seven silver altars to the Lateran church and a silver ciborium. These were solid silver, not thin revetments. He also gave 200 silver objects consisting of liturgical utensils and lighting equipment.[25] Hagia Sophia had 40,000 Roman pounds of silver in its sanctuary.[26] A better comparison is the donations made to the church of St Sergios in the village of Kaper Koraon. The Kaper Koraon Treasure consists of more than fifty silver objects, including patens, chalices and other liturgical utensils and objects used inside the church. There are seven chalices, seven patens, two flabella, five crosses, three ewers, four book covers, two lampstands, thirteen spoons, two strainers, two ladles, three ewers, two lamps, one mirror and one bowl. All in all, this is close to the number of objects in the Sion Treasure, though there are differences in the types of vessel. The Sion Treasure does not contain strainers, spoons, flabella and ladles; the Kaper Koraon Treasure does not include censers,

---

The Byzantine and Early Islamic Near East: Elites Old and New in the Byzantine and Early Islamic Near East *(Princeton, 2004), 149–78; Rapp,* Holy Bishops in Late Antiquity*, 23.*

22 Rapp, *Holy Bishops in Late Antiquity*, 178–9.

23 Apostolic Constitutions II. 24.7, cited in Rapp, 'Charity and piety as episcopal and imperial virtues in late antiquity', in M. Frenkel and Y. Lev (ed.), *Charity and Giving in Monotheistic Religions*, SGKIO, 22 (Berlin, 2009), 80.

24 S.A. Boyd, 'A "metropolitan" treasure from a church in the provinces: an introduction to the study of the Sion Treasure', in *Ecclesiastical Silver Plate*, ed. Boyd and Mango, 17–18; Mango, 'The monetary value of silver revetments and objects', 132.

25 *Le Liber Pontificalis*, 172–4, 177, 179, 182, 183, 232, 244, ed. L. Duchesne (Paris, 1886), cited in Mango, 'The monetary value of silver revetments and objects', 127, 132, 134.

26 Procopius, *Περι Κτισμάτων (De Aedificiis*), I.i.65, ed. tr. H.B. Dewing, *Procopius VII: Buildings,* Loeb Classical Library, 343 (Cambridge, MA, 1940), 29, tr. C. Mango, *Art of the Byzantine Empire*, 76; see also M. Mango, 'The monetary value of silver revetments and objects', 128.

polycandela, or silver sheeting for the altar table and columns for lampstands. The Attarouthi Treasure, dated again to the sixth century and again from Byzantine Syria, has ten chalices, three censers and a representation of the dove of the Holy Spirit. Whether these differences are due to the chance of survival or a different idea of relevant fixtures and fittings for a church, or different levels of wealth among the donors is unclear. What perhaps matters more are questions about the value of the silverware to each individual church, why it might have been given and how it was used, even what role the 'extra' vessels might have played. Some items might not have been in continual use, but were perhaps used for special occasions. Size makes a difference: the Sion church was a large three-aisled basilica with a large triconch apse and a rectangular baptistery and a reliquary chapel attached to it, so needing a great deal of lighting.[27]

In addition, the silver was a form of capital. Monasteries needed wealth to carry out the appropriate social actions expected of them – feeding the hungry, caring for the poor for example. The *Vita* of St Nicholas of Sion tells us that when Nicholas went to the shrine of the archangel Gabriel in Karkabo in Lycia, to make offering during the plague, he brought with him nomismata, wine and grain which he took from the monastery. He then 'slaughtered three oxen and summoned all the people of the place. And they all ate and were filled'.[28] He also travelled to the other places and made offering and people gathered and made merry, then he arrived at his monastery after twenty-five days of this journey of offering and helping people.[29] In the *Vita* we are also told that, 'the sanctuary of St Daniel in Sabandos was about to collapse on account of old age'. When Nicholas heard and saw this, he gave 'eighty and a half nomismata' for restoring the place and 'he gave orders that the provisions be supplied from the monastery'.[30] The monastery of Sion was not only a place for monastic life; it was also a place that supported the villages around it.

Bishop Eutychianos and the other donors of silver were surely aware of their duties, aware that Christian gift-giving to God included giving money to the poor as charity, or gifting things that were needed, like ecclesiastical silverware, to churches and holy places. These were a form of practising 'philanthropy', a quality given by God to individuals, which obliged Christian donors to give to the poor and make offerings to the church. To

27 R.M. Harrison, 'Churches and chapels of central Lycia', *Anatolian Studies*, 13 (1963), 131–5. For up-to-date plans also see; B. İşler, 'Likya Bölgesi'ndeki Karabel-Asarcık yerleşimi yapılarının plan ve işlev özellikleri üzerine gözlemler', *International Young Scholars Conference I: Mediterranean Anatolia Symposium Proceedings 4–7 November 2009* (İstanbul, 2012), 173.

28 Nicholas of Sion, *Βίος τοῦ 'Αγίου Νικολάου τῆς 'Αγίας Σιών*, c. 56, ed. tr. I. Ševčenko and N.P. Ševčenko, *The Life of Saint Nicholas of Sion* (Brookline, MA, 1984), 89.

29 Nicholas of Sion, c. 57, ed. tr. Ševčenko and Ševčenko, 90.

30 Nicholas of Sion, c. 58, ed. tr. Ševčenko and Ševčenko, 91.

do these things was important since it was what was expected by God. This is more than an idea of reciprocity in gift-giving, the idea put forward by Marcel Mauss that giving a gift puts the recipient under an obligation.[31] In Christianity, the virtuous individual was already under an obligation to give gifts, almost with thought of no return.[32] The fundamental intention was to please God, not human individuals, very different from the case when secular gifts were given.[33] Religious gifts did not serve to underline the relationship between the power of the giver over the receiver. According to Christian belief, God is the source of all power and worldly matters, and he gives wealth and poverty to people according to his will. The gift is to show one's respect to God.[34] Thus, Eutychianos had no need to display his wealth or his authority to God in the manner emperors did when giving gifts to other rulers. Eutychianos received or expected blessings in return for his gifts, not reciprocation in material form.[35] The act of gifting involved a sacrificing of his wealth, which God had bestowed in the first place, taking the form of thanks. So, the vessels of the Sion monastery were not gifts for reciprocation, they functioned as items to show their respect and piety towards God. The donor requested help and salvation not as a return for the silver but for his piety.

All of which means that there was almost an imperative for gifts to be given to God. Eutychianos must have been well aware of the writings of the Church Fathers and Councils. As the Fourth Church Council of Chalcedon (448), explains, 'We were made by God for works of philanthropy'.[36] In giving silver, he and other donors believed they were making offerings to God so as to fulfil God's expectations of them, as Christian and bishops, deacon and priest alike.[37] They would have also been aware of Paul's writings in the *Epistles* to the Corinthians which made the point that these offerings were not for worldly returns, but rather for spiritual returns, and most importantly

31 M. Mauss, 'Gifts and the obligation to return gifts', in F. Candlin and R. Guins (ed.), *The Object Reader* (London, 2009), 23.

32 R. Franses, *Donor Portraits in Byzantine Art: The Vicissitudes of Contact between Human and Divine* (Cambridge, 2018), 177.

33 A. Cutler, 'Significant gifts: patterns of exchange in late antique, Byzantine and early Islamic diplomacy', *Journal of Medieval and Early Modern Studies,* 38.1 (2008), 79–85.

34 Franses, *Donor Portraits in Byzantine Art,* 177.

35 D. Caner, 'Alms, blessings, offerings: the repertoire of Christian gifts in early Byzantium', in M.L. Satlow (ed.), *The Gift in Antiquity*(Oxford, 2013), 29.

36 Rapp, 'Charity and Piety', 75.

37 I. Drpić, *Epigram, Art, and Devotion in Later Byzantium* (Cambridge, 2016), 249–51; also see Mauss, *The Gift: The Form and Reason for Exchange in Archaic Societies* (London, 2002); Mauss, 'Gifts and the obligation to return gifts', 21–31; D. Caner, 'Towards a miraculous economy: Christian gifts and material "blessings" in late antiquity', *JEChS,* 14 (3) (2006), 329–77; Caner, 'Alms, Blessings, Offerings', 25–44; V. Dimitropoulou, 'Giving gifts to God: aspects of patronage in Byzantine art', in L. James (ed.), *A Companion to Byzantium* (Oxford, 2010), 161–70.

people should make offerings cheerfully, 'not reluctantly or under compulsion'. It is the 'expression of thanks to God', and a way of showing how grateful they are for the good given by God. Further, Byzantine Christians believed that God loved people who gave and showed respect.[38] It was in this context that Caesarius of Arles instructed his congregants that gift-giving was an obligation, and that it was equal to doing other good works.[39] All of these circumstances lie behind the Sion Treasure and explain something of the motive forces behind their creation: they represented a sacrifice of the donor's wealth, a proper fulfilment of his vows, a gift to God; but also, a request for help, protection and salvation for the individuals and for their church and congregation.

As commodities, the initial reason behind the creation and the decoration of the Sion silver was the demand of its commissioners, influenced by cultural and religious demands – what the church needed, what was expected of the bishop. Therefore, the primary aim of producers was to please the clients, who were the donors of these objects. The initial consideration of producers of Sion objects was a categorisation of the item according to expected physical and functional features. One craftsman's polycandelon or paten might differ from others, but their function was the same. The decoration or form of objects depended on both these cultural norms and the intention of producers shaped according to the availability of the material, the tools used for the production and the shape of the object during production.[40] We might equally explain the differences between the decorations, weights and forms of patens, polycandela and lamps as arising from the craftsman's choice, rather than their skill or the products of different workshops. Each of the objects Eutychianos gave was equally successful, as he liked them enough to buy and give them to the Sion monastery.

The material used for the production of object also had to be appropriate to use inside the church – materials as well as donors needed to be pure and respectable. In the *Life* of St Theodore of Sykeon, we are told that Theodore sent his deacon to the capital to buy a fine silver chalice and a paten. When the deacon presented the items for use in the Eucharist, Theodore told him that they were unsuitable. The archdeacon, indicating the five imperial stamps and good workmanship of the objects, argued that they were made from pure silver. Theodore told him that, while this might be so, they were nonetheless damned because of their previous use. When Theodore filled the chalice, the liquid became black. Then the archdeacon

38 2 Corinthians, 9: 7, 8, 12 and 14, cited in Caner, 'Towards a miraculous economy', 337.

39 Caesarius, *Sermo 16*, cc 103, 77; tr. D. Ganz, 'Giving to God in the Mass: the experience of the offertory', in P. Fouracre and W. Davies (ed.), *The Languages of Gift in the Early Middle Ages* (Cambridge, 2010), 21.

40 Leeuw, 'Agency, networks, past and future', 220; Knappett, *Thinking Through Material Culture*, 22; Malafouris, 'At the potter's wheel', 23.

went back to the capital to find out why and the silversmith explained that the set had been refashioned from a chamber-pot used by a prostitute.[41] Here, the expectations of the users of the religious objects were crucial. Theodore was less concerned with the cost of the silverware but its purity in terms of its previous usage.

Another story that explains the importance of the purity of materials is a passage taken from the *History* of Theophylact Simocatta. It tells the story of a Constantinopolitan named Paulinos who had indulged in witchcraft and sold a silver bowl that he had used to collect the blood of his sacrifices to some dealers. When this silver object was recycled, and the other object made from the same material was displayed in the silver shop, the bishop of Thracian Herakleia purchased it and presented it to the shrine of St Glykeria in place of a copper bowl, which had previously been used for collecting sacred aromatics. Because of the new object's former use the sacred aromatics disappeared.[42] Again, the object was not spiritually pure and consequently could not be used as a sacred object. Indeed, the conversion from one form of vessel to another seems not to have mattered – once a prostitute's chamber pot, it seems that the silver was contaminated forever. In this context, we can only presume that Eutychianos and other patrons of the Sion Treasure paid some attention to the silver as silver and its possible previous lives.

Rather than founding a church with money, they gave sacred silver to it to fulfil a functional purpose, and also for their protection or to gain rewards from God. By giving these gifts to the monastery, they both gave offerings to God and helped the monastery to have enough equipment to celebrate the liturgy, lighting the church and covering its altar table, and furthermore ensured their own protection and salvation, or so they hoped. The idea of philanthropy was an important one in Christian culture and people gave offerings to the church. They actually gave these offerings to God, through the agency of sacred places.

It is this environment that puts Sion silverware into a commodity context. Once they were commissioned, the intention of the donors affected the ways in which the vessels were made and decorated. Their future contexts, as gifts to God or objects to be used inside the church, brought them to life. They were in this commodity context to become sacred gifts and provide some income to the producer. Cultural and religious needs converted them from silver sheets to vessels to be used inside the church.

41 Theodore of Sykeon, *Βίος Τοῦ Ὁσίου Πατρὸς Ἡμῶν Θεοδώρου Ἀρχιμανδρίτου Συκεών*, c. 42, ed. A. Festugière, *Vie de Théodore de Sykeon: Texte Grec* 1, SH 48 (Brussels, 1970), 37, tr. E. Dawes and N.H. Baynes, *Three Byzantine Saints: Contemporary Biographies Translated from the Greek* (Oxford, 1948), 118.

42 Theophylact Simocatta, *Ἱστορία,* I.11–12, ed. C. de Boor, *Theophylacti Simocattae Historiae* (Leipzig, 1887), 60–4, tr. Michael and Mary Whitby, *The History of Theophylact Simocatta* (Oxford, 1986), 34–7.

The Sion Vessels as Gifts

The next stage of the silver vessels was their life as gifts to God. The inscriptions on the vessels took the donors' names inside the church and kept them present there, even after their death. These inscriptions, written on silver used inside the church, were visible to the wider users of the church in which they were displayed and employed. They were a public statement of the objects' role as gifts to God. They also said something about the donors' hopes and fears. The inscriptions on the objects indicate how materiality of objects – their functions to carry these inscriptions – can affect their intended functions and biography.

Table 2.1 in chapter 2 details the motives and hopes of the donors of the objects, which formulae were used on which type of object and the extent of the different wishes and prayer on each object. The words used make it clear that the objects were seen by their donors as gifts: 'this was presented in the time of', 'presents this/offers this to the Lord/Great God/Christ/Mother of God' (nos 1 and 2). Some were for the fulfilment of a vow (nos 10–12). Some of these formulae was followed by the wishes of their donors such as 'forgiveness of sins' (nos 1 and 2), and some ask for salvation, help and mercy (nos 10–12, 13–18 and 43). Some vessels were given for the memory of the individuals whose names appear on them (nos 4–8). These phrases mostly include the names of the donors except the ones applied on the chalices (nos 22, 25 and 26) on which the inscription reads; 'A vow/a prayer of those whose names are known to God' and 'Having given thanks I made (it)'. None of the formulae is unique; indeed, they are quite common expressions of pious wishes, implying that there were acceptable and unacceptable, or perhaps appropriate and inappropriate ways for donors to express themselves.[43] These formulae on the Sion objects can be examined in four headings; protection, forgiveness and salvation, memory and fulfilment of a vow. These headings will indicate that Sion silver both worked as gifts and carried the wishes of donors and memory of the individuals as specified on the inscriptions.

Protection

Protection is apparent in several inscriptions on the Sion silverware which directly asks for help from God or Holy Sion. The formula 'Thrice-Holy Lord help' can be seen on three cruciform polycandela (nos 7–9), 'Holy Sion help' can be seen on six rectangular polycandela (nos 13–18) and on two amphorae (nos 28 and 29). Requesting help and protection from God is a common formula also used on other Byzantine objects. People used the

43 For other examples of these same formulae on silverware, see, for example, M.M. Mango, *Silver from Early Byzantium: The Kaper Koraon and Related Treasures* (Baltimore, MD, 1986), nos 1, 2, 5, 9, 10, 14, 15, 18, 27, 29, 33, 34, 42, 61, 62.

formula of 'help' on their marriage rings to protect their marriage, as with a sixth-century ring from Dumbarton Oaks.[44] An inscription from a sixth-century floor mosaic from Kourion in Cyprus bears formulae to 'help' and 'protect'.[45] The formula was used to protect individuals' houses from natural disasters, and many carried amulets to receive miraculous healing. It was common to use the same phrase on magical amulets, as it was believed to protect people from the evil eye. Two gold amulets from Dumbarton Oaks (dated to the third and sixth centuries) bear inscriptions requesting help and protection from God.[46] The evil eye was believed, according to church Fathers such as St Basil and St John Chrysostom, to derive from the envious eyes of others, which then caused bad things to happen to people. Fear of the evil eye was very common in the Late Antique and Byzantine worlds.[47] It is clear that objects with the inscription 'Lord help' were used to obtain miraculous healing and protection, as votive objects presented to the shrine of St Symeon the Younger demonstrate.[48] All of this is linked to the simple word 'help' on the Sion objects. Just as with magical amulets, seals and tokens, so too Eutychianos sought help and protection for himself and for the church through the church silver. 'Help!' was surely a prayer for protection and invocation in the same way that it was used on rings and amulets.

The monastery itself was also seen as a place of protection and safety as the inscription on rectangular polycandela (nos 13–18) says: 'Holy Sion, help'. It was seen as the counterpart of Jerusalem, its local counterpart for forgiveness and salvation.[49] Nicholas had 'produced many miraculous signs and cures for those who believed through him in holy Sion'.[50] Those who believed in St Nicholas of Sion and his miraculous healings through holy Sion could expect to gain salvation and protection.

Holy Sion was not the only agency Eutychianos sought help and protection from. The formula on the cruciform polycandela (nos 7–9), 'Thrice-holy Lord help', was used in the liturgies of St Mark and St James and in Syrian liturgies.[51] A stone door lintel found in Syria where near the

44 For the example of a marriage ring and its inscription which can be read as; 'Lord help Maria', as well as its counterparts, see M.C. Ross, *Catalogue of the Byzantine and Early Medieval Antiquities in the Dumbarton Oaks Collection 2: Jewelry, Enamels and Art of the Migration Period* (Washington, DC, 1965), nos 6, 36, 63, 69.

45 G. Osbourne, 'Mosaics of power: superstition, magic and Christian power in early Byzantine floor mosaics' (PhD Dissertation, University of Sussex, 2014), 147.

46 Ross, *Catalogue of the Byzantine and Early Medieval Antiquities,* nos 28, 30.

47 M.W. Dickie, 'The Fathers of the church and the evil eye', in H. Maguire (ed.), *Byzantine Magic* (Washington, DC, 1995), 9–35.

48 G. Vikan, 'Art, medicine and magic in early Byzantium', *DOP,* 35 (1984), 65–86.

49 Nicholas of Sion, c. 10, ed. tr. Ševčenko and Ševčenko, 31.

50 Nicholas of Sion, c. 14, ed. tr. Ševčenko and Ševčenko, 35.

51 W.K. Prentice, 'Fragments of an Early Christian liturgy in Syrian inscriptions' *TAPA*, 33 (1902), 82.

church door was inscribed with 'Thrice-holy have mercy on us'.[52] A story from the *Miracles* of St Artemios explains that when a man named Polychronios came to the saint for healing, he heard Artemios say, 'The Holy Trinity which created all things visible and invisible, which preserves all men and watches over the diseased and sick, will cure you itself'.[53] The story is a suggestive indication of the power of this formula and why Eutychianos might have inscribed his objects as demanding help from the 'Thrice-holy'. In Nikephoros Kallistos's *Ecclesiastical History* there were natural disasters and earthquakes that caused many people to die in fifth-century Constantinople. Further, people prayed to God by saying the hymn of the Thrice Holy.[54] An amulet from Anemourion inscribed with the Trisagion also shows that the Trisagion was used for protection from the evil eye.[55] Eutychianos too wanted protection from the disasters or demons for himself and for the monastery.

Forgiveness and Salvation

Eutychianos also chose to put his wish for forgiveness and salvation on three patens (nos 1–3), three circular polycandela (nos 10–12), a censer (no. 20), and on the reverse side of the suspension bracket to hold lamps (no. 43). Again, this is not an unusual wish. On the atrium of the church of the Holy Apostles in Anemourion, there is an inscription written on the floor mosaic; 'O Lord … With thanksgiving I have brought you these gifts; accept them for the forgiveness of my sins.'[56] Similarly in the Treasury of San Marco in Venice, there is a ciborium from the sixth century found in Constantinople. On the left, right and front faces of the arches is an encircling inscription, which reads; 'in fulfilment of a vow and for the salvation of the most glorious Anastasia'.[57] Here, she claimed that she had both fulfilled her vow by giving the gift and also wanted salvation from God in exchange for it. These examples show the sorts of pleas and prayers that were common practice in Byzantium. Some people carried their prayers on their person in the form of amulets; others inscribed them on their offerings or placed them in churches and holy places.

52 Prentice, 'Fragments of an Early Christian liturgy', 81.

53 Miracles of St Artemios, *Διήγησις των Θαυμάτων Του Αγίου Και Ενδόξου Μεγαλομάρτυρος Και Θαυματουργού Αρτεμίου*, 41, ed. tr. V.S. Crisafulli and J.W. Nesbitt, *The Miracles of St. Artemios: A Collection of Miracle Stories by an Anonymous Author of Seventh-Century Byzantium,* TMM, 13 (Leiden and New York, 1997), 213–5.

54 Nikephoros Kallistos, *Εκκλησιαστικής Ιστορίας,* XIV, 46, PG 146: 1215–21; cited and tr. Prentice, 'Fragments of an early Christian liturgy', 83.

55 J. Russell, 'The archaeological context of magic in the early Byzantine period', in *Byzantine Magic,* ed. Maguire, 39.

56 Russell, *The Mosaic Inscriptions of Anemurium*, ETAM, 13 (Vienna, 1987), 53.

57 D. Buckton, *The Treasury of San Marco, Venice* (New York, 1984), 96.

The word ‘humble’, followed by the words ‘forgiveness’ and ‘salvation’ was also used on the objects given by Eutychianos. Eutychianos here, by accepting he was a sinner, placed his prayer on his offering. It is also the common ritual when someone prays before God. Romanos’s hymns taught people how to pray through a number of biblical stories. When judging himself, Romanos considered himself a sinner in front of the congregants; this act was an act of confession and was ritually performed in the liturgy.[58] When accepting himself as a sinner and praying for forgiveness, he uses humble language, followed by a prayer for forgiveness and salvation.[59] Romanos here makes a point that everyone should confess and accept themselves as sinners. By doing this everyone should pray for sinner. So Eutychianos also accepted himself as a sinner and prayed for the forgiveness of his sins by using humble language on his vessels.

Memory

Some donors, as we can see in the inscriptions on patens (nos 4–6), openwork lamps (nos 39 and 40) and the pair of book covers (no. 45) from the Sion Treasure, mention explicitly their hopes of their family or relatives being remembered – by God and possibly by the congregation. We read ‘for the repose and memory of Maria the illustrious’, ‘for the memory and repose of John’, ‘for the memory and repose of Angeleuos Roufinos’, ‘for the memory and repose of Himeria’, ‘for the memory and repose of Eutychianos’. These inscriptions state that these prayers were for the memory of someone’s family and relatives, not for themselves. This same formula was also used in the Liturgy: during the Great Entrance, worshippers prayed ‘Lord remember me in your kingdom’.[60] Amy Papalexandrou interpreted this as a central motivating factor for every Byzantine that they be remembered by God himself for eternity.[61] This remembrance might also help with their eternal salvation after death. The remembrance by God was important in the orthodox faith to gain salvation, so people prayed for their own remembrance and of their relatives as well, especially for those who died before them. In his fifth lecture on the mysteries, Cyril of Jerusalem asserted that in the congregation, ‘we pray for all the sick, poor and needy and all who have gone from us, since we believe that it is of the greatest help to those souls for whom the prayer is offered’. He continues: ‘then we commemorate also those

58 D. Krueger, *Liturgical Subjects: Christian Ritual, Biblical Narrative, and the Formation of the Self in Byzantium* (Philadelphia, PA, 2014), 11.

59 Krueger, *Liturgical Subjects*, 33.

60 A. Papalexandrou, ‘The memory culture of Byzantium’, in *A Companion to Byzantium*, ed. James, 110.

61 Papalexandrou, ‘The memory culture of Byzantium’, 110.

who have fallen asleep'.[62] These examples show that praying for oneself and for others, and commemorating people who are dead, were common rituals.

For the donors of the Sion Treasure, these objects then were valued for their multi-functionality. The objects were intermediaries to be used as objects carrying prayers and wishes. They were used for magical protection, salvation, forgiveness and memory.

Fulfilment of a Vow

Some of Eutychianos's silver was explicitly given to fulfil his vow (polycandela nos 10–12, censer no. 20, openwork lamp no. 38, suspension bracket for lamps no. 43). Gifts for the fulfilment of a vow were slightly different than giving devotional gifts.[63] It was the responsibility of donors to fulfil their vows after their expectations had been granted: not fulfilling a vow was a sin and burden.[64] Failure to fulfil a vow as a result of giving the wrong object or not giving anything caused difficulties and problems. There is a story explains what happened when the donor's gift was not compatible to the standards of his vow. In the *Life* of St Niketas, written in the sixth century, a donor promised to donate two silver chalices to the church as a transaction for his safety during a military campaign. However, he actually gave one chalice and one cloth for covering an altar to replace the second chalice. Afterwards he experienced difficulties and troubles in his life. The saint appeared to him in his dream and pointed out his failure to keep his vow. After this he fulfilled his vow.[65] It was vital, given these beliefs, that Eutychianos kept his promise.

There are also important examples showing the importance of fulfilling a vow, even though it is from later centuries. In an epigram from the twelfth century in *the Anthologia Marciana,* we are told that Gerasimos asked for a cure from St Panteleimon and made a vow to decorate the icon of the saint with a textile hanging if he was healed. He was healed but failed to fulfil his vow and then the saint appeared in his dreams to warn him.[66] Gerasimos responded:

62 Cyril of Jerusalem, *Κατήχησις Μυσταγωγική* (*Catechesis Mystagogica)*, V.8-9, PG 33: 1115, tr. L.P. McCauley and A.A. Stephenson, *The Works of Saint Cyril of Jerusalem,* 2, The Fathers of the Church, 64 (Washington, DC, 1970), 197.

63 Drpić, *Epigram, Art and Devotion*, 257.

64 S.V. Leatherbury, 'Textiles as gifts to God in late antiquity: Christian altar cloths as cultic objects', in C. Brøns and M. Nosch (ed.), *Textiles and Cult in the Ancient Mediterranean* (Oxford, 2017), 252.

65 Gregory of Tours, *Vitae Patrum*, 8. 11, tr. E. James, *Gregory of Tours: Life of the Fathers*, TTH, 1 (Liverpool, 1991), 62–3; see also Leatherbury, 'Textiles as gifts to God', 252.

66 Drpić, *Epigram, Art and Devotion*, 259; F. Spingou, 'Words and artworks in the twelfth century and beyond: the thirteenth century manuscript Marcianus gr. 524 and the twelfth-century dedicatory epigrams on works of art' (PhD diss., University of Oxford, 2012), 123.

> In the past, you conferred your grace for free; and now, not because you long for silver or gold, but because you do not want to see me punished for lying to you, you disturb me during the night when <in my dream> I appear to kiss your icon and to hold a veil, together with a special bond, until I remember the debt which I have had for the past three years, and which I, your Gerasimos, now settle by bringing this adornment to you, O blessed Panteleimon.[67]

The objects inscribed with the formula 'fulfilment of a vow' also indicate the role of silver. These objects were for fulfilling Eutychianos's vow as he felt obliged to give them. For him, these objects were materials helping him to keep his promise and also add his prayers, as can be seen on some objects (nos 10–12), while the others only bear the formula of fulfilment of a vow.

Prayer and Identity inside the Church with the Sion Silver

Because they were inside the holy places, the Sion silver also perpetuated the prayers and names of donors. The inscriptions were written on silver vessels that were visible to the wider users of the church in which they were displayed and employed – they were a public statement of the objects' role as gifts to God, whilst also lighting the church, carrying the Eucharistic elements, burning incense, etc. The Sion donors surely intended that their silver vessels would be placed and used in holy places, and because they presumably expected the gifts to outlive themselves, they reported that their continued survival would guarantee continued intercessory prayers. All the vessels in the Treasure were designed for use inside the churches. Polycandela and lamps were used for lighting; chalices, patens, book covers and censers were used in the liturgy. But none are static objects. All of the vessels that bear donors' names were objects that could – and presumably were – moved about from place to place within the church and so came into contact with a range of users.

Writing down one's intentions in a manner that was also visible to other people made the vows, devotions and wishes public. Pulcheria, sister of Theodosios II, decided to remain a virgin. To prove her resolve, she 'wished to make God Himself, the clergy and all the subjects witnesses to her decisions. She, therefore, dedicated on behalf of her virginity a holy table to the church of Constantinople … . Upon the front of the table she wrote down these things that they may be known to everyone.'[68] On the lintel inscription in the church of Rhodiapolis in Lycia, 'Deacon Epigoros presented (one and

67 *Anthologia Marciana*, no. 368, ed. tr. Spingou, 'Words and artworks', 123; also tr. in Drpić, *Epigram, Art, and Devotion*, 258.

68 Sozomen, *Εκκλησιαστική Ιστορία*, IX, 1, PG 67: 1593–8, tr. Mango, *Art of the Byzantine Empire,* 51.

three-quarters gold coins) in fulfilment of his vow'.[69] There is an inscription from the wall of a fifth-century church in Aphrodisias which reads: 'Tatianos made this vow, to be seen and admired by all'.[70] Names on the inscriptions confirm their donations to God, and make them public in the eyes of people.

Amy Papalexandrou argued that inscriptions on monumental buildings were there to be seen by other people, and outlined the donor's hopes. She argued that people walked around the church and engaged with the inscriptions, and that the people who were able to read these inscriptions read them out loud so that others understood.[71] These texts were not to be read silently, but aloud, and that this meant that the message was made more public through being heard. Reading these inscriptions audibly made the donors' hopes audible to listeners, made the buildings animated and kept the donors' hopes alive. Bissera Pentcheva also suggested that when prayers on icons were read by other people, then the hopes of donors were repeated by those people, and thereby increased the power of their prayers.[72]

So, the donor's name was kept alive in the congregation, as was his or her name, prayers and hopes. The presence of a name placed on the altar table, covered with the bread or wine of the Eucharist (as with patens and chalices), or enclosing the books of the Gospel brought that name and perhaps the individual also closer to God, to protection and salvation. And of course, having vessels with inscriptions circulating in the congregation, with the emphasis on forgiveness of sins, gaining salvation and protection and being commemorated might also have encouraged people to make donations so that their names too could be part of the ritual.

What then of anonymous inscriptions? Why did some donors choose to have their names and/or monograms inscribed on silver vessels? And why did others choose to appear anonymously? None of the inscribed chalices (nos 22, 23, 25 and 26) bears the names of their donors. On two of the three inscribed chalices there is the phrase: 'a vow of a prayer of those whose names are

69 A. Tiryaki, 'A group of parapet slabs from the Rhodiapolis episcopal church', *Olba,* 20 (2012), 501, plate 2.

70 C. Roueché, *Aphrodisias in Late Antiquity: The Late Roman and Byzantine Inscriptions Including Texts from the Excavations at Aphrodisias Conducted by Kenan T. Erim*, JRSM, 5 (London, 1989), 63.

71 Papalexandrou, 'Text in context: eloquent monuments and the Byzantine beholder', *Word and Image: A Journal of Verbal/Visual Enquiry*, 17.3 (2001), 259–83; Papalexandrou, 'Echoes of orality in the monumental inscriptions of Byzantium', in L. James (ed.), *Art and Text in Byzantine Culture* (Cambridge, 2007), 161–87; for the discussion of inscriptions on the walls and their possibility to be read or perceived as art see A.M. Yasin, 'Prayers on site: the materiality of devotional graffiti and the production of early Christian sacred space', in A. Eastmond (ed.), *Viewing Inscriptions in the Late Antique and Medieval Worlds* (Cambridge, 2015), 36–60; A. Rhoby, 'Text as art? Byzantine inscriptions and their display', in I. Berti et al. (ed.), *Writing Matters: Presenting and Perceiving Monumental Inscriptions in Antiquity and the Middle Ages*(Berlin, 2017), 265–83.

72 B.V. Pentcheva, 'Epigrams on icons', in *Art and Text*, ed. James, 120–38.

known to God', and on one chalice the inscription reads: 'having given thanks I made it'. The phrase 'known only to God' may be a sign of self-effacement.[73] This formula was common in Byzantine inscriptions. It is used, for example, on a paten from the F. Alouf Collection: 'in fulfilment of a vow and for the salvation of him whose name God knows'.[74] It is also found on fifth- and sixth-century wall and floor mosaics and baptismal fonts.[75] In the third miracle of St Demetrios, when Demetrios was restoring the church, he prayed to God for help; saying 'this is the praying of names God knows'.[76] The faithful believed that God already knew who they were and hoped to gain a new name written in the book of the elect. It is also the possibility that the donors of these objects might have not wanted their names were revealed, because they want to be humble.

Clearly, the objects in the Sion Treasure performed various roles in their time in the church. They were their donors' gift to God and to the church, but also their prayer for salvation and help – for themselves, for their church, for their relatives and presumably the whole congregation, illuminated by the lamps they carried, receiving the wine and bread of the Eucharist from the patens and chalices, listening to the scriptures covered with the silver wrappers. Their life story as gifts reminds us of the conceptual importance of gifts for giver and audience alike.

The Sion Silver at Work

However, once inside the church, the Sion silverware had another life beyond that of being either a commodity or a gift to God. It also carried out a practical role, carrying wine, holding bread and lighting the church. Moreover, the Sion monastery, like other churches and monasteries, is also a place where objects would have come into contact with a range of users – from clergy and worshippers to those who lit the lamps, consecrated the wine and bread of Eucharist or polished the silver. All of these interacted with and experienced the vessels in the Treasure in very different ways as the accessibility of the silverware and the visibility of its inscriptions would have changed according to how and where they were used inside the church. Though knowing where

73 I. Ševčenko, 'The Sion Treasure: the evidence of the inscriptions', in *Ecclesiastical Silver Plate*, ed. Boyd and Mango, 42; also see L. Brubaker, 'Elites and patronage in early Byzantium: the evidence from Hagios Demetrios at Thessalonike', in J. Haldon and L.I. Conrad (ed.), *The Byzantine and Early Islamic Near East: Elites Old and New in the Byzantine and Early Islamic Near East* (Princeton, 2004), 63–90.

74 Mango, *Silver from Early Byzantium*, cat. no. 74.

75 Ševčenko, 'The Sion Treasure: the evidence of the inscriptions', 42; Brubaker, 'Elites and patronage in early Byzantium', 84.

76 *Miracula S. Demetrii*, mir. 3, tr. ed. P. Lemerle, *Les plus anciens recueils des miracles de Saint Démétrius et la pénétration des Slaves dans les Balkans*, vol. 1 (Le Texte) (Paris, 1979), 197; see also Ševčenko, 'The Sion Treasure: the evidence of the inscriptions', 42.

exactly inside the church these objects were used and how and when people interacted with them is a matter of some conjecture.

Perhaps the lighting devices and revetments had the widest circulation. Harrison's and İşler's plans of the Sion monastery in Karabel show that it was a large building with a three aisled naos. Two of the aisles terminate in barrel-vaulted passages leading into the north and south apses, respectively.[77] The sanctuary was probably closed off with stone blocks used for the templon screen. A further door in the north apse gives access to the adjoining baptistery, which is rectangular and has one apse. The roof of the sanctuary with its triconch apse is demolished, but it is clear from the remains of large blocks on the sanctuary that it was surmounted with a dome. The naos has six doors. Three lead to an atrium at the south end of the church, and two lead to a reliquary chapel and mausoleum attached to the east wall of the church. The final door on the north leads to the baptistery. The reliquary chapel attached to the south side of the church includes three sarcophagi, an apse and a stone altar 1.30 m by 0.53 m. It is entered through the door in the south aisle. The mausoleum on the west side of the reliquary chapel can also be entered from the door in the south aisle. The mausoleum has no apse or altar.[78] There are also six other rooms attached to the walls of the church but it is not known what they were used for. There are no pastophorion rooms in this church, so possibly some of these rooms functioned as storage rooms for the valuable vessels of the church or the personal items of the clergy.[79]

The plan allows some assumptions to be made about where the altar table revetments, lampstands, polycandela and other lighting devices were used. The altar revetments must have been used on the altar inside the sanctuary of the church rather than the altar in the east chapel which is too small – it is 1.30 m in length, while the rim sheeting in the Sion Treasure is 2.25 m in length. Since they were used inside the sanctuary, the clergy would have been able both to see and touch them at close range; the congregation would have been set a considerable distance away. The lampstand sheeting in the shape of a column was possibly used inside church possibly inside the sanctuary to cover stone columns, rather than in the reliquary chapel.[80] It is possible that

77 İşler, 'Sionlu Aziz Nikolaos'un Batı Asarcık yerleşimindeki mezar yapısı', in S. Doğan and M. Kadiroğlu (ed.), *Bizans Ve Çevre Kültürler: Prof. Dr. S. Yıldız Ötüken'e Armağan* (İstanbul, 2010), 187; Harrison, 'Churches and chapels of central Lycia', 132.

78 Harrison, 'Churches and chapels of central Lycia', 132–4; İşler, 'Sionlu Aziz Nikolaos'un Batı Asarcık yerleşimindeki mezar yapısı', 186–90.

79 Harrison, 'Churches and chapels of central Lycia', 133; İşler, 'Sionlu Aziz Nikolaos'un Batı Asarcık yerleşimindeki mezar yapısı', 187

80 As suggested by accounts of the sanctuary of Hagia Sophia. Paul the Silentiary mentions the silver columns of the chancel screen with capitals and above their capitals they carry the lamplighters. See Paul the Silentiary, *Έκφρασις τοῦ ναοῦ τῆς Άγίας Σοφίας* lines 871–875, ed. P. Friedländer, *Johannes von Gaza und Paulus Silentiarius* (Leipzig 1912), 250–6, tr. Mango, *Art of the Byzantine Empire*, 80–96.

the silver standing lamps were placed on the silver lampstands to provide light during the Eucharist or in other liturgical ceremonies, since they lack the hoops to be hung by chains. The scene of the communion of the apostles depicted on the Riha paten shows standing lamps similar in shape to the standing lamps from the Sion treasure placed on the ciborium.[81] If so, it would again have restricted access to the silver to the clergy.

The other silver openwork lamps (both standing and hanging), the suspension bracket for hanging lamps and the polycandela would have been used anywhere inside the church. Some will have hung in the sanctuary and on or near the altar.[82] Others may have had a role as portable lighting within the monastery, where such lighting was always needed. During the Easter vigil, for example, the newly-baptised moved in procession from the baptistery to the church and portable lights were needed for this procession to light the church during the dark hours.[83] Lamps were used in the healing shrines of monasteries during the night to provide light to sick people.[84] It is possible that there was a healing shrine in the Sion monastery, since there are passages in *The Vita of Nicholas of Sion* that mention that certain villagers visited the monastery to be healed by Nicholas of Sion.[85] The hanging lamps from the Sion treasure might have also been used as portable lights and carried in the baptistery and used in the shrine or chapels. Therefore, they might have had contact with a range of users or viewers more than they did inside the sanctuary. The polycandela presumably hung from the roofs of the aisles. Indeed, in the ruins of the Karabel church and chapel, there were consoles with rivets attached that the polycandela could have been attached to.[86] The polycandela would have been hard to remove, and would not have been carried about the church, unlike the lamps which could have been used anywhere in the church. They might only have been removed for cleaning and restoration, as examples of other polycandela indicate that they were removed for restoration (Figure 5.1). In addition to cleaners and people who restored the polycandela, person who lit the lamps and fill the candles with oils always engaged with these objects.

In contrast to the polycandela, the liturgical vessels had a function somewhere between clergy and laity – they were under the control of the clergy but used with the laity. The Sion treasure has six patens, seven chalices, two amphorae, a ewer, and three book covers. These were mostly used for the

81 Mango, *Silver from Early Byzantium*, no. 35.
82 B. Caseau, 'Objects in churches: the testimony of inventories', in L. Lavan, E. Swift, T. Putzeys (ed.), *Objects in Context, Objects in Use: Material Spirituality in Late Antiquity* (Boston, 2007), 560.
83 Caseau, 'Objects in churches', 560.
84 Caseau, 'Objects in churches', 559.
85 Nicholas of Sion, c. 66, ed. tr. Ševčenko and Ševčenko, 101.
86 C. Foss, 'Cities and villages of Lycia in the Life of Saint Nicholas of Zion', *GOTR*, 36 (1991), 309.

Figure 5.1 Detail of cruciform polycandelon (No. 7) showing ancient restoration by silver soldering. Antalya Museum, Turkey (1051).

Source: Photograph by the author.

Eucharist. There are sources explaining how communion was held and where people stayed during the communion.[87] It took place according to rules and hierarchy. The *Apostolic Constitution*, written in 380 CE, stated: 'let the bishop communicate, then the presbyters and the deacons and the sub-deacons and the readers and the cantors and the ascetics and, from among the women, the deaconess and the virgins and the widows, then the children and finally all people, in order'.[88] Pseudo-Dionysios in his *Ecclesiastical Hierarchy* explains the same order of taking communion; 'Having himself partaken of and imparted the divine communion, the hierarch concludes the ceremony with a sacred thanksgiving together with the entire sacred assembly'.[89] The clergy took their communion in the sanctuary and the laity outside the sanctuary.

The chalices were meant to hold the wine of the Eucharist. It is not known whether all seven chalices and six patens were used in the Eucharist at once. It is possible that some of them might have been kept for special occasions or

87 R.F. Taft, *A History of the Liturgy of St John Chrysostom. Vol. 6: The Communion, Thanksgiving, and Concluding Rites*, OCA, 281 (Rome, 2008).

88 Taft, *A History of the Liturgy of St John Chrysostom,* 81.

89 Pseudo-Dionysios the Areopagite, *Της Ἐκκλησιαστικῆς Ἱεραρχίας* (Ecclesiastica Hierarchia), 3.3.14 in *Τὰ Σωζόμενα Πάντα (Opera Omnia),* PG 3: 443–6; tr. C. Luibheid and P. Rorem, *Pseudo Dionysius: The Complete Works* (New York, 1987), 223.

used when there was a larger congregation. But presumably, over time, all were used. The clergy physically engaged with them close up, carrying them, filling them and taking bread or drinking from them. The laity may have seen them close up when the patens were used for offering bread or the chalices were offered for drinking, but we do not know if they took the vessels into their own hands at this point, or even whether the paten was left on the altar table.[90] The weight of the Sion patens is considerable: between 4 and 8 kg each (specifically 4300, 4500, 5400 and 8000 g), making it really challenging to carry them. It is even possible that the congregation received the bread and wine via a spoon from the hands of a deacon – the rite known as Intinction.[91] It is, however, worth noting that no spoons were found in the Sion Treasure, though that is not conclusive evidence either way.

The amphora, which can also be described as a 'ewer', was a part of the washing set in the liturgy. It carried the water used for purifying the hands of the priest before the Eucharistic service. It is possible that the three objects in the Sion Treasure used to carry the water for the priest were mostly seen by the clergy inside the sanctuary and those who kept them safe and cleaned them (presumably also monks).

The censers were also used in the Eucharist, and at other liturgical hours. They were carried by the deacon to provide the smell of incense inside the church, baptistery or shrines. There are two censers in the Sion Treasure (nos 19 and 20), inscribed in niello technique, and with decorations encircling their bodies. They were designed to be hung from three chains, and would have carried burning incense, used for censing the altar and Eucharistic vessels during the communion. Unlike standing censers, which were placed on the altar, these censers were carried by deacons during the Eucharistic services or hung on the walls near the altar or in the church.[92] The censers might have also been carried by deacons beyond the sanctuary into the aisles to provide the smell of incense inside the church.

Finally, the book covers, like the censers, had a role in the Eucharist and other liturgical hours. During the processions in the liturgy the deacon would take the gospel in its silver cover and process around the altar, go outside the sanctuary and bless the entrance of the church. This is the opportunity of people to see and interact with these covers. The books, such as gospels with their silver covers, were carried by deacons inside the church during reading

90 Taft, *A History of the Liturgy of St John Chrysostom*, 249–51.

91 J. Meyendorff, *Imperial Unity and Christian Divisions: The Church 450–680 AD, Church History* (Crestwood, 1989), 74.

92 For instance, see the mosaic depiction of the Death of the Virgin in the Chora Monastery from the fourteenth century; and for the usage of early examples, see Caseau, 'Incense and fragrances: from house to church. A study of the introduction of incense in the early Byzantine Christian churches', in Michael Grünbart et al. (ed.), *Material Culture and Well-Being in Byzantium (400–1453)*, (Vienna, 2007), 75–92; Caseau, 'Objects in churches', 551–79.

times and processions which makes them visible to visitors. There are also other possibilities that people moved inside the church during processions.[93]

In the first instance therefore, monks and priests came into closest contact with the silver vessels. The laity could experience them mostly from a distance, though taking communion offered the possibility of a closer contact. Within the church setting, presumably there were those monks whose task it was to clean and look after the silver, perhaps moving it about within the church.[94] Some of the silver was unlikely to be removed from the church – the sheeting for the lampstands and the altar table silver soldered and nailed in place – but was presumably cleaned in situ. It would have been someone's job to fill the lamps. What these made of that contact is unknown: was it a role to be performed reverently or a job to be done quickly?

There were also other possibilities for contact with the silver.[95] Processional liturgies moved between places and churches.[96] Outsiders could be taken into the monastery. A man named Paul was possessed with an evil spirit and Nicholas prayed over him, 'and the unclean spirit was put to flight'. After this Paul stayed in the monastery and 'performed the functions of reader at Matins and Vespers, and sang psalms and recited the readings, giving thanks to God'.[97] These visitors might have been in contact with some of the silver. Paul presumably had contact with the book covers inside the church when he was reading books which these objects covered.

Whilst the clergy using the silver had every opportunity to examine it in detail and be familiar with it, this is less true of the laity. This will have affected their experience of the silver vessels, and especially of the writing on them. Experiments show that if the paten were placed on a table (supposing that the height of the altar was close to the height of this table, which is approximately 1 m), it is likely that only one part of the object could be seen, the rim (Figure 5.2). It is unlikely that the congregation was ever in a position to read the inscriptions encircling the vessels. Even if they were literate, they would only have seen part of the inscription, that closest to them, and they would not have been in a position to turn the chalice, for example, in order to see the whole. The size of the letters does not help. On the two chalices from the Antalya museum the letters encircle the rim, which is between 21 and 23 cm in diameter. The size of the letters varies; the letters on the rim of the chalice (no. 26) are 1.2 cm high and encircled with lines in relief, while the others are 1.5 in high (no. 25), and one of the chalices from Dumbarton Oaks is also inscribed with engraving, and the

93 Papalexandrou, 'Text in Context', 267.

94 A.M. Talbot, 'Byzantine monasticism and the liturgical arts', in O.Z. Pevny (ed.), *Perceptions of Byzantium and its Neighbors (843–1261)* (New York, 2000), 31.

95 Papalexandrou, 'Text in context', 267.

96 C. Eaton, 'Byzantine church in procession: stational liturgy evidenced at Decapolis Abila', *Stone-Campbell Journal,* 16 (2013), 49–61.

97 Nicholas of Sion, c. 64, ed. tr. Ševčenko and Ševčenko, 97.

height of the letters varies between 1.2 and 1.3 (no. 22). The engraving makes it even harder to read the inscription.

There are similar issues with the censers, where the inscriptions were only partially visible (Figures 1.19 and 21). A very similar issue applies to the amphora and the ewer. Both were used in the sanctuary of the church, so only the priest and the clergy engaged with it. Even the altar table sheet, which was also inscribed with the hopes of donors and their names was not wholly public. Again, it was in the sanctuary, perhaps covered by altar cloths, or by other objects such as the paten and chalice. And indeed, the writing on the rim sheeting cannot be seen or read, even when standing near the altar table – I have tried this (Figure 5.2).

Nor are the inscriptions on the standing lamps visible. Both standing and hanging lamps (which means they may be used either by hanging or by standing) are decorated as openwork, and some of their inscriptions are also openwork, with the other inscriptions being in niello technique. These objects are also circular, and the inscriptions encircle their rims. This makes it hard to read them. The inscriptions on the polycandela would have been equally inaccessible to casual observers. The polycandela hung from the

Figure 5.2 Photo showing the designated altar table with sheeting for altar table, lamps, patens, chalice, censer and book covers possibly from 3 m away. Dumbarton Oaks, Byzantine Collection, Washington, DC.

Source: Photograph by the author.

roofs of the churches. The inscriptions on the polycandela from the Sion Treasure encircle their centre on the upper face with the monogram of the donor. If they were used in the church aisles, and were accessible to the faithful, the reading of the inscriptions on polycandela would be easy for them. Even though they were hung from possibly 2 or 3 m, it is possible to read the inscriptions. As the photo of the Dumbarton Oaks polycandelon shows, when the objects are hung we need to look up to see the inscription, although it is hard to read it clearly. It is also similar for a hanging lamp; if the lamp was hung on aisles of the church it is possible for people to see the inscriptions. But if they were hung on the ciborium of the altar, standing far away from the object makes it impossible for the laity to read the inscription. Moreover, the objects are circular, and if they were hung on the altar table or ciborium, it would be impossible to walk around the object to read the inscription (Figure 5.2).

So whilst it is possible that the inscriptions on the Sion silver vessels were regularly read by their users or viewers, it is also possible that they were not. Not all inscriptions were visible or accessible. Some of the Sion silver was used inside the sanctuary where the laity was not allowed to enter (nos 47, 51, 53 and 54). Not everyone would have read the inscriptions, although they would not have required a high degree of literacy to make sense of them, either because they were illiterate or because they did not bother. The literate population in Lycia and especially in monastery of Sion is unknown, but there seems to have been a high level of functional literacy in the Byzantine world – monasteries needed literate monks.[98] The occasion of reading the inscription aloud on the silverware might not have been common, but there may have been times, such as when the vessels were donated, that they were read aloud.[99] But if people knew what the inscriptions said, this could change their perception of the object – not simply a polycandelon but Eutychianos's polycandelon, his gift to God.

To see the decorations on the patens, the bread would have to be removed; the cross decorating the objects would then be visible. However, the point of communion was not to admire the paten or chalice and read their inscriptions. The focus of the worshipper, clerical or lay person, would have been the bread and wine, not the vessels, which were a mere side-show in proceedings,

98 For important examinations on Byzantine literacy, see M. Mullett, 'Writing in early mediaeval Byzantium', in R. McKitterick (ed.), *The Uses of Literacy in Early Mediaeval Europe* (Cambridge, 1990), 156–85; R. Browning, 'Literacy in the Byzantine World', *BMGS*, 4 (1978), 39–54; M. Jeffreys, 'Literacy', in E. Jeffreys, J. Haldon and R. Cormack (ed.), *The Oxford Handbook of Byzantine Studies* (Oxford, 2008), 796–802; A. Giannouli, 'Education and literary language in Byzantium', in M. Hinterberger (ed.), *The Language of Byzantine Learned Literature*, SBHC, 9 (Turnhout, 2014), 52–71; A. Markopoulos, 'Education', in Jeffreys, Haldon and Cormack (ed.), *The Oxford Handbook of Byzantine Studies*, 785–95; R. Betancourt, *Sight, Touch, and Imagination in Byzantium* (Cambridge, 2018), 10–20.

99 Drpić, *Epigram, Art and Devotion*, 61.

however lavish and costly. The chalice and paten were designed to carry the bread and wine, but inside the church they actually carried the blood and body of Christ during the Eucharist. The silver vessels first mattered for their primary use in the church – their appropriateness for use in carrying wine and bread for example. Similarly, the altar sheets needed to fit well as they were protecting the Holy Table. And the lamps needed to light the church sufficiently. Other than the paten and chalice, the altar revetments and lighting vessels, amphorae carried the holy water to purify the hands of the priest and censers carried the incense and produced a pleasant fragrance inside the church. But if the silver did its job well, no one would notice it; the congregation might be aware that the church was appropriately lit without looking at the polycandela and the smell of incense spread over the church without their seeing the censer.

However, the Sion silver had values which secular silver would never have.[100] The visible performance of the silverware was part of the ceremony within the church which aimed to make the invisible present. Marbles, mosaics and other decoration imbued the church with heavenly and corporeal light. The sound and echoes of the church were also important. Hymns were sung, psalms were and prayers were made. It was a multi-sensory experience in which the silver vessels had a role to play.[101] When describing the church of Hagia Sophia, Paul the Silentiary observed: 'everything is clothed in beauty, everything fills the eye with wonder'.[102] When people entered the church, their five senses were activated. An interior of marble and gold provides shimmer and reflection, and these marbles acoustically reflect sounds. They heard the hymns and music, they touched the marble, and smelt the incense, and they saw the light of many candles. John Chrysostom tried to explain how the eyes of the worshippers inside the church seek the divine presence, but that sight alone is not enough, and worshippers must also use their other senses to reach the divine. He claimed that 'through these gates and doors Christ entered into us, whensoever we communicate. Who partake of the mysteries understand what I say'.[103] The church context offered worshippers

100 For the context and its multisensory experiences see B. Pentcheva, 'Hagia Sophia and multisensory aesthetics', *Gesta*, 50.2 (2011), 93–111; L. James, 'Senses and sensibility in Byzantium', *ArtH*, 27 (2004), 522–37; B. Caseau, 'Christian bodies: The senses and early Byzantine Christianity', in L. James (ed.), *Desire and Denial in Byzantium: Papers from the 31st Spring Symposium of Byzantine Studies, Brighton, March 1997*, SPBS, 6 (Aldershot, 1999), 101–9.

101 James, 'Senses and Sensibility in Byzantium', 524–5.

102 Mango, *The Art of the Byzantine Empire*, 89.

103 John Chrysostom, *Υπόμνημα εις τὴν πρὸς Κορινθίους Δευτέραν ἐπιστολήν*, 30.2, PG 61, (Paris, 1862) 607–8, tr. P. Schaff, *Saint Chrysostom: Homilies on the Epistles of Paul to the Corinthians*, NPNF 12 (Grand Rapids, MI, 1889), 418; also cited in Caseau, 'Experiencing the sacred', in C. Nesbitt and M. Jackson (ed.), *Experiencing Byzantium: Papers from the 44th Spring Symposium of Byzantine Studies, Newcastle and Durham, April 2011*, SPBS, 18 (Farnham, 2013), 69.

the space to reach the heavenly realm from the earthly realm: 'the church is an earthly heaven in which super celestial God dwells and walks about'.[104] In this environment, the Sion vessels, in their materials, shining surfaces, and their sensual impact engaged with the senses in different ways for everybody.

In the Eucharistic context, worshippers, while drinking wine from the chalice, imagined themselves drinking the blood of Christ and kissing and touching the holy object. The same applies to the paten. It was a sacred vessel because it was carrying the body of Christ. Christians also touched and kissed the holy bread as if they were kissing and touching Christ.[105] The stories of the lives of the saints underline how people valued the objects used in the Eucharist. In *The Spiritual Meadow*, John Moschos told the story of children who played at the Holy Eucharist. One of them became a bishop, another became a priest, another became a deacon, and the other remained a lay person. They set out everything for the Eucharist, including a paten and chalice.[106] People in Byzantium grew up with these stories and this learning process. Even without seeing or sensing these objects, they knew that holy mysteries could not be conducted without them. Another story also told by Moschos describes how people from a town called Romilla went to the pope in Rome and complained about their bishop, accusing him of eating from the consecrated paten. After finding out that the story was true, the pope jailed the bishop.[107] The paten had been consecrated and was holy; therefore, it could only be used for the Holy Eucharist and to carry the holy bread, and the townspeople knew this and were appalled by the divergence from proper behaviour. The paten was holy and could not be used for other purposes.

The silver perhaps functioned rather as icons did. People used their senses to engage with icons.[108] The tactile surfaces and textures of icons meant they could be experienced by touch and sight. Furthermore, the light-reflective surfaces, gold colour and the texture of the icons caused people to engage with their materiality, which was seen to embody the divine. The material and gilded surfaces of the chalice and paten too embodied the divine. The silver had to be, and be seen to be, a fit place for the body of Christ to rest on; the chalice as worthy of his blood. The light-reflective qualities of such vessels, derived from their gold and silver surfaces, were understood not to reflect the sun but to emit a divine light of their own, a light which helped worshippers engage with the divine presence.[109]

104 Germanos of Constantinople, *Ἐκκλησιαστική Ἱστορία καί Μυστική Θεωρία*, 1, ed. tr. P. Meyendorff, *St Germanus of Constantinople on the Divine Liturgy* (New York, 1984), 57.

105 Caseau, 'Experiencing the sacred', 74.

106 John Moschos, *Pratum Spirituale*, c.196, PG 87: 3079–84, tr. J. Wortley, *The Spiritual Meadow (Pratum Spirituale) by John Moschos* (Kalamazoo, MI, 1992), 172–4.

107 Moschos, c. 150, PG 87: 3013–6, tr. Wortley, 122–4.

108 Pentcheva, 'The performative icon', *ArtB*, 88(4) (2006), 631.

109 H. Hunter-Crawley, 'Embodying the divine: the sensational experience of the sixth-century

That sense of divine light was as apparent in the silver polycandela and other lamps.[110] Light was an important element inside the church, for example, Pseudo-Dionysios wrote that light is both important for pleasing the eye and 'provoking associations with the divine'.[111] By equating intelligible beauty and understanding the divine with knowledge, Pseudo-Dionysios associated light with the divine. He also claimed that seeing divine light through celestial light depends on the intelligence of the viewer, stating that divine light 'generously grants the beneficent rays of its own light to whoever views it with the eyes of intelligence'. Furthermore, that 'the divine light, out of generosity, never ceases to offer itself to the eyes of the mind, eyes which should seize upon it for it is always there'.[112] Therefore, in Pseudo-Dionysios's writings, the light symbolised God and the way people reach the divine presence. Light also had an important role in Byzantine aesthetic experience, associated with the divine, a spiritual function as well as its physical function. For both Procopius of Caesarea and Paul the Silentiary, light was important in understanding the significance and beauty of buildings.[113] Light was considered important to reaching the divine. As Paul put it:

> … everything clothed in beauty; everything fills the eye with wonder. But no words are sufficient to describe the illumination in the evening: you might say that some nocturnal sun filled the majestic temple with light. … And to each chain he has attached silver discs suspended circle-wise in the air around the central confines of the church. Thus, descending from their lofty course, they float in a circle above the heads of men. The cunning craftsman has pierced the discs all over with his iron tool so that they may receive shafts of fire-wrought glass and provide pendent sources of light for men at night. … thus hangs the circling choir of bright lights. You might say you were gazing on the effulgent stars of the heavenly Corona close to Arcturus and the head of Draco.[114]

Some of the Sion vessels – the chalices – were more tactile. Others – the censers – engaged with smell rather than sight or tactility. When a deacon

---

Eucharist', in J. Day (ed.), *Making Senses of the Past: Toward a Sensory Archaeology* (Carbondale, 2013), 163–70.

110 James, 'Senses and sensibility in Byzantium', 528. Hunter-Crawley, 'The cross of light: experiencing divine presence in Byzantine Syria', in *Experiencing Byzantium*, ed. Nesbitt and Jackson, 177–81.

111 N. Schibille, *Hagia Sophia and the Byzantine Aesthetic Experience* (Farnham, 2014), 177.

112 Pseudo-Dionysios the Areopagite, *Τῆς Ἐκκλησιαστικῆς Ἱεραρχίας* 2.3.3, PG 3: 417–8, tr. Luibheid and Rorem, 205.

113 Procopius, I.i.27–78, ed. tr. Dewing, 13–31; Paul the Silentiary, lines 806–920, ed. P. Friedländer, 250–6, tr. Mango, *Art of the Byzantine Empire*, 80–96.

114 Paul the Silentiary, lines. 806–33, ed. Friedländer, 250, tr. Mango, *Art of the Byzantine Empire,* 89–90.

carried a censer he held it with his hands and swung it between his knees. Censers were also hung on the walls and ciborium at a distance from the congregation. The function of the censer to create a smell was more important than its tactility. The mother of Symeon Stylites the Younger used a censer to burn incense and make the church full of scent while she was praying.[115] For Christians, the smell of incense symbolised Paradise. With the fragrance of incense, people felt that they were in Paradise. Furthermore, 'to encounter a scent was to encounter proof of a material presence' – Christians felt that the presence of a smell indicated the presence of God.[116] Therefore, the censer as an object used inside the church functioned as a vessel for carrying the holy incense and creating the fragrance associated with Paradise.

Each part of the Sion Treasure brought its own sensual affordances to bear in creating the atmosphere of the church and triggering the senses of those within. Worshippers did not have to touch the chalice to know its symbolism or receive the blood of Christ from it. Knowing that these objects had sensual affordances, the important question here is whether people knew these affordances of these objects would reach the divine presence before they engaged with them or they came to that knowledge after they experienced the objects. In the previous section I discussed where these objects could be used and who could and could not see them or experience them by touching or kissing. Those facts led me to ask what happened when they could not touch them. I argue that the experience and valuing of the objects was similar even though they did not touch them or kiss them. Here, cognition and imagination play a part. As I discussed earlier, cognition and imagination are triggered by the environment of the church. Even though they do not touch the objects directly, they were in touch through other parts of the church, smelling incense and hearing sound. Their prior knowledge of what objects can do triggered them to use their inner senses. They did not value or see the objects as we do now. Indeed, my examination of the objects in Antalya and Dumbarton Oaks revealed that touching a chalice and holding it reveals the object's characteristics, how heavy it is, and the texture which makes it tactile. However, in the museum context, this experience is not the same as that of people in the sixth century within the context of the church. Their background knowledge and the idea of seeking the divine presence through the materiality of silver combined with their imagination led them to perceive these objects in different ways. How they would have experienced silver tableware and silver church vessels also differed – here function and setting – social environment – come into play.

115 Cited in B. Pentcheva, *The Sensual Icon: Space, Ritual, and the Senses in Byzantium* (University Park, PA., 2010), 37.

116 Caseau, 'The senses in religion: liturgy, devotion, and deprivation', in R.G. Newhauser (ed.), *A Cultural History of the Senses in the Middle Ages* (New York, 2014), 93.

Inside the church, Christians combined their mind and sight. They were encouraged to use their inner senses and imagination.[117] John of Damascus stated that the form and presence of something can be understood by the combination of our mind and sight. When these are combined with the other senses and experienced, 'we come to an understanding of these things'.[118] This highlights the importance of knowledge gained prior to sensing objects to reaching the divine presence. People were already aware of the divine presence before they touched or did not touch the objects. They were aware that the divine was already inside the church and they were experiencing it, since the Christian church was perceived as a place which combined the earthly and heavenly worlds; that is, the church was perceived to include both the visible and the invisible world.[119] And people reached the understanding of this invisible world via their inner senses and spiritual eyes. In Byzantium, the emotional and cognitive pathways inside the church were enhanced by other aspects, such as using all senses and having a knowledge of being inside a holy place, and made people gave these objects different biographies. Hearing the hymns and smelling the incense or fragrance of the oils may have been pleasing and made people feel as though they were in Heaven. Therefore, in this environment full of holy and divine experiences, although people did not touch and read the inscriptions of the objects, they perceived them in different ways. They became holy objects inside the holy place, gifts from donors to God, transacting Eucharistic and lighting processes, and they were defined as holy objects since they carried out holy transactions.

When a person inside the church was situated far from the paten, he was not able to see its visuality, could not read its inscriptions, and could not touch it. However, he knew that the paten was carrying the body of Christ and doing important and holy work. Therefore, their understanding of the object was not gained through the use of the senses, but through their imagination. Prior knowledge of the objects' functions and what they can do affected their perception. As Chris Gosden has shown, 'the locus of sensory activity is as much cultural as bodily, so that various cultures apprehend the world in different ways'.[120] Users may have known that these objects had sensual affordances without experiencing them directly. Moreover, they knew these objects were used inside the church and therefore that they were holy

117 For this see P.C. Miller, *The Corporeal Imagination: Signifying the Holy in Late Ancient Christianity* (Philadelphia, PA, 2009); Betancourt, *Sight, Touch, and Imagination in Byzantium*, 116–87.

118 John of Damascus, *Λόγος Τρίτος πρὸς τοὺς Διαβάλλοντας τὰς Ἁγίας Εικόνας* 3.24, PG 94: 1344, tr. A. Louth, *St John of Damascus: Three Treatises on the Divine Images* (New York, 2003), 100–1.

119 H.G. Saradi, 'Space in Byzantine thought', in S. Ćurčić and E. Hadjitryphonos (ed.), *Architecture as Icon: Perception and Representation of Architecture in Byzantine Art* (New Haven, 2010), 99.

120 Gosden, 'Making sense: archaeology and aesthetics', *World Archaeology*, 33(2) (2001), 163.

objects. As people's knowledge influenced them before they had seen the objects, their perception may have remained abstract had they not touched them. This imagination and abstraction were also applied in the Eucharist. In his *Mystagogical Catecheses*, Cyril of Jerusalem advised 'Do not then think of the elements as mere bread and wine. Instead of judging the matter by taste, let faith give you an unwavering assurance that you have been privileged to receive the Body and Blood of Christ'.[121] The importance of seeing with the eyes of the faith was also evident in the writings of John Chrysostom. For Chrysostom, the spiritual seeing 'makes the unseen visible from the seen', and he encouraged his audience to see the objects with the 'eyes of the spirit'.[122] Theodore of Mopsuestia said that before ordering the sacrifices, everyone should look at the objects placed on the altar, and the priest should command them to 'lift up your minds'.[123] As I suggested earlier when discussing the importance of light inside the church, the 'eyes of the intellect' refers to the ability of the person to see it. Seeing or embodying the divine through touch or seeing the tactile surfaces did not only happen by experiencing it but also by using the imagination triggered by prior knowledge and environment. According to Ambrose, the bishop of Milan, 'to see the unseen required another set of eyes, the eyes of the heart'.[124] By knowing how to approach the silver wares and how to sense them, worshippers at the Sion church perceived them or defined them as holy, as they were used in the Eucharist to carry the body and blood of Christ, for covering the altar and for lighting the church. Previous knowledge of an object's affordances and knowing that they were inside the holy place enabled people to interpret the many meanings of the vessels. Byzantine people inside the Sion monastery knew how to experience the object, then they were aware what these objects could do whether they saw it or not.[125]

121 Cyril of Jerusalem, *Κατήχησις Μυσταγωγική*, 4.6, PG 33: 1101–2; cited and tr. in G. Frank, '"Taste and see": the Eucharist and the eyes of the faith in the fourth century', *CH*, 70.4 (2001), 628.

122 John Chrysostom, *Κατήχησις Δεύτερα*, 2.28, ed. Fr. tr. A. Wenger, *Jean Chrysostome: Huit Catéchèses Baptismales Inédites*, SC, 50 (Paris, 1957), 149; cited and tr. in Frank, 'Taste and see', 636.

123 A. Mingana, *Commentary of Theodore of Mopsuestia on the Lord's Prayer and on the Sacraments of Baptism and the Eucharist*, Woodbrooke Studies, 6 (Cambridge, 1933), 97–9.

124 Frank, 'Taste and see', 620.

125 For modern theories on how prior knowledge about the functions of objects leads people to use their assumptions and imaginations to perceive them and give them conceptual meaning, see W.P. Seeley, 'Naturalizing aesthetics: art and the cognitive neuroscience of vision', 5(3) (2006), 198; O. da Silva et al., 'Beauty in efficiency: an experimental enquiry into the principle of maximum effect for minimum means', *Empirical Studies of the Arts*, 35(1) (2017), 95; Da Silva et al., 'Maximum effect for minimum means: the aesthetics of efficiency', *Design Issues* 32(1) (2016), 42; A.M. Barry, 'Perceptual aesthetics: transcendent emotion, neurological image', *Visual Communication Quarterly*, 13(3) (2006), 137; Knappett, *Thinking through Material Culture*, 65; T. Ingold, 'Materials against materiality', *Archaeological Dialogues*, 14(1) (2007), 13; T. Van Gelder and R.F. Port, 'It's about time:

The Afterlives of the Sion Vessels

The fifty-seven Sion objects have had long and interesting lives. They started as raw silver, a commodity changed into a gift through the desires of the donor and the skill of the craft workers. As gifts to God, they had a home in the Sion monastery, where they fulfilled different roles: as functional objects (bearing lights or holding wine); as sacred vessels, consecrated to God; as prayers and requests for salvation. Inside the church, different audiences perceived and experienced the silverware in a variety of ways, with their senses and emotions.

But their stories do not end inside the church. The Treasure was found in 1963 as a hoard. This might have been because the monks tried to keep their valuable objects safe from the Arabs when they attacked the southern coast of Anatolia. Most of the objects, such as chalices, the ewer and standing lamps were folded and rolled up. They were folded intentionally, possibly to be fitted inside some sort of box or case for safekeeping during or before the burial of the objects. They were carried from the monastery to another, safer, place – Korydalla is located 40 km away from the Sion monastery. The hope was surely that they would one day be replaced in the church, though that did not happen.

In the twentieth century the silverware was found and perceived as a collection of objects to be sold to and by collectors. To the finders and the sellers, the Treasure once more was a commodity, a way of earning money. The vessels now in Dumbarton Oaks, Geneva and London were sold. Other vessels were saved to be valued as part of the museum collection in Antalya. There is no difference between the objects which were sold and those saved by the police and the museum director in Antalya in terms of measurements or decoration which might make one object more valuable than another. Simply, some ended by sold privately and some ended up in a public museum. Both collectors and museum officials however valued the Sion Treasure as 'works of art'. Now most of the Treasure is displayed inside museum cases as 'works of art', remote and removed from human touch – regarded as damaging to the objects. But they are also representatives of Byzantine history. Visitors reading the labels gain knowledge about how these objects were used in the past but can only imagine what they might have been. The labels still privilege the names of the original donors – Eutychianos is still mentioned. Perhaps then the silver retains something of its role as a gift to God with their inscriptions. Even though we cannot sense them or we have no chance to use them inside the church, we are still aware that these objects

an overview of the dynamical approach to cognition', in R. F. Port and T. Van Gelder (ed.), *Mind as Motion: Explorations in the Dynamics of Cognition* (Cambridge, 1995), 2–4; A. Maihoub, 'Thinking through the sociality of art objects', *JAC*, 7 (2015), 1; M. Svašek, *Anthropology, Art and Cultural Production* (London, 2007), 63; A. Sheppard, 'The role of imagination in aesthetic experience', *JAE*, 25.4 (1991), 35–42.

were created to be used inside the church, not on the dining table or for lighting private houses. So the silver constantly gains new biographies from century to century, but its previous biographies still remain and should not be forgotten.

Bibliography

Primary Sources

Cyril of Jerusalem, *Κατήχησις Μυσταγωγική (Catechesis Mystagogica)*, PG 33: 1059–1132, tr. L.P. McCauley and A.A. Stephenson, *The Works of Saint Cyril of Jerusalem,* vol. 2, The Fathers of the Church, 64 (Washington, DC, 1970).

Cyril of Scythopolis, *Βίος Τοῦ Ὁσίου Πατρὸς Ἡμῶν Σάββα*, ed. E. Schwartz, *Kyrillos von Skythopolis*, TU, 49:2 (Leipzig, 1939), tr. R.M. Price, *Cyril of Scythopolis: Lives of the Monks of Palestine* (Kalamazoo, MI, 1991).

Germanos of Constantinople, *Ἐκκλησιαστική Ἱστορία καί Μυστική Θεωρία*, ed.tr. P. Meyendorff, *St Germanus of Constantinople on the Divine Liturgy* (New York, 1984).

Gregory of Tours, *Vitae Patrum*, tr. E. James, *Gregory of Tours: Life of the Fathers*, TTH, 1 (Liverpool, 1991).

John Chrysostom, *Κατήχησις Δεύτερα*, ed.tr. A. Wenger, *Jean Chrysostome: Huit Catéchèses Baptismales Inédites*, SC, 50 (Paris, 1957).

John Chrysostom, *Υπόμνημα εις τὴν πρὸς Κορινθίους Δευτέραν ἐπιστολήν,* PG 61: 9–611, tr. P. Schaff, *Saint Chrysostom: Homilies on the Epistles of Paul to the Corinthians*, NPNF, 12 (Grand Rapids, MI, 1889).

John Moschos, *Pratum Spirituale*, PG 87(3): 2851–3112, tr. J. Wortley, *The Spiritual Meadow (Pratum Spirituale) by John Moschos* (Kalamazoo, MI, 1992).

John of Damascus, *Λόγος Τρίτος πρὸς τοὺς Διαβάλλοντας τὰς Ἁγίας Εικόνας* 3.24, PG 94: 1227–1421, tr. A. Louth, *St John of Damascus: Three Treatises on the Divine Images* (New York, 2003).

John of Ephesus, *Historiae Ecclesiasticae*, ed.tr. E.W. Brooks, *Iohannis Ephesini, Historiae Ecclesiasticae Pars Tertia*, CSCO, Scriptores Syri, 55 (Louvain, 1936), tr. R.P. Smith, *The Third Part of the Ecclesiastical History of John Bishop of Ephesus* (Oxford, 1860).

Justinian, *Novellae Constitutiones*, tr. Scott, *Justinian, The Civil Law*, 17 vols (Cincinnati, 1932), vols 16 and 17.

Miracles of St Artemios, *Διήγησις των Θαυμάτων τοῦ Ἁγίου καί Ἐνδόξου Μεγαλομάρτυρος* καί *Θαυματουργοῦ Αρτεμίου*, ed.tr. V.S. Crisafulli and J.W. Nesbitt, *The Miracles of St. Artemios: A Collection of Miracle Stories by an Anonymous Author of Seventh-Century Byzantium*, TMM, 13 (Leiden and New York, 1997).

Miracula S. Demetrii, ed.tr. P. Lemerle, *Les plus anciens recueils des miracles de Saint Démétrius et la pénétration des Slaves dans les Balkans*, 2 vols (Paris, 1979).

Nicholas of Sion, *Βίος τοῦ Ἁγίου Νικολάου τῆς Ἁγίας Σιών*, ed.tr. I. Ševčenko and N.P. Ševčenko, *The Life of Saint Nicholas of Sion* (Brookline, MA, 1984).
Nikephoros Kallistos, *Ἐκκλησιαστικῆς Ἱστορίας*, PG 146: 1095–1288.
Paul the Silentiary, *Ἔκφρασις τοῦ ναοῦ τῆς Ἁγίας Σοφίας*, ed. P. Friedländer, *Johannes von Gaza und Paulus Silentiarius* (Leipzig, 1912).
Procopius, *Ἀπόκρυφη Ἱστορία (Historia Arcana)*, ed. B.G. Niebuhr, *Procopius, vol. 3,* CSHB 42 (Bonn, 1838), tr. H.B. Dewing, *Procopius Vol. 6: Anecdota or Secret History,* Loeb Classical Library, 290 (London and Cambridge, MA, 1935).
Procopius, *Περι Κτισμάτων, (De Aedificiis)*, ed.tr. H. B. Dewing, Procopius VII: *Buildings,* Loeb Classical Library, 343 (London and Cambridge, MA, 1940).
Pseudo-Dionysios the Areopagite, *Τῆς Ἐκκλησιαστικῆς Ἱεραρχίας, Τὰ Σωζόμενα Πάντα (Opera Omnia)*, PG 3: 369–586, tr. C. Luibheid and P. Rorem, *Pseudo Dionysius: The Complete Works* (New York, 1987).
Severus of Antioch, *Homiliae Cathedrales*, ed. and Fr. tr. I. Guidi, *Les Homiliae Cathedrales de Sévère d'Antioche. Homelies XCIX à CIII*, PO 22 (Paris, 1930).
Sozomen, Εκκλησιαστική Ιστορία, PG 67: 843–1630.
St. Jerome, *Letter 52*, tr. P. Schaff and H. Wace, *A Select Library of Nicene and Post-Nicene Fathers of the Christian Church*, s. 2, vol. 6 (New York, 1893), 94.
Theodore of Sykeon, *Βίος Τοῦ Ὁσίου Πατρὸς Ἡμῶν Θεοδώρου Ἀρχιμανδρίτου Συκεών*, ed. A. Festugière, *Vie de Theodore de Sykeon: Texte Grec* 1, SH, 48 (Brussels, 1970), tr. E. Dawes and N.H. Baynes, *Three Byzantine Saints: Contemporary Biographies Translated from the Greek* (Oxford, 1948).
Theophanes, *Χρονογραφία*, ed. C. de Boor, *Theophanis Chronographia*, 1 (Leipzig, 1883), tr. C. Mango and R. Scott, *The Chronicle of Theophanes Confessor* (Oxford, 1997).
Theophylact Simocatta, *Ἱστορία,* ed. C. de Boor, *Theophylacti Simocattae Historiae* (Leipzig, 1887), tr. Michael and Mary Whitby, *The History of Theophylact Simocatta* (Oxford, 1986).

Secondary Sources

Acara, M. 'Kumluca/Corydalla definesi', *Sanat Tarihi Araştırmaları Dergisi*, 6 (1989), 74–6.
Acara-Eser, M. *Bizans Maden Sanatı: Dini Törenlerde Kullanılan (Litürjik) Eşyalar* (Ankara, 2020).
Alkan, M. 'Parerga to the Stadiasmus Patarensis (8): On the named places in the journeys of sacrifice recorded in the Vita of Saint Nicholas of Holy Sion', *Gephyra*, 8 (2011), 99–124.
Appadurai, A. 'Introduction: commodities and the politics of value', in A. Appadurai (ed.), *The Social Life of Things: Commodities in Cultural Perspective* (Cambridge, 1986), 3–63.
Ari, A. 'Byzantine control stamps applied on the silver objects from the Sion Treasure', *Nevşehir Hacı Bektaş Veli Üniversitesi SBE Dergisi*, 12.1 (2022), 34–55.
Arıkan, C. 'Lykia'da erken Bizans devri'ne ait bir define: Korydalla Hazinesi', in N.E. Akyürek Şahin and A.V. Çelgin (ed.), *Eskiçağ Yazıları* (İstanbul, 2012), 129–87.
Barry, A.M. 'Perceptual aesthetics: transcendent emotion, neurological image', *Visual Communication Quarterly*, 13.3 (2006), 134–51.
Betancourt, R. *Sight, Touch, and Imagination in Byzantium* (Cambridge, 2018).
Bloom, P. 'Intention, history, and artifact concepts', *Cognition*, 60 (1996), 1–29.

Boyd, S.A. 'A "metropolitan" treasure from a church in the provinces: an introduction to the study of the Sion Treasure', in Boyd and Mango (ed.), *Ecclesiastical Silver Plate*, 5–38.

Boyd, S.A. 'A bishop's gift: openwork lamps from the Sion Treasure', in F. Baratte (ed.), *Argenterie romaine et byzantine: Actes de la table ronde* (Paris, 1988), 191–209.

Boyd, S.A. and M.M. Mango (ed.), *Ecclesiastical Silver Plate in Sixth-Century Byzantium* (Washington, DC, 1992).

Browning, R. 'Literacy in the Byzantine world', *BMGS*, 4 (1978), 39–54.

Brubaker, L. 'Elites and patronage in early Byzantium: the evidence from Hagios Demetrios at Thessalonike', in J. Haldon and L.I. Conrad (ed.), *The Byzantine and Early Islamic Near East: Elites Old and New in the Byzantine and Early Islamic Near East* (Princeton, 2004), 63–90.

Buckton, D. *The Treasury of San Marco, Venice* (New York, 1984).

Cameron, A. and P. Garnsey. (ed.), *Late Antiquity: Empire and Successors, A.D. 425–600*, CAH, 14 (Cambridge, 2000).

Caner, D. 'Alms, blessings, offerings: the repertoire of Christian gifts in early Byzantium', in M. L. Satlow (ed.), *The Gift in Antiquity* (Oxford, 2013), 25–44.

Caner, D. 'Towards a miraculous economy: Christian gifts and material blessings in late antiquity', *JEChS*, 14.3 (2006), 329–77.

Caseau, B. 'Christian bodies: the senses and early Byzantine Christianity', in L. James (ed.), *Desire and Denial in Byzantium: Papers from the 31st Spring Symposium of Byzantine Studies*, Brighton, March 1997, SPBS, 6 (Aldershot, 1999), 101–09.

Caseau, B. 'Experiencing the sacred', in C. Nesbitt and M. Jackson (ed.), *Experiencing Byzantium: Papers from the 44th Spring Symposium of Byzantine Studies*, Newcastle and Durham, April 2011, SPBS, 18 (Farnham, 2013), 59–77.

Caseau, B. 'Incense and fragrances: from house to church. A study of the introduction of incense in the early Byzantine Christian churches', in Michael Grünbart et al. (ed.), *Material Culture and Well-Being in Byzantium (400–1453)* (Vienna, 2007), 75–92.

Caseau, B. 'Objects in churches: the testimony of inventories', in L. Lavan, E. Swift and T. Putzeys (ed.), *Objects in Context, Objects in Use: Material Spirituality in Late Antiquity* (Boston, 2007), 551–79.

Caseau, B. 'The senses in religion: liturgy, devotion, and deprivation', in R.G. Newhauser (ed.), *A Cultural History of the Senses in the Middle Ages* (New York, 2014), 89–110.

Ćurčić, S. and E. Hadjitryphonos (ed.), *Architecture as Icon: Perception and Representation of Architecture in Byzantine Art* (New Haven, 2010).

Cutler, A. 'Significant gifts: patterns of exchange in late antique, Byzantine and early Islamic diplomacy', *Journal of Medieval and Early Modern Studies*, 38(1) (2008), 79–85.

Cutler, A. and A. Kazhdan. 'Comes Sacrarum Largitionum', in A. Kazhdan (ed.), *ODB*, 3 vols (Oxford, 1991), vol. 1, 486.

Da Silva, O. et al. 'Beauty in efficiency: an experimental enquiry into the principle of maximum effect for minimum means', *Empirical Studies of the Arts*, 35.11 (2017), 93–120.

Da Silva, O. et al. 'Maximum effect for minimum means: the aesthetics of efficiency', *Design Issues*, 32.1 (2016), 41–51.

Dickie, M.W. 'The Fathers of the church and the Evil Eye', in H. Maguire (ed.), *Byzantine Magic* (Washington, DC, 1995), 9–35.

Dimitropoulou, V. 'Giving gifts to God: aspects of patronage in Byzantine art', in L. James (ed.), *A Companion to Byzantium* (Oxford, 2010), 161–70.

Dodd, E.C. 'The location of silver stamping: evidence from newly discovered stamps', in Boyd and Mango (ed.), *Ecclesiastical Silver Plate*, 217–24.

Dodd, E.C. 'The question of workshop: evidence of the stamps on the Sion Treasure', in Boyd and Mango (ed.), *Ecclesiastical Silver Plate*, 57–64.

Dodd, E.C. *Byzantine Silver Stamps* (Washington, DC, 1961).

Drpić, I. *Epigram, Art and Devotion in Later Byzantium* (Cambridge, 2016).

Eastmond, A. 'Consular diptychs, rhetoric and the languages of art in sixth-century Constantinople', *ArtH*, 33.5 (2010), 742–65.

Eaton, C. 'Byzantine church in procession: stational liturgy evidenced at Decapolis Abila', *Stone-Campbell Journal*, 16 (2013), 49–61.

Edmondson, J.C. 'Mining in the later Roman empire and beyond: continuity or disruption?' *JRS*, 79 (1989), 84–102.

Feissel, E. 'Le Préfet de Constantinople, les poids étalons et l'estampillage de l'argenterie au VIe et au VIIe siècle', *RN*, 28 (1986), 119–42.

Fıratlı, N. 'Un trésor du VIe siècle à Kumluca en Lycie', *Akten des VII. Internationalen Kongresses für Christliche Archäologie*, Trier 5–11 September 1965 (Vatican City, 1969), 523–25.

Foss, C. 'Cities and villages of Lycia in the Life of Saint Nicholas of Zion', *GOTR*, 36 (1991), 303–39.

Foss, C. 'The Lycian coast in the Byzantine age', *DOP*, 48 (1994), 1–52.

Frank, G. '"Taste and see": the Eucharist and the eyes of the faith in the fourth century', *CH*, 70.4 (2001), 619–43.

Franses, R. *Donor Portraits in Byzantine Art: The Vicissitudes of Contact between Human and Divine* (Cambridge, 2018).

Ganz, D. 'Giving to God in the Mass: the experience of the offertory', in P. Fouracre and W. Davies (ed.), *The Languages of Gift in the Early Middle Ages* (Cambridge, 2010), 18–32.

Gell, A. *Art and Agency: An Anthropological Theory* (Oxford, 1998).

Giannouli, A. 'Education and literary language in Byzantium', in M. Hinterberger (ed.), *The Language of Byzantine Learned Literature*, SBHC, 9 (Turnhout, 2014), 52–71.

Gosden, C. 'Making sense: archaeology and aesthetics', *World Archaeology*, 33.2 (2001), 163–67.

Gosden, C. 'What do objects want?' *JAMT*, 12.3 (2005), 193–211.

Harrison, R.M. 'Churches and chapels of central Lycia', *Anatolian Studies*, 13 (1963), 117–51.

Harrison, R.M. *Mountain and Plain: From the Lycian Coast to the Phrygian Plateau in the Late Roman and Early Byzantine Period* (Ann Arbor, MI, 2001).

Hellenkemper, H. 'Ecclesiastical silver hoards and their findspots: implications for the treasure found at Korydella, Lycia', in Boyd and Mango (ed.), *Ecclesiastical Silver Plate*, 65–70.

Hendy, M.F. 'The administration of mints and treasuries, fourth to seventh centuries, with an appendix on the production of silver plate', in M.F. Hendy (ed.), *The Economy, Fiscal Administration and Coinage of Byzantium* (Northampton, 1989), 1–18.

Hendy, M.F. *Studies in the Byzantine Monetary Economy 300–1450* (Cambridge, 1985).

Hunter-Crawley, H. 'Embodying the divine: the sensational experience of the sixth-century Eucharist', in J. Day (ed.), *Making Senses of the Past: Toward a Sensory Archaeology* (Carbondale, 2013), 160–76.
Hunter-Crawley, H. 'The Cross of Light: experiencing divine presence in Byzantine Syria', in Nesbitt and Jackson (ed.), *Experiencing Byzantium*, 177–81.
Ingold, T. 'Materials against materiality', *Archaeological Dialogues*, 14.1 (2007), 1–16.
İşler, B. 'Karabel Asarcık'taki Sion Manastırı Mezar Odası Ve Bizans Lahitleri, (the burial chamber and early Byzantine sarcophagi in the Sion monastery at Karabel Asarcık)', *Seleucia*, 7 (2017), 161–82.
İşler, B. 'Likya bölgesi Karabel Asarcık'taki erken Bizans dönemi yerleşimi' (PhD diss. Hacettepe University, 2009).
İşler, B. 'Likya Bölgesi'ndeki Karabel-Asarcık yerleşimi yapılarının plan ve işlev özellikleri üzerine gözlemler', *International Young Scholars Conference I: Mediterranean Anatolia Symposium Proceedings,* 4–7 November 2009 (İstanbul, 2012), 161–73.
İşler, B. 'Sionlu Aziz Nikolaos'un Batı Asarcık yerleşimindeki mezar yapısı', in S. Doğan and M. Kadiroğlu (ed.), *Bizans Ve Çevre Kültürler: Prof. Dr. S. Yıldız Ötüken'e Armağan* (İstanbul, 2010), 186–96.
James, L. (ed.), *Art and Text in Byzantine Culture* (Cambridge, 2007).
James, L. 'Senses and sensibility in Byzantium', *ArtH*, 27 (2004), 522–37.
Jeffreys, M. 'Literacy', in E. Jeffreys, J.F. Haldon and R. Cormack (ed.), *The Oxford Handbook of Byzantine Studies* (Oxford, 2008), 796–802.
Jones, A.H.M. *Later Roman Empire 284–602: A Social, Economic, and Administrative Survey*, 3 vols (Oxford, 1964).
Kitzinger, E. 'A pair of silver book covers in the Sion Treasure', in U.E. McCracken et al. (ed.), *Gatherings in Honour of Dorothy E. Miner* (Baltimore, 1974), 3–17.
Klingshirn, W.E. and L. Safran (ed.), *The Early Christian Book* (Washington, DC, 2007).
Knappett, C. and L. Malafouris (ed.), *Material Agency: Towards a Non-Anthropocentric Approach* (New York, 2008).
Knappett, C. and L. Malafouris. 'The neglected networks of material agency: artefacts, pictures and texts', in Knappett and Malafouris (ed.), *Material Agency*, 139–56.
Knappett, C. *Thinking Through Material Culture: An Interdisciplinary Perspective* (Philadelphia, PA, 2005).
Kopytoff, I. 'The cultural biography of things: commoditization as process', in Appadurai (ed.), *The Social Life of Things*, 64–91.
Krueger, D. *Liturgical Subjects: Christian Ritual, Biblical Narrative, and the Formation of the Self in Byzantium* (Philadelphia, PA, 2014).
Küchler, S. and T. Carroll. *A Return to the Object: Alfred Gell, Art, and Social Theory* (New York, 2021).
Laiou, A.E. (ed.), *The Economic History of Byzantium: From the Seventh through the Fifteenth Century*, 3 vols, DOS, 39 (Washington, DC, 2002).
Leatherbury, S.V. 'Textiles as gifts to God in late antiquity: Christian altar cloths as cultic objects', in C. Brøns and M. Nosch (ed.), *Textiles and Cult in the Ancient Mediterranean* (Oxford, 2017), 243–57.
Lowden, J. 'The Word made visible: the exterior of the early Christian book as visual argument', in Klingshirn and Safran (ed.), *The Early Christian Book*, 28–29.
Maguire, H. (ed.), *Byzantine Magic* (Washington, DC, 1995).

Maihoub, A. 'Thinking through the sociality of art objects', *JAC*, 7 (2015), 1–9.
Malafouris, L. 'At the potter's wheel: an argument for material agency', in Knappett and Malafouris (ed.), *Material Agency*, 19–36.
Mango, C. *The Art of the Byzantine Empire: 312–1453, Sources and Documents* (Toronto, 1986).
Mango, M.M. 'The monetary value of silver revetments and objects belonging to churches A.D. 300–700', in Boyd and Mango (ed.), *Ecclesiastical Silver Plate*, 123–36.
Mango, M.M. 'The purpose and places of Byzantine silver stamping', in Boyd and Mango (ed.), *Ecclesiastical Silver Plate*, 203–16.
Mango, M.M. 'Three illuminating objects in the Lampsacus Treasure', in C. Entwistle (ed.), *Through a Glass Brightly: Studies in Byzantine and Medieval Art and Archaeology Presented to David Buckton* (Oxford, 2003), 64–75.
Mango, M.M. 'Tracking Byzantine silver and copper metalware, 4th–12th centuries', in M.M. Mango (ed.), *Byzantine Trade, 4th–12th Centuries: The Archaeology of Local, Regional and International Exchange*, SPBS, 14 (Farnham, 2009), 221–36.
Mango, M.M. *Silver from Early Byzantium: The Kaper Koraon and Related Treasures*, (Baltimore, MD, 1986).
Markopoulos, A. 'Education', in Jeffreys, Haldon and Cormack (ed.), *The Oxford Handbook of Byzantine Studies*, 785–95.
Martiniani-Reber, M (ed.), *Byzance en Suisse* (Milan and Geneva, 2015).
Mauss, M. 'Gifts and the obligation to return gifts', in F. Candlin and R. Guins (ed.), *The Object Reader* (London, 2009), 21–31.
Mauss, M. *The Gift: The Form and Reason for Exchange in Archaic Societies* (London, 2002).
Meyendorff, J. *Imperial Unity and Christian Divisions: The Church 450–680 AD, Church History* (Crestwood, 1989).
Meyers, P. 'Elemental compositions of the Sion Treasure and other Byzantine silver objects', in Boyd and Mango (ed.), *Ecclesiastical Silver Plate*, 169–90.
Miller, P.C. *The Corporeal Imagination: Signifying the Holy in Late Ancient Christianity* (Philadelphia, PA, 2009).
Mingana, A. *Commentary of Theodore of Mopsuestia on the Lord's Prayer and on the Sacraments of Baptism and the Eucharist*, Woodbrooke Studies, 6 (Cambridge, 1933).
Morphy, H. 'Art as a mode of action: some problems with Gell's *Art and Agency*', *JMC*, 14.1 (2009), 5–27.
Mullett, M. 'Writing in early mediaeval Byzantium' in R. McKitterick (ed.), *The Uses of Literacy in Early Mediaeval Europe* (Cambridge, 1990), 156–85.
Nesbitt, J.W. 'Some observations on Byzantine control stamps', in Boyd and Mango (ed.), *Ecclesiastical Silver Plate*, 225–27.
Newman, R. and H. Lie 'The technical examination and conservation of objects in the Sion Treasure', in Boyd and Mango (ed.), *Ecclesiastical Silver Plate*, 77–88.
O'Malley, M. 'Altarpieces and agency: the altarpiece of the Society of the Purification and its "invisible skein of relations"', *ArtH*, 28.4 (2005), 417–41.
Oransay, A. 'Arykanda Antik Kenti'nde 1971–2002 kazı sezonlarında ele geçen madeni buluntular ve madencilik faaliyetleri' (PhD diss., Ankara University, 2006), 19–25.
Osbourne, G. 'Mosaics of power: superstition, magic and Christian power in early Byzantine floor mosaics' (PhD diss., University of Sussex, 2014).

Papalexandrou, A. 'Echoes of orality in the monumental inscriptions of Byzantium', in James (ed.), *Art and Text in Byzantine Culture*, 161–87.
Papalexandrou, A. 'Text in context: eloquent monuments and the Byzantine beholder', *Word and Image: A Journal of Verbal/Visual Enquiry*, 17.3 (2001), 259–83.
Papalexandrou, A. 'The memory culture of Byzantium', in James (ed.), *A Companion to Byzantium*, 108–22.
Parani, M.G. and L. Bouras, *Lighting in Early Byzantium* (Washington, DC, 2008).
Pearce, M.T. et al., 'Neuroaesthetics: The cognitive neuroscience of aesthetic experience', *Perspectives on Psychological Science*, 11.2 (2016), 265–79.
Pentcheva, B.V. 'Epigrams on Icons', in James (ed.), *Art and Text in Byzantine Culture*, 120–38.
Pentcheva, B.V. 'Hagia Sophia and multisensory aesthetics', *Gesta*, 50.2 (2011), 93–111.
Pentcheva, B.V. 'The Performative Icon', *ArtB*, 88.4 (2006), 631–55.
Pentcheva, B.V. *The Sensual Icon: Space, Ritual, and the Senses in Byzantium* (University Park, PA, 2010).
Prentice, W.K. 'Fragments of an early Christian liturgy in Syrian inscriptions', *TAPA*, 33 (1902), 81–100.
Preston, B. 'The functions of things: a philosophical perspective on material culture', in P.M. Graves-Brown (ed.), *Matter, Materiality and Modern Culture* (London, 2000), 22–49.
Rapp, C. 'Bishops in late antiquity: a new social and urban elite?' in J. Haldon and L.I. Conrad (ed.), *The Byzantine and Early Islamic Near East: Elites Old and New in the Byzantine and Early Islamic Near East* (Princeton, 2004), 149–78.
Rapp, C. 'Charity and piety as episcopal and imperial virtues in late antiquity', in M. Frenkel and Y. Lev (ed.), *Charity and Giving in Monotheistic Religions*, SGKIO, 22 (Berlin, 2009), 75–88.
Rapp, C. 'The elite status of bishops in late antiquity in ecclesiastical, spiritual and social context', *Arethusa*, 33.3 (2000), 377–99.
Rapp, C. *Holy Bishops in Late Antiquity: The Nature of Christian Leadership in an Age of Transition* (London, 2005), 178–79.
Rhoby, A. 'Text as art? Byzantine inscriptions and their display', in I. Berti et al. (ed.), *Writing Matters: Presenting and Perceiving Monumental Inscriptions in Antiquity and the Middle Ages* (Berlin, 2017), 265–83.
Robb, J. 'Beyond agency', *World Archaeology*, 42.4 (2010), 493–520.
Robb, J. 'What do things want? Object design as a middle range theory of material culture', *Archaeological Papers of the American Anthropological Association*, 26.1 (2015), 166–80.
Ross, M.C. *Catalogue of the Byzantine and Early Medieval Antiquities in the Dumbarton Oaks Collection 2: Jewelry, Enamels and Art of the Migration Period*, (Washington, DC, 1965).
Roueché, C. *Aphrodisias in Late Antiquity: The Late Roman and Byzantine Inscriptions Including Texts from the Excavations at Aphrodisias Conducted by Kenan T. Erim*, JRSM, 5 (London, 1989).
Russell, J. 'The archaeological context of magic in the early Byzantine period', in Maguire (ed.), *Byzantine Magic*, 35–50.
Russell, J. *The Mosaic Inscriptions of Anemurium*, ETAM, 13 (Wien, 1987).

Schibille, N. *Hagia Sophia and the Byzantine Aesthetic Experience* (Farnham, 2014).
Schiffer, M.B. *Behavioral Archaeology: First Principles* (Salt Lake City, 1995).
Seeley, W.P. 'Naturalizing aesthetics: art and the cognitive neuroscience of vision', *Journal of Visual Art Practice*, 5.3 (2006), 195–213.
Ševčenko, I. 'The Sion Treasure: the evidence of the inscriptions', in Boyd and Mango (ed.), *Ecclesiastical Silver Plate*, 46–58.
Sheppard, A. 'The role of imagination in aesthetic experience', *JAE*, 25.4 (1991), 35–42.
Skibo, J.M. and M.B. Schiffer, *People and Things: A Behavioral Approach to Material Culture* (New York, 2008).
Snow, C.E. 'From ingot to object: fabrication techniques used in the manufacture of the Hama Silver', in Boyd and Mango (ed.), *Ecclesiastical Silver Plate*, 197–201.
Spingou, F. 'Words and artworks in the twelfth century and beyond: the thirteenth-century manuscript Marcianus gr. 524 and the twelfth-century dedicatory epigrams on works of art' (PhD diss., University of Oxford, 2012).
Stock, W.-M. 'Theurgy and aesthetics in Dionysios the Areopagite', in S. Mariev and W.-M. Stock (ed.), *Aesthetics and Theurgy in Byzantium* (Berlin, 2013), 13–30.
Svašek, M. *Anthropology, Art and Cultural Production* (London, 2007).
Taft, R.F. *A History of the Liturgy of St John Chrysostom. Vol. 6: The Communion, Thanksgiving, and Concluding Rites*, OCA, 281 (Rome, 2008).
Talbot, A.M. 'Byzantine monasticism and the liturgical arts', in O.Z. Pevny (ed.), *Perceptions of Byzantium and its Neighbors (843–1261)* (New York, 2000), 27–31.
Tiryaki, A. 'A group of parapet slabs from the Rhodiapolis episcopal church', *Olba*, 20 (2012), 493–514.
Van der Leeuw, S.E. 'Agency, networks, past and future', in Knappett and Malafouris (ed.), *Material Agency*, 217–46.
Van Gelder, T. and R.F. Port. 'It's about time: an overview of the dynamical approach to cognition', in R.F. Port and T. Van Gelder (ed.), *Mind as Motion: Explorations in the Dynamics of Cognition* (Cambridge, 1995), 1–43.
Vikan, G. 'Art, medicine and magic in early Byzantium', *DOP*, 35 (1984), 65–86.
Yasin, A.M. 'Prayers on site: the materiality of devotional graffiti and the production of early Christian sacred space', in A. Eastmond (ed.), *Viewing Inscriptions in the Late Antique and Medieval Worlds* (Cambridge, 2015), 36–60.
Yener, K.A. 'Byzantine silver mines: an archaeometallurgy project in Turkey', in Boyd and Mango (ed.), *Ecclesiastical Silver Plate*, 155–67.

Index

Note: **Bold** page numbers refer to tables and figures and *italic* page numbers refer to footnotes.

Adeos (CSL) 115
agency 2, 164; of sacred places 162; human 152–153; material 152–153
Anastasius I (emperor) 122, 132
Angeleuos Roufinos, memory of 16, **35**, 102, **105**, 145, 149, **151**, 166
Anemourion, Isauria (Turkey) 165
Anthologia Marciana 167
Aphrodisias 169
Arabissus (native town of emperor Maurice, Cappadocia, Turkey) 156
Archaeological museum, Istanbul (Turkey) 120, 147
Areobindus (Consul) 148
asterisk 6n4, 7, 16, **35**, **46**, *50*
Attarouthi Treasure 159

Battle of Masts 12
Black Sea 140
Bliss, Robert Woods 5
Bliss, Mildred Barness 6
Bolkardag Valley *see* Taurus Mountains
Buyuk Asar Hill, Kumluca (Antalya-Turkey) 1, 10, 11

Caesarius of Arles 161
chief finance officer 123
Christogram 15, 16, **35**, *47*, *48*, 144
Church of St Sergios in Kaper Koraon Village 158
Cognition 2, 154, 181
Comes Sacrarum Largitionum (CSL) 121–123, 127, 129, 130, 132, 141–142, 146
Commodity 154, 154n7, 162, 170, 184
Constans II (emperor) 132
Constantine (emperor) 150, 158
Constantinople 130, 132–133, 140–143, 145–147, 158, 165, 168
Cultural biography 2, 2n5, 4, 152
Cyril of Jerusalem 167, 183

Digby-Jones, Kenelm 1n2, 26n54
Digby-Jones Collection, London 1, 1n2, 7, 7n8, 26, 26n54, 27, **42**, 119, 126, **138**

elemental composition 2, 13, 14, 16–20, 22, 23, 25, 26, 28, 29, 141, 144
Elias (CSL) 122, 130
Ernst Kitzinger Collection 8n8
Eutychianos (bishop, donor) 8, 14, 17, 18, 21, 24, 28, **35–43**, 103, **104–116**, 119, 133, 141–144, 147–50, **151**, 157–62, 164–168, 177, 184; memory of 28, 42, 103, 149

F. Alouf Collection 170

Gerasimos *see* Anthologia Marciana
George Ortiz Collection, Geneva 1, 2n3, 7, 7n8, 14, 15n37, **35**
gifts to God 3, 153–155, 162–163, 168, 184
Goldsmith 143, 148

Hagia Sophia (Church) 150, 158, 178; sanctuary of 171n80
Hama 34
Harun Al Rashid 12

Heraclius (emperor) 140
Hermitage Museum (Russia) 128, 130
Hewett, Kenneth John 1n2
Hewett Collection, London 1, 1n2, 7, 7n8, 24, 24n49, 27, 27n57, 28, **40–42**, **46**
Himeria 28, 102; memory of 28, **42**, 103, **115**, 149, **151**, 166
Holy Sion 11, 163, 164; Church of 3, 11; formula 9, 11, 102, 108–12, 163, 164; in Jerussalem 9

imagination 155, 181–183, 183n125
inner sense 181–182
Iohannes of Palestine (CSL) 130

John 102; for the memory of 16, **35**, 102, **105**, 145, **150**, 166
John Chrysostom 164, 178, 183
John of Damascus 182
John of Ephesus 148, 156
John Moschos 143, 148, 179
Julianus (CSL) 122, 128–131
Justinian I (emperor) 11, 119, 122–125, 127–130, **135–139**, 147, 147n26, 150, 157
Justin II (emperor) 122, 130

Kaper Koraon Treasure 132, 143, 149, 158
Karabel-Asarcık, Antalya (Turkey) 9, 10, 11, 171, 172
Konon (deacon) **43**, 102, **116**, 149, **151**
Korydalla, Antalya (Turkey) 1, 5, 184
Kumluca, Antalya (Turkey) 1, 10–12

Lateran Church, Rome (Italy) 150, 158
Lead Isotope Analysis 140
Liber Pontificalis 150, 150n41, 158n25
Lycia (region) 1, 9, 12, 142–143, 145–146, 159, 168, 177

magical amulets 164
Maria 103, 133; for the memory of **36**, **105**, 133, 145, 147–149, **151**, 166
Martyrium of St Drosis 157
mausoleum in Sion Monastery 10, 10n17, 171
Ministry of Culture, Ankara (Turkey) 6
Monastery of Nicholas of Myra, Antalya (Turkey) 10
Monogram 8, 17, 19–21, 36–38, 106–10, 121, 125, 126, 127, 128, 130; of Adeos 125, 126, 135–139; of emperor 121; of Eutychianos (bishop) 18–20, 131; of Iohannes 127, 135, 136, 138; of Julianus 128; of Justinian 11, 119, 123, 124, 125, 126, 127, 129, 135–139; secondary 121, 123, 125–127; of senior official 121, 124, 129, 132; of Theodoros 130
Myra, Antalya (Tukey) 10, 12

Nicholas of Sion, (St) 9, 9n11, 9n13, 10, 10n17, 159, 172; Vita of 9–11, 10n14, 159, 172
Nikephoros Kallistos 165

Openwork 17, 18, 19, 27, 28; lamp 1, 5, 7–9, 14, 26, 27, 27n57, 28, **41–3**, *82–7*, 102–3, **114–15**, 122–123, 126–28, 131–132, **138–139**, 149, **151**, 166–67, 172, 176; inscription 5, 28, **43**, *87–8*; monograms 18, 19, 36–38

Paregoros (bishop) 8, 33, **45**, 103, **117–118**, 149, **151**, 157
Petrus Barysimes (CSL) 122, 130
Paulinos *see* Theophylact Simocatta
Paul the Silentiary 171n80, 178, 180
philanthropy 158–160, 162
Phoenix, Lycia 12
Prinkipios (deacon), for the memory of **43**, 102, **116**, 149, **151**, 157
Procopius of Caesarea 180
Pseudo-Dionysios 173, 180
Pulcheria (sister of Theodosios II, emperor) 168

reliquary chapel in Sion Monastery 10, 159, 171
Rhodiapolis, Antalya (Turkey) 168
Riha 130, 132, 172
Romanos the Melodist 166

Sakellarios 122
Sanctuary of St Daniel in Sabandos 159
sarcophagi 10, 10n17, 171
Senior official 121, 123–125
Severus of Antioch 157
Shrine of the archangel Gabriel, Karkabo (Lycia) 159
Shrine of St Glykeria 162
Shrine of St Symeon the Younger 164

Silversmith 132, 141–147, 162
Sion Monastery 9, 11, 12, 103, 150, 157, 160, 161, 170–172, 183, 184
Stamps: imperial 11, 14, 17–19, 22, 24–26, 34, **35–45**, *68*, *101*, 121, 122, *124–129*, 125, 132, 141, 147, 161; irregular or non-imperial *120*, 122, **139**, 141, 143; secondary 121n9
St Artemios 165
St Basil 164
St Demetrios 156, 170
St Jerome 157
St Niketas 167
St Pankratios 156
St Panteleimon *see* Anthologia Marciana
St Sabas 143
Strategius (CSL) 130
Stuma 130, 147

Taurus Mountains (Turkey) 140, 141, 143
Theodore (bishop) 8, **44**, 102, **117**
Theodore of Mopsuestia 183
Theodore of Sykeon 150, 161
Theophylact Simocatta 162
Treasury of San Marco, Venice 165

XRF 13, 14, 14n35, 20, 22, 25

Zacharias (priest) 8, 33, **45**, 102, **118**, 149, **151**, 157
Zacos, George 5